CLEVELAND

Discovery
Guide

2nd Edition

CLEVELAND
Discovery
Guide

·· **2nd Edition** ··········

Jennifer Stoffel *&* Stephen Phillips

GRAY & COMPANY, PUBLISHERS
CLEVELAND

Gray & Company, Publishers
1588 E. 40th Street
Cleveland, Ohio 44103-2302
email: info@grayco.com

Library of Congress Cataloging-in-Publication Data
Stoffel, Jennifer, 1955-
Cleveland Discovery Guide / by Jennifer Stoffel & Stephen Phillips.—2nd ed.
First ed. of this book published in 1994.
Includes bibliographical references and index.
1. Cleveland (Ohio)—Guidebooks. 2. Family recreation Ohio—Cleveland—Guidebooks. I. Phillips, Stephen, 1959- .
II. Title.
F499.C63S76 1997
977.1'32—dc21   97-4718

This guide was prepared on the basis of the authors' best knowledge at the time of publication. However, because of constantly changing conditions beyond their control, the authors disclaim any responsibility for the accuracy and completeness of the information in this guide. Users of this guide are cautioned not to place undue reliance upon the validity of the information contained herein and to use this guide at their own risk.

ISBN 1-886228-04-3

Printed in the United States of America
10 9 8 7 6 5 4 3 2 1

Contents

Preface

As new parents and newcomers to Cleveland, we needed help to guide us through the many decisions we faced. We had no family nearby, no friends in the city. Yet we realized we were not alone.

That was 1989 and the beginning of *Cleveland Parent*. Several years later, thanks to our own discoveries, tips from friends, and ideas from families all over Northeast Ohio, we now know *a lot* about this area's offerings for families. We are glad to be able to share that knowledge with other Clevelanders in this guide.

Our goal is to make Cleveland more accessible to all of us—especially those with kids. We know, and we hear from other parents—and not just two-career parents—that time is becoming more and more precious. That's why we made sure to include details, details, details to help make your outing choices easier. We scouted the city so that you can spend less time searching and more time discovering. So get out and enjoy!

For this **second edition**, we set out to explore Akron, Canton, and other destinations a bit farther from home. In the process, we also broadened our discussion of area libraries to include computer resources for families; added to the chapter on sports; and updated information wherever we found changes.

There are bound to be some places we overlooked. If you know of something we should include in future editions, or if you have comments about any of our listings, please write to us at *Cleveland Parent*, Box 40056, Cleveland, Ohio 44140.

Acknowledgements

This book couldn't have been written without help—lots of it! Particular thanks go to Aura Ensley, senior editor for *Cleveland Parent*, and to our son Alex, age 7, for his willingness to give everything a try.

Jennifer Stoffel & Stephen Phillips

Introduction

•••

Family Time, Cleveland-Style

Nothing is more fun than a successful family outing—one that parents and children alike can truly enjoy; one you all will remember fondly, talk about, and want to do over again.

Sound impossible?

It's not, really—especially here in Greater Cleveland. Because we're fortunate: this is a wonderful place for families.

The best news is that our community is paying more attention to the educational and recreational needs of children than ever before. A whole generation of interactive museums is dramatically changing the profile of our local institutions. "Please touch" hands-on exhibits are fast replacing the roped-off, glassed-in displays. And this trend isn't just limited to museums. Now, children's activities are being planned nearly everywhere, libraries are setting aside areas for noisy youngsters, and theaters are offering special children's series.

Cleveland boasts a history of well-established family favorites, too. Just five miles east of downtown, University Circle, the city's cultural heart, has been home to world-class museums, renowned performing arts groups, and eclectic galleries for decades. An "Emerald Necklace" of Metroparks and state parks surrounds the city with a wealth of green open spaces and plenty of opportunity for nature education and outdoor recreation. Many amusement parks—some big, some little, and all within easy reach—offer lively fun for a full range of ages. Historical sites and small museums scattered throughout the area provide quieter, more educational recreation. Sporting opportunities range from major league baseball, basketball, and soccer to instructional programs at civic recreation centers. A far-reaching system of libraries brings a convenient range of thoughtful family entertainment to every community.

In fact, Greater Cleveland offers so much for families that a lot of exploring is required to really know the area well. This is true even for natives—especially so when we become parents (when we're suddenly challenged to discover the city all over again!). For newcomers and visitors to Cleveland, there's so much to discover that it can be hard even to decide where to start.

That is why this book exists. We've done the work of researching, collecting, and compiling information about all the best family recreation opportunities in Greater Cleveland—so you can concentrate on the most important part: having fun together.

Planning for Quality Time

Fun and learning can sometimes happen spontaneously. But you can't count on them being a part of your next outing unless you do a little planning ahead of time.

Find out about the place you will be visiting before you go. For example, does it mix hands-on and hands-off activities? What age children is it most appropriate for? Match its features with the needs and interests of your family members.

Discuss expectations with your children. Find out what subject they want to focus on. Will it be dinosaurs or Gothic armor? You may want to select one or two specific areas or exhibits for a visit—especially at larger attractions. (Even adults get over-stimulated!)

Choose the right time, and the right amount of time. Avoid scheduling visits for the end of a hectic day of errands or sightseeing, or during naptimes or mealtimes. If you will be taking a long car ride, plan to let the kids blow off some steam after they arrive and before asking them to sit quietly at a performance or walk obediently through an exhibit.

Perhaps most importantly, plan activities appropriate to your kids. As experts and parents alike will attest, all kids—younger ones most of all—do not like just to watch and sit. They like to move and do. This is not something you should fight. Experts point to hands-on activities as the best use of our children's time; that is how kids really learn.

One of the nicest things about exploring together as a family is that if the outing is set up right, your kids can make their own discoveries. It can be a relief to find that as a parent you don't have to be constantly involved. Where does this leave you? Your biggest role is setting up those opportunities for discovery. There are plenty of things that parents and children can do together—a bookful in fact!

Using this Book
....

Especially for Families
We have included all the best family-oriented attractions in Greater Cleveland and gathered information specifically on child- and family-related offerings. Keep in mind that each entry will not necessarily cover the entire attraction; exhibits and events geared only toward adult audiences are not typically included.

At a Glance
For easy reference, each entry starts with a few basic facts about the attraction, including its general location, a suggested age range for which it is appropriate, and a general cost range. These can help you decide which attractions are worth a closer look.

Description
Our descriptions tell what families can expect—and what they should look out for—at each attraction. We have visited and reviewed these places with an eye out for what makes them notable or special for families. Descriptions include major features, unusual offerings, and seasonal highlights.

Specifics
Then, we list the information you are going to need to get there: address, phone number, season, hours of operation, actual prices and directions (or sources that can provide them).

Helpful Details
Because outings with children involve so many details, we have tried to help families plan some of the basic mechanics of a visit by answering the following questions: Are strollers allowed? Are there diaper-changing facilities? Is there food service, or food available nearby? Is parking provided, or is there access to public transportation? Can groups be accommodated? These items are noted with bullet points as follows:

● Strollers	● Groups	● Food Serv.	● Parking	● Birthdays
● Diap. Chg.	● Picnic	● Food Nearby	● Pub. Trans.	● Handicap. Access

Call Ahead

The information in this book was current and accurate at the time it went to press. But information like this—especially prices, dates, and times—is always subject to change. We strongly recommend that you call first before departing on your outing.

We also suggest you call for special events, classes, and other programs that may be offered on an irregular basis. (We have found that some programs are so popular, you need to call on the first day of registration just to get in.)

To make this process easier, we have included phone numbers for each entry. Most are general information numbers, some of which connect you with computerized switchboards. If you reach a computer, don't be too upset; most will let you speak with a real person if your inquiry doesn't fit into one of their preprogrammed categories.

Area Code Change

As of April 1998, telephone exchanges in the outer suburbs of Cuyahoga County, as well as in contiguous Northeast Ohio counties, will change from the 216 area code to the 440 area code. Phone numbers affected by this change are designated as (216[†]).

Costs

Our cost rating system is as follows: $ for under $6; $$ for under $12 and $$$ for over $12. Each of these costs is rated on a per-person basis. (Some attractions are free only at certain times or for certain ages; we have listed as free in the Cost section only those attractions that, at one time or another, can be visited totally free by the whole family.)

Directions

Directions were provided by each organization listed and were confirmed using the most current AAA/Ohio Motorist Association maps. Directions generally start from the nearest major highway and use main roads, to make following them easier. However, it is always a good idea to call ahead and confirm directions, especially for longer drives or trips to unfamiliar places. Travel conditions, road closings, construction detours, and even street names are subject to continual change. Call ahead to avoid any confusion!

Areas Covered in This Book

We have divided Greater Cleveland into sections so that you can tell from a glance at the *Area* and *City* categories at the top of each listing approximately where any attraction is located. *Area* is indicated at the top of each listing. At the end of the listing we provide street address information and directions, as well as phone numbers so you can call for more information.

Areas Covered in This Book:

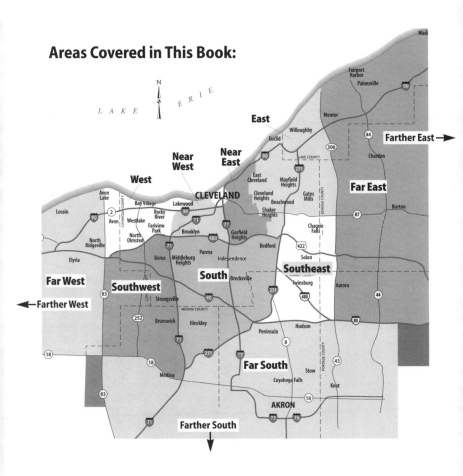

CLEVELAND

Discovery
Guide

2nd Edition

Amusements

••

Theme parks recognize that parents with younger children are important customers. In recent years, offerings for kids have been expanded and improved to include easier access, better prices and, simply, more to do. Bear Country at Cedar Point is delightful. The sand, sun, and swimming at Turtle Beach in Geauga Lake are just the right combination for youngsters. And the slides and rope climbing at Sea World's Happy Harbor can easily occupy a whole day's visit. Discovery Zone adds a convenient indoor option.

These are not places you want to visit without some preparation, though. Crowds can be daunting, and the day can become quite expensive. But take heart, use our lists and access information to help plan, and enjoy.

To give you the widest choice of amusements, we've included both the large, well-recognized theme parks and the smaller, neighborhood family fun centers.

Brookpark Fun and Games Emporium

Area: **West**   City: **Cleveland**   Ages: **All**   Cost: **$–$$$**

This formerly all-outdoor fun center has added an indoor playground. Outside, there are two 18-hole miniature golf courses, go-carts, and batting cages. Inside are a video arcade, skee ball machines, and a two-level romp-around room with tubes and balls (restricted to folks under 4-1/2 feet tall). There is also a small collection of indoor kiddie rides, including a mechanical boat, motorcycle, and horses. Several different birthday party group event packages are available.

Address:	6770 Brookpark Rd.
Phone:	(216) 351-1910
Season:	Year-round (indoor), seasonal for outdoor activities
Hours:	Summer: Mon–Thu 11 a.m.–10 p.m., Fri–Sat 11 a.m.–11 p.m., Sun noon–10 p.m.; Winter: Fri 4 p.m.–10 p.m., Sat–Sun 11 a.m.–11 p.m. (closing times vary)
Prices:	$5 for 25 tokens; group rates available; go-carts: $4 for 5 min.; batting cages: $5 for 7 tokens
Direct.:	I-480 to Exit 15 (Ridge Rd.); south on Ridge to Brookpark Rd.; left (east) on Brookpark; on left (north) side.

AMUSEMENTS

- Strollers   • Groups   • Food Serv.   • Parking   • Birthdays
- Diap. Chg.   • Picnic   • Food Nearby   • Pub. Trans.   • Handicap. Access

Buzzard Cove
Area: **South**   City: **Hinckley**   Ages: **3 & up**   Cost: **$–$$$**

This family funland is equipped with miniature golf, bumper boats, go-carts, and a video game arcade. In addition to the two 18-hole miniature golf courses, there is a lighted driving range with covered tees. Golf instruction is available. Adjacent is Hinckley Lake, with picnic pavilions, boating, swimming, and fishing. The *Hinckley Queen* lake boat is available for rides.

During the month of October, Buzzard Cove features a 100-year-old Haunted Barn (a covered waiting area is provided for any not-so-nice fall weather).

Address: 1053 Bellus Rd. (near Hinckley Lake Dam)
Phone: (216†) 278-2384
Season: Apr–Oct
Hours: Daily 10 a.m.–11 p.m.
Prices: Vary
Direct.:   I-71 to Exit 226; east on SR 303; located at the intersection of Hinckley Hills Rd. (SR 606) and Bellus Rd.

Strollers   • Groups   • Food Serv.   • Parking   • Birthdays
Diap. Chg.   • Picnic   • Food Nearby   Pub. Trans.   Handicap. Access

Cedar Point
Area: **Farther West**   City: **Sandusky**   Ages: **1-1/2 & up**   Cost: **$$$**

You name it, Cedar Point has it: water rides, live shows, merry-go-rounds. A new multi-million-dollar ride seems to be added each season to the more than 50 other rides, which make up the largest collection of roller coasters in the country. One of the state's most popular tourist attractions, this place can be a madhouse during July and August. If you don't like crowds, go early or late in the season.

To ride the real thrillers you must be at least 48 inches tall, but there is an area with rides for younger visitors located off the main drag. Bear Country is specifically designed for toddlers and preschoolers. Based on the Berenstain Bears stories, it is a first-rate playground complete with shady trees, piped-in music by Raffi, and child-scale buildings in which to run and hide. There are also plenty of benches for parents. Kiddie Kingdom is another popular destination for the youngest children.

Given the size of Cedar Point (it covers 364 acres) and the large crowds, you will have a better trip if on entering the park you take the

AMUSEMENTS

time to plan what you most want to do and see. Better yet, call ahead for a map and visitor's information packet. A drawback that cannot be avoided at peak season is the lines—the most popular roller coasters can require more than an hour's wait!

There is more to Cedar Point than rides (a sandy Lake Erie beach, for example), and if you want to stay more than a day there are hotels and a campground on the premises. Next door to Cedar Point is the separate (costs extra) Challenge Park, home to Soak City water park, miniature golf, and a raceway.

Address: SR 2/One Causeway Dr. (on the Sandusky Peninsula)
Phone: (419) 627-2350; (419) 626-0830
WWW: http://www.cedarpoint.com/
Season: May–Oct
Hours: Vary throughout season; gates open one hour before rides begin
Prices: Varied prices for different ages and dates, multi-day passes, and combination packages. Separate admission for Soak City and Challenge Park (Cedar Point admission not required). Fee for parking.
Direct.: Ohio Turnpike (I-80/90) to Exit 7; north on US 250, follow signs; or take exit 6A; north on SR 4 north. Routes are marked once in Sandusky.

- Strollers   - Groups   - Food Serv.   - Parking   Birthdays
- Diap. Chg.   - Picnic   - Food Nearby   Pub. Trans.   - Handicap. Access

Conneaut Lake Park
Area: **Farther East**   City: **Conneaut Lake, PA**   Ages: **All**   Cost: **$–$$$**

This small amusement park is just one of several attractions surrounding Conneaut Lake, Pennsylvania's largest natural lake. Conneaut Lake Park looks like an old-time park because it is one—with all the typical rides: merry-go-round, dodgems, inner tube ride, Tilt-a-Whirl. The Blue Streak, a small wooden roller coaster, is meaner than it looks. There is also a water slide.

On the waterfront there are motorboat and pontoon boat rentals, and there is a playground area on the beach. Other activities available nearby include swimming, boating, golf, and sternwheeler sightseeing cruises on the lake. (Conneaut Lake is also one of the only lakes in the area with no limit on horsepower, making it very popular with speedboaters and water-skiers.)

Annual events draw crowds. The biggest are fishing tournaments, music festivals, a frog-jumping contest, and, for winter visitors, a snowball festival.

Address: SR 618
Phone: Hotel Conneaut: (814) 382-5115
Season: Memorial Day–Labor Day
Hours: Mon–Fri 11 a.m.–9 p.m., Sat–Sun 11 a.m.–10 p.m.; water park: noon–dusk
Prices: $6–$16

AMUSEMENTS

Direct.:   I-90 to Exit 241 (SR 7); south on SR 7; left (east) on US 6 through Linesville; left (north) on PA SR 618 for 3 miles.

● *Strollers*   ● *Groups*   ● *Food Serv.*   ● *Parking*   *Birthdays*
● *Diap. Chg.*   ● *Picnic*   ● *Food Nearby*   *Pub. Trans.*   ● *Handicap. Access*

Discovery Zone
(See following listings for location information)

Discovery Zone has figured out how to bring the popular "Chutes and Ladders" game to life: kids playing pirate scale hanging nets; cylindrical slides hasten transport from high vantage points back to earth. Expect some chaos—the shrieks never stop in the main play area.

With 30 separate areas, each offering several activities, there is plenty to do here.

A Micro Zone is geared to toddlers, with mini-slides and crawl-in coves. A quiet area is set aside upstairs for parents who need to feed babies or just catch their breath.

Several Kid Coaches patrol all areas to make sure the playing is safe. The "adults play free" policy also helps ensure safety—a parent's presence seems to prevent total anarchy.

Discovery Zone occasionally schedules arts and crafts classes and scavenger hunts; they also do birthday parties by special arrangement.

Discovery Zone, Akron
Area: **South**   City: **Akron**   Ages: **1-1/2 to 12**   Cost: **$–$$**

(See main listing for description.)

Address: 1952 Bucholzer Blvd. (Chapel Hill Square)
Phone: (330) 630-0133
Season: Year-round
Hours: Sun–Thu 10 a.m.–8 p.m.; Fri–Sat 9 a.m.–9 p.m.
Prices: $5.99 ages 3–12, $3.99 ages 2 & under, no charge for adults and infants under 12 months
Direct.:   SR 8 to exit for Howe Ave.; east on Howe; right (south) on Bucholzer Blvd.

● *Strollers*   ● *Groups*   ● *Food Serv.*   ● *Parking*   ● *Birthdays*
● *Diap. Chg.*   *Picnic*   ● *Food Nearby*   ● *Pub. Trans.*   ● *Handicap. Access*

Discovery Zone, Mayfield Hts.
Area: **East**   City: **Mayfield Hts.**   Ages: **1-1/2 to 12**   Cost: **$–$$**

(See main listing for description.)

Address: 6420 Mayfield Rd.
Phone: (216) 461-8887

Season: Year-round
Hours: Sun–Thu 10 a.m.–8 p.m.; Fri–Sat 9 a.m.–9 p.m.
Prices: $5.99 ages 3–12, $3.99 ages 2 & under, no charge for adults and infants under 12 months
Direct.: I-271 to Exit 34 (Mayfield Rd.); 1/2 mile west on Mayfield; on left.

- Strollers   • Groups   • Food Serv.   • Parking   • Birthdays
- Diap. Chg.   Picnic   • Food Nearby   • Pub. Trans.   • Handicap. Access

Erieview Park
Area: **Farther East**   City: **Geneva-on-the-Lake**   Ages: **All**   Cost: **$–$$**

Not much has changed here over the past 35 years. Located right on the "strip" in Geneva-on-the-Lake, this small park hugs the Lake Erie shoreline only a short walk from the video arcades, tee-shirt boutiques, and other diversions that have made this mile-long stretch of Lake Rd. so popular for decades.

Erieview Park can be busy on summer weekends. All the typical rides are here: Tilt-a-Whirl, Ferris wheel, fun house, bumper cars, and carousel. There are several kiddie rides suitable for toddlers and preschoolers. The bumper cars are popular with older kids, as is the water slide (for which riders must be 42 inches tall).

Address: 5483 Lake Rd.
Phone: (216†) 466-8650
Season: Memorial Day–Labor Day
Hours: Daily to 10 p.m.; opening varies
Prices: $1 per ride, $10.25 day-long ride & slide pass, group rates available
Direct.: I-90 to Exit 218 (SR 534); north on SR 534 to Lake Rd. in Geneva-on-the-Lake.

- Strollers   • Groups   • Food Serv.   Parking   Birthdays
  Diap. Chg.   • Picnic   • Food Nearby   Pub. Trans.   • Handicap. Access

Fun N Stuff
Area: **South**   City: **Macedonia**   Ages: **2 & up**   Cost: **$$–$$$**

If you're hankering for a go-cart race or some putt-putt golf and it's February, it's time to try this place; there is even an on-site tanning center. Complete with covered batting cages, bumper boats, and video games, this place translates indoor fun into outdoor play with the seasons. Fun N Stuff is scheduled to open its Laser Tag arcade in 1997.

Address: 661 E. Highland Rd.
Phone: (216†) 467-0820
Season: Year-round
Hours: Mon–Thu 4 p.m.–8 p.m., Fri 4 p.m.–midnight, Sat 11 a.m.–midnight, Sun noon–8 p.m. Summer hours (Memorial Day–Labor Day): daily noon–10 p.m., weekends until 1 a.m.

AMUSEMENTS

Prices: Each attraction is priced separately. Special group rates for youth programs from January through March include free go-cart rides or a game of miniature golf.

Direct.: I-271 to Exit 18 for SR 8 (Boston Hts./Akron); south on SR 8; right on Highland Rd. for 3/4 mile; on right.

- Strollers
  Diap. Chg.
- Groups
- Picnic
- Food Serv.
- Food Nearby
- Parking
- Pub. Trans.
- Birthdays
- Handicap. Access

Geauga Lake
Area: **Southeast**   City: **Aurora**   Ages: **All**   Cost: **$$$**

Roller coasters, live entertainment, and extensive water play areas make Geauga Lake a popular summertime destination for families.

There are plenty of water-based activities. The Wave, a two-million-gallon, two-and-a-half-acre pool, boasts surfs cresting up to six feet. There are four water chutes and wet slides.

As at many large amusement parks, the real thrill rides (the Big Dipper, Corkscrew, and Neptune's Falls) require that riders be at least a certain height—42, 48, or 54 inches tall. Other rides merely require that smaller children be accompanied by an adult. On busy summer weekends and holidays, don't be surprised if there are waits of an hour or so for the most popular rides, such as Raging Wolf Bob's roller coaster.

For littler folks, Turtle Beach and Rainbow Island create an aquatic playground equipped with waterfalls and water slides. (You'll want to head directly here if you have preschoolers.)

Courtesy of Geauga Lake

10 Great Things to Do...

For First-Time Visitors:

◉ Visit Tower City and check out the view from the Terminal Tower observation deck. (p. 205)

◉ Tour the Cuyahoga River and view the Lake Erie skyline on the *Goodtime III*. (p. 202)

◉ Shop for goodies and groceries at the West Side Market. (p. 207)

◉ Get stuck in a "rainstorm" at the Cleveland Metroparks Zoo RainForest. (p. 80)

◉ Cruise around downtown and see the sights from aboard Lolly the Trolley. (p. 203)

◉ Check out the new Rock and Roll Hall of Fame and Museum. (p. 60)

◉ Tour Wade Oval and visit the sculpture gardens and the current exhibits at the Cleveland Museum of Art. (p. 36)

◉ Take in a concert by the Cleveland Orchestra at Severance Hall or Blossom Music Center. (p. 143)

◉ Take in a play or special performance at one of the area's theaters.

◉ Reinvent the wheel at Inventure Place. (p. 50)

AMUSEMENTS

In recent years, the management has been working hard to make your stay more pleasant by adding numerous conveniences. There are lockers, life jackets, towels for rent, fitting rooms, and even swimwear for sale in the shops in case you forgot yours. (Proper swimming attire is required; tee-shirts and cut-offs are not permitted.) Near Turtle Beach there is a diaper-changing facility complete with a microwave, bassinets, high chairs, and ready-to-feed juice and milk bottles.

The food here is basic park fare—burgers, hot dogs, ice cream, pizza. It is also pricey. You'll do much better to bring your own meal in a cooler and park it in one of the nicely shaded picnic areas.

Address: 1060 N. Aurora Rd.
Phone: (216†) 562-7131
Season: May–Oct
Hours: 10 a.m.–10 p.m.; hours vary early & late in season
Prices: $20.99, $7.99 under 48 inches, $11.99 seniors, Free for kids under 2, no added charge for water park; stroller rental $5; wagon rental $7
Direct.: I-271 to Exit 27 (US 422); east on US 422; south on SR 91; left on SR 43 (becomes N. Aurora Rd.); on left.

- Strollers
- Diap. Chg.
- Groups
- Picnic
- Food Serv.
- Food Nearby
- Parking
- Pub. Trans.
- Birthdays
- Handicap. Access

Goodtimes
Area: **Far West**   City: **Avon**   Ages: **All**   Cost: **$–$$$**

This seasonal outdoor family fun center has plenty of activities for kids of all ages. There are bumper boats, bumper-style cars, and race cars (some designed for parent and tot). Preschoolers can play two 18-hole miniature golf courses with special clubs for pint-sized players. Facilities for older kids include a video arcade and batting cages.

Address: 33777 Chester Rd.
Phone: (216†) 236-6601; (216†) 937-6210 (Lorain)
Season: May–Oct
Hours: Vary throughout season: call for times
Prices: $6–$20 for ticket packs (rides and games require 2–4 tickets); play-all-day wristbands available
Direct.: I-90 to exit for SR 83; north on SR 83; right on Chester Rd.; on right.

- Strollers
- Diap. Chg.
- Groups
- Picnic
- Food Serv.
- Food Nearby
- Parking
- Pub. Trans.
- Birthdays
- Handicap. Access

I-X Center Indoor Amusement Park
Area: **West**   City: **Brook Park**   Ages: **All**   Cost: **$$–$$$**

This indoor amusement park began operation at the I-X Center in 1989 and has grown to include over 150 rides, games, and live entertainment shows, with special events scheduled each weekend. A roller coaster, video arcade, laser karaoke, and miniature golf course are among the 20-acre indoor park's popular attractions.

For younger kids, there is a kiddie area with motorcycles, fire engines, and trains to ride, as well as a petting zoo. There are also plenty of rides for parents to enjoy with their kids.

The setting is rather like a big garage. The cavernous exhibit floor and metal siding create weird acoustics and lighting. In other words, it is dark and loud. Still, with Cleveland's spring weather, it's no surprise that the indoor park has become a popular destination—particularly on weekend evenings for teenagers and young adults.

The food is what you might expect: hot dogs, popcorn, pizza. An expanded food pavilion can accommodate lunch or dinner.

One of the biggest hits is the world's tallest indoor Ferris wheel. At 10 stories high, it literally pops out of the roof (the top is enclosed in a glass atrium). From the top of the wheel you get a good view of nearby Hopkins airport and the downtown skyline. (There is often a 20- to 30-minute wait to board the wheel.)

Address: 6200 Riverside Dr. (the I-X Center, adjacent to Cleveland-Hopkins Int'l Airport)
Phone: (216) 676-6000
Season: Late Mar–early May (exact dates vary)
Hours: Vary
Prices: $14; $9 seniors; Free 2 and under
Direct.: I-480 to exit for SR 237 (Berea Freeway); south on SR 237; right on I-X Center Dr.; follow signs.

- *Strollers*
- *Diap. Chg.*
- *Groups*
- *Picnic*
- *Food Serv.*
- *Food Nearby*
- *Parking*
- *Pub. Trans.*
- *Birthdays*
- *Handicap. Access*

Courtesy of I-X Indoor Amusement Park

AMUSEMENTS

Jumping Jolly Jambers
Area: **South**   City: **Northfield**   Ages: **3 & up**   Cost: **$-$$**

Billed as "10,000 square feet of challenging fun," Jumping Jolly Jambers is sort of a rubber room. All play areas are covered in foam and vinyl for soft landings, and all areas are large and open to prevent kids from feeling lost. They are also easily accessible to parents and supervised by staff to keep things from getting out of hand.

Address: 10333 Northfield Rd. (Northfield Plaza)
Phone: (216†) 468-3505
Season: Year-round
Hours: Tue–Thu 10 a.m.–8 p.m., Fri–Sat 10 a.m.–10 p.m., Sun 11 a.m.–8 p.m. (open Mon for special holidays)
Prices: $5.75, $3 under 3, parents free
Direct.: I-271 to Exit 18 (SR 8); north on SR 8 (becomes Northfield Rd.); on right.

- Strollers   ● Groups   ● Food Serv.   ● Parking   ● Birthdays
- Diap. Chg.   ● Picnic   ● Food Nearby   ● Pub. Trans.   ● Handicap. Access

Memphis Kiddie Park
Area: **South**   City: **Brooklyn**   Ages: **1-1/2–8**   Cost: **$$**

Memphis Kiddie Park has been a Cleveland institution since its opening in 1952. Many local youngsters have met their first roller coaster here. (With seats just big enough to accommodate an adult companion, the ride is certainly tame enough for a first-timer.) All the typical rides are here—in miniature versions. There's a Ferris wheel, a pony cart, rocket rides, and a merry-go-round. A mini-train circles the park with a short detour through some trees. And, for older kids, there is an 18-hole miniature golf course.

Address: 10340 Memphis Ave.
Phone: (216) 941-5995
Season: Mid-May–mid-Sep
Hours: Daily 10 a.m.–9 p.m. (June–Aug)
Prices: $7 for 10 tickets, $13 for 25 tickets (1 ticket per ride); group rates available
Direct.: I-71 southbound to Fulton Rd.; left (south) on Fulton; right on Memphis Ave. I-71 northbound to exit for Bellaire Rd./W. 105; left off freeway; right on Memphis Ave.

- Strollers   ● Groups   ● Food Serv.   ● Parking   ● Birthdays
- Diap. Chg.   ● Picnic   ● Food Nearby   ● Pub. Trans.   ● Handicap. Access

Mr. Divot's Sports Park
Area: **Southwest**   City: **North Royalton**   Ages: **3 & up**   Cost: **$-$$**

This family fun center is equipped with an 18-hole miniature golf course, a driving range, bumper boats, batting cage, and a tennis-ball target shoot.

Address: 13393 York Rd.
Phone: (216†) 237-2226
Season: Mid-Mar–Oct (weather permitting)
Hours: Daily 10 a.m.–11 p.m.
Prices: Vary; group rates available
Direct.: I-71 to Exit 231; east on SR 82 (Royalton Rd.); left (north) on York 1/2 mile.

• *Strollers*	• *Groups*	• *Food Serv.*	• *Parking*	• *Birthdays*
Diap. Chg.	• *Picnic*	• *Food Nearby*	*Pub. Trans.*	• *Handicap. Access*

Pioneer Waterland
Area: Far East   **City: Chardon**   **Ages: All**   **Cost: FREE—$$$**

Pioneer Waterland offers wet and dry activities as well as ample shaded and grassy picnic areas.

Four killer water slides—the twin Banzai Speed Slides and two giant Spiraling Waterslides—share one six-story tower and act as a magnet for pre-teens and other daredevils. But smaller kids fare well too, especially on the Elephant Slide in the Kiddie Waterpark. There is also a kiddie train and a mini–go-cart track— mighty popular with the age 3–8 grand prix set.

This water park has a large natural lake for paddleboats, a three-acre cement activity pool with water volleyball and basketball, and a lazy inner tube ride for all ages that gently flows through the middle of the park around Adventure Island.

Elsewhere on the grounds are a Grand Prix Supertrack (go carts), batting cages, an 18-hole miniature golf course, golf cages, and an indoor game arcade.

Companies often reserve pavilions in the Group Picnic Grove for corporate picnics on weekends. Expect larger crowds on these days. There are also other activities exclusively for groups, including the Fort Pioneer Play Area, horseshoes, sand volleyball, bocce, shuffleboard, and more.

Tee-shirts and shorts are permitted in all water attractions. Pioneer Waterland has a raincheck policy, so don't worry if your trip is cut short by a summer rainstorm.

Address: 10661 Kile Rd.
Phone: (216†) 951-7507, 285-0909; group sales (216†) 951-7227
WWW: http://www.virtcity.com/business/waterland
Season: Early June–Labor Day
Hours: Daily 10 a.m.–8 p.m. (Sat–Sun only before 2nd week of June)
Prices: Activity admission $11.95; Sportsland admission $9.95; children under 40" Free; free parking

AMUSEMENTS

Direct.:   I-271 to Exit 34 (US 322); east on US 322 past SR 608; left (north) on Kile Rd. (follow signs); on right (east) side.

Strollers	• Groups	• Food Serv.	• Parking	• Birthdays
• Diap. Chg.	• Picnic	• Food Nearby	Pub. Trans.	• Handicap. Access

Sea World of Ohio
Area: **Southeast**   City: **Aurora**   Ages: **All**   Cost: **$$$**

Each summer, this 90-acre marine-life theme park fills with families in search of Shamu the "Killer Whale" and his aquatic pals. Sea World, brought to you by the same folks who run Busch Gardens in Tampa, Florida, and Colonial Williamsburg, Virginia, is a slick and impressive operation—from its water shows to its playground area.

An athletic dolphin act showcases the grace and power of these mammals. Another show, featuring sea lions, penguins, otters, and walruses, plays it strictly for laughs. Other shows, featuring water-skiers and high divers, are scheduled throughout the day. To catch the most popular attractions (Shamu and Namu the killer whales, and the dolphin shows), be sure to line up early. (Oh, and if you don't want to get wet, don't sit in the front rows.) The down side of this strategy is that kids get fidgety listening to the shameless promotions that run before performances.

Shark Encounter, a recent addition, features an impressive tank that bends overhead, making it look like sharks are surrounding you. Interactive exhibits teach about sharks, including how they swim.

Courtesy of Sea World of Ohio

A big hit with children is Shamu's Happy Harbor, a three-acre nautical playground. It is complete with boat deck (with water cannons), a huge net to climb on, clear plastic tubes to crawl through (with water cascading over them), and air mattresses to fall on. Even toddlers will find some entertainment here. Parents can and often do squeeze through the tubes and clamber up the rope ladders themselves.

Don't miss the World of Sea Aquarium. It is small, but it is Northeast Ohio's best aquarium, complete with a touch pool filled with starfish, jellyfish, anemones, crabs, and coral reef fish. Another popular new exhibit, Dolphin Cove, allows kids to get personal with dolphins (fish food is sold at posted intervals).

As at other theme parks, food and drink—while plentiful—are not cheap. So, if you are willing to carry them, bring your own.

Address: 1100 Sea World Dr.
Phone: (800) 63-SHAMU; (216†) 562-8101
WWW: http://www.SeaWorld.org
Season: May–Sep (weekends only in Sep)
Hours: Daily 10 a.m.–7 p.m. (closes at 11 p.m. early Jun–late Aug)
Prices: $27.95, $19.95 ages 3–11, no charge under age 3; parking: $4 per vehicle; strollers and wagons available for rental. Discounts for seniors
Direct.: I-480 to exit for US 422; east on 422; south on SR 91; east on SR 43 (becomes N. Aurora Rd.); left on Sea World Dr.

| ● Strollers | ● Groups | ● Food Serv. | ● Parking | Birthdays |
| ● Diap. Chg. | ● Picnic | ● Food Nearby | ● Pub. Trans. | ● Handicap. Access |

Swings-N-Things Family Fun Park
Area: **Southwest**   City: **Olmsted Twp.**   Ages: **All**   Cost: **$$$**

Swings-N-Things is a popular destination both for families with small children and for those with older school-age children. While there is an indoor video arcade and an ice-cream parlor, the best action is really outside. There are two miniature golf courses, complete with short clubs for short kids, and a cordoned-off area, Fun Kiddie Junction Park, for small children, where they can ride in electric-powered cars, bumper boats, and a very tame roller coaster, and take a short train ride. If smaller kids stick with a parent, they can also get wet in gasoline-powered bumper boats and yell at their parents to outmaneuver wily teens in two-person go-carts that never go quite as fast as the single person versions.

Address: 8501 Stearns Rd.
Phone: (216†) 235-4420
WWW: http://clevernet/realpages/swingsandthings
Season: Year-round
Hours: Vary
Prices: Vary
Direct.: I-480 to exit for Stearns Rd.; south on Stearns for 1-1/2 miles.

| ● Strollers | ● Groups | ● Food Serv. | ● Parking | ● Birthdays |
| ● Diap. Chg. | ● Picnic | ● Food Nearby | Pub. Trans. | ● Handicap. Access |

Wildwood Water Park

Area: **Southwest**   City: **Columbia Station**   Ages: **All**   Cost: **$$**

This water park, located in 65 acres of woods, has been a neighborhood favorite for more than 50 years, especially for older school-age kids. The main attractions are the sandy beach (great for sunning) and 11 water slides. There are also paddle boats, miniature golf, canoes, and a large picnic area.

Address: 11200 E. River Rd. (SR 252)
Phone: (216†) 236-3944
Season: Mid-Jun–Labor Day
Hours: Daily 10:30 a.m.–8 p.m.; water slides: 11 a.m.–7 p.m.
Prices: $10, no charge age 4 & under
Direct.: I-480 to Exit 6 (SR 252); south on SR 252 for 7.5 miles (becomes E. River Rd.)

| *Strollers* | ● *Groups* | ● *Food Serv.* | ● *Parking* | ● *Birthdays* |
| *Diap. Chg.* | ● *Picnic* | ● *Food Nearby* | *Pub. Trans.* | ● *Handicap. Access* |

10 Great Things to Do...

On Lake Erie:

- Fly a kite (or just watch others fly them) at Edgewater Park. (p. 90)

- Walk the boardwalk and tour the rose gardens at Lorain Lakeview Park. (p. 111)

- Board the *Steamship William G. Mather* Museum. (p. 68)

- Pilot a ship's wheel and play captain at the Fairport Marine Museum. (p. 43)

- Stroll along a mile-long stretch of sand at Headlands Beach State Park. (p. 102)

- Tour the lakefront (and the Cuyahoga River) aboard the *Goodtime III*. (p. 202)

- Climb atop the tower at the Inland Seas Maritime Museum and watch the sailboats. (p. 50)

- Take the ferry to the Lake Erie Islands. (p. 106)

- Unwind on the beach after riding roller coasters at Cedar Point. (p. 16)

- Visit the United States Coast Guard station and see the icebreaker *Neah Bay*. (p. 206)

Museums & History

You might think of museums as difficult to visit with young children. Think again. True, some youngsters wouldn't pick a museum exhibit over their favorite video. But if they've been to a museum before and had a good time, they will probably want to go back. It's up to parents, though, to ensure a successful visit by planning ahead.

Be aware when visiting large institutions with children that weekends can be quite crowded. If weekends are your only opportunity, try to go first thing in the morning and quit by lunchtime. You may not see the entire collection in one visit, but that's okay; you can come back.

If you find yourself returning again and again to a particular museum, look into becoming members. Memberships often include free or reduced admission prices, preferred enrollment in classes (a chance to sign up before the general public), and savings in gift shops (often stocked with unusual toys and games).

African American Museum

Area: **Near East**	City: **Cleveland**	Ages: **5 & up**	Cost: **$**

Founded in 1953, the African American Museum was one of the first museums of its kind to open in the U.S. Its special offerings for school-age children include a Saturday "Shule" (school) during the school year that focuses on African history and heritage, and activities in the arts, history, and dance. Annual celebrations of particular interest to families include Black History Month (February) and the Carter G. Woodson celebration in December.

Address: 1765 Crawford Rd. (between Chester & Hough Aves.)
Phone: (216) 791-1700
Season: Year-round
Hours: Tue–Fri 10 a.m.–3 p.m., Sat 11 a.m.–3 p.m.; closed Sun–Mon
Prices: $3 adults; $2 students 17 & under, $2.50 seniors
Direct.: I-90 eastbound to Exit 173B (Chester Ave./US 322); east on Chester past E. 82; left on Crawford; on right.
I-90 westbound to Exit 175 (E. 55); south on E. 55; left (east) on Chester past E. 82; left on Crawford; on right.

Strollers	● *Groups*	*Food Serv.*	● *Parking*	*Birthdays*
Diap. Chg.	*Picnic*	● *Food Nearby*	● *Pub. Trans.*	*Handicap. Access*

MUSEUMS &
HISTORY

Akron Art Museum

Area: **Far South**   City: **Akron**   Ages: **All**   Cost: **FREE**

This smaller museum has shown a consistent ability to line up first-class art exhibitions that other museums in the area overlook. Housed in an Italian Renaissance Revival structure built in 1899, the museum was extensively renovated in 1981. Dedicated to modern art produced since 1950, its permanent collection boasts works by Frank Stella and Andy Warhol. In the courtyard there is a modern sculpture collection, which was a big hit and conversation-starter with our family. Arts festivals and a regular Saturday family workshop series blend exhibits with hands-on creative activities.

Address: 70 E. Market St.
Phone: (330) 376-9185
WWW: http://www.winc.com/~aam
Season: Year-round
Hours: Tue–Fri 11 a.m.–5 p.m., Sat 10 a.m.–5 p.m., Sun noon–5 p.m.
Prices: FREE (donations accepted); on-site parking available
Direct.:   I-77 to exit for SR 59/downtown; stay in left lane until freeway ends; right on High St. 1 block; left on E. Market St.; on right, use Wheeler Ln. entrance. SR 8 to exit for Perkins St.; west on Perkins; left (south) on High St.; left on E. Market; on right, use Wheeler Ln. entrance.

● *Strollers*   ● *Groups*   *Food Serv.*   ● *Parking*   *Birthdays*
  Diap. Chg.   *Picnic*   ● *Food Nearby*   ● *Pub. Trans.*   ● *Handicap. Access*

Allen Memorial Art Museum, Oberlin College

Area: **Far West**   City: **Oberlin**   Ages: **Preschool & up**   Cost: **FREE**

Opened in 1917, Oberlin College's Allen Memorial Art Museum contains one of the finest college or university collections in the nation, including some 14,000 objects ranging from Modigliani's *Naked Woman* to Japanese woodblocks, Islamic carpets, and Old Master prints. Also, it always seems to have an interesting temporary exhibition. Special children's programs, including art workshops and art appreciation tours, are scheduled throughout the year, after school and on Saturdays.

Address: 87 N. Main St. (across from Tappan Square)
Phone: (216†) 775-8665
WWW: http://www.oberlin.edu
Season: Year-round
Hours: Tue–Sat 10 a.m.–5 p.m., Sun 1–5 p.m. (closed major holidays)
Prices: FREE
Direct.:   I-480 west to SR 10/US 20 west; exit at SR 511 (Oberlin); west on SR 511; on left at intersection of SR 511 and SR 58 (N. Main St.)

● *Strollers*   ● *Groups*   *Food Serv.*   ● *Parking*   *Birthdays*
● *Diap. Chg.*   *Picnic*   ● *Food Nearby*   *Pub. Trans.*   ● *Handicap. Access*

Ashtabula, Carson & Jefferson Scenic Line
Area: **Farther East**   City: **Jefferson**   Ages: **All ages**   Cost: **$$**

On summer and fall weekends, this year-round, fully operating freight line becomes a six-mile-long scenic rail ride operated by engineer Bob Callahan and his daughter Heather. There are three partially restored passenger cars, one dating from 1922, the other two from 1926. The trip, aside from crossing a couple of streams, is mostly through old country farms, fields, and woods. A fun, educational family adventure.

Special events include Family Halloween Theme Trains in October and murder mysteries several times a year. Fall rides when the leaves change are especially beautiful.

Address: 160 E. Walnut St.
Phone: (216†) 576-6346
Season: Jun–Oct
Hours: Sat–Sun 12:30 p.m., 2 p.m., 3:30 p.m. (no reservations in the summer)
Prices: $7 adults, $6 seniors, $5 ages 3-12, under 3 Free when held
Direct.: I-90 to Exit 229 (SR 11); south on SR 11; south on SR 46 into Jefferson; left on E. Walnut at 2nd light, 2 blocks to tracks, park at Douglass Lumber.

● Strollers	● Groups	Food Serv.	● Parking	Birthdays
Diap. Chg.	Picnic	● Food Nearby	Pub. Trans.	Handicap. Access

Century Village
Area: **Far East**   City: **Burton**   Ages: **All**   Cost: **$**

Century Village is a great place for an afternoon of playing pioneer. Created by the Geauga Historical Society, it includes 21 reassembled buildings from the Western Reserve era (1798–1900), complete with antiques in and around the buildings, and a working farm with barn, orchards, fields, and animals.

Any one of the society's annual festivals will whisk you back to "Little House on the Prairie" days as people dressed in period costume go about their business.

In the center of the town square, a log cabin offers craft boutiques, maple sugar samples, or hot apple butter depending on the season. Food always seems to motivate our family, so, not surprisingly, our favorite event here is the Apple Butter Festival. Held at the peak of apple-picking season, usually in late September, it coats the village with the scent of cinnamon-spiced apples. You can watch volunteers stir the tangy brown concoction in huge wooden barrels over open-flame pits. But the best part is not visual: slices of warm, freshly baked bread are for sale, topped with ladles full of hot apple butter.

If your children are interested in getting more than just a taste of this village, Pioneer School Camp is held each summer in July for ages 9–11.

MUSEUMS & HISTORY

Workshops include whitewashing, ink making, gingerbread baking, jam making, and square dancing.

Other events of special interest include a Civil War show. Tours through the schoolhouse, stores, and other buildings are usually available during the events, but don't expect to climb cannons or practice sharpshooting; most of the exhibits are set up for looking, listening, and, well, eating.

Address: 14653 E. Park St. (on the Square in Burton)
Phone: (216†) 834-4012
Season: May 1–Oct 31
Hours: Tue–Fri: 9:30 a.m.–4 p.m., tours at 10:30 a.m., 1 p.m., and 3:30 p.m.; Sat–Sun: 9:30 a.m.–4 p.m., tours at 1 p.m. and 3 p.m.
Prices: $3, $2 ages 6–12, Free for ages 5 & under
Direct.: I-271 to Exit 29 (SR 87); east on SR 87 for 35 miles to Burton.

Strollers	● Groups	Food Serv.	● Parking	Birthdays
Diap. Chg.	● Picnic	● Food Nearby	Pub. Trans.	Handicap. Access

Courtesy of Century Village / Geauga Co. Hist. Society

Cleveland Botanical Garden
Area: **Near East**   City: **Cleveland**   Ages: **All**   Cost: **FREE–$$**

Founded in 1930, this is the oldest civic garden in the United States. (The name was changed from The Garden Center of Greater Cleveland in 1994.) Wildflower, herb, rose, perennial, and Japanese gardens are included among the 3,000 meticulously maintained plants and shrubs on the Cleveland Botanical Garden's 7.5 acres. Inside is one of the country's largest garden libraries—including a special children's section.

Throughout the year, special classes for ages 3 and up are offered with either a garden theme or make-and-take project. Library story sessions for preschoolers usually have a nature theme. A gardening program for school-age children is offered each spring.

Annual events at Valentine's Day, Easter, and Christmas are especially popular and fill up fast, so register early. The annual winter holiday show here is especially nice and typically includes special children's activities as well as entertainment.

Address: 11030 East Blvd.
Phone: (216†) 721-1600
Season: Year-round
Hours: Building: Mon–Fri 9 a.m.–5 p.m., Sat noon–5 p.m., Sun 1–5 p.m.; grounds: daily dawn–dusk
Prices: FREE; fees for special events
Direct.:   I-90 to exit 177; south on Martin Luther King, Jr. Blvd. across E. 105 St.; bear left around traffic circle; right on East Blvd.

● Strollers   ● Groups   Food Serv.   ● Parking   Birthdays
   Diap. Chg.   ● Picnic   ● Food Nearby   ● Pub. Trans.   ● Handicap. Access

Cleveland Center for Contemporary Art
Area: **Near East**   City: **Cleveland**   Ages: **3 & up**   Cost: **$–$$**

Founded in a dry cleaner's storefront in 1968, the Cleveland Center for Contemporary Art is now part of the Cleveland Play House complex. This is not a place for permanent exhibits, so each trip offers a chance to see something different. Past exhibits have ranged from life-size porcelain pigs facing a lectern to television monitors chanting "wal, wal, wal … nut, nut, nut …." With children in tow, be prepared for plenty of questions—answering them can be an interesting lesson in art. And be forewarned that the Center's commitment to the new can also be shocking. Exhibits here are well marked, and as a rule you are your own guide. The staff can be helpful or not so helpful. On one visit, they volunteered stories about the artists and their works while answering odd questions from our then-toddler son. But on a recent excursion we were shadowed by staff, making us feel about as welcome as the flu.

There is also a fine gift shop (with some fun children's items), an art rental program (for members), organized lectures, school programs, outdoor sculptures, and occasional special events suitable for family outings.

Address: 8501 Carnegie Ave. (adjacent to the Cleveland Play House complex)
Phone: (216) 421-8671
WWW: http://www.cybergate.net/~ccca
Season: Year-round
Hours: Wed–Fri 11 a.m.–6 p.m.; Sat–Sun noon–5 p.m.
Prices: FREE
Direct.:   I-90 eastbound to exit for Carnegie Ave.; right (east) on Carnegie; on left.
               I-90 westbound to exit for E. 55; south on E. 55; left (east) on Carnegie Ave.; on left (north) side of Carnegie.

   Strollers   ● Groups   Food Serv.   ● Parking   Birthdays
   Diap. Chg.   Picnic   ● Food Nearby   ● Pub. Trans.   ● Handicap. Access

MUSEUMS & HISTORY

Cleveland Institute of Art
Area: **Near East**   City: **Cleveland**   Ages: **5 & up**   Cost: **FREE–$$$**

The Cleveland Institute of Art is a professional college of fine arts, crafts, and design. For the general public there are exhibits, films, lectures, and classes through the continuing education program. For school-age children (grades 3–12) the Institute also offers a year-round schedule of classes in arts basics, drawing, painting, fiber, book making, photography, computer graphics, and more.

The special "Saturdays with the Children" series—offered twice a year, in fall and spring—is a wonderful introduction to the arts for younger children (ages 5–8) accompanied by parents. Activities cover a wide variety of arts, including collage, masks, and simple sculpture. Class size is limited, so reserve a spot early.

Address: 11141 East Blvd.
Phone: (216) 421-7000
WWW: http://www.zdepth.com/cia/
Season: Year-round
Hours: Gallery: Mon 9:30 a.m.–4 p.m., Tue–Sat 9:30 a.m.–9 p.m., Sun 1–4 p.m.
Prices: FREE; fee for classes
Direct.:   I-90 to Exit 177; south on Martin Luther King, Jr. Blvd. across E. 105 St.; bear left around traffic circle; right on East Blvd.

- Strollers   • Groups   Food Serv.   • Parking   Birthdays
  Diap. Chg.   Picnic   • Food Nearby   • Pub. Trans.   • Handicap. Access

Cleveland Museum of Art
Area: **Near East**   City: **Cleveland**   Ages: **All**   Cost: **FREE–$$**

Visiting the Cleveland Museum of Art is like going on a treasure hunt: if you are good with maps, lucky, or both, you will discover one of the finest collections of art in the country. But make a wrong turn and it is easy to get lost in the maze of galleries. Acknowledging this, museum officials have spruced up their map, "Finding Your Way," which you can find at the information desk as well as in several major corridors. (The guards are also friendly and helpful.) Two educational workbook packets published by the museum ("Looking Together: Introducing Young Children to the Cleveland Museum of Art" and the "Museum Sleuth" workbook) are for sale.

Still, we recommend having a plan of attack. For example, if medieval battle gear or Egyptian artifacts are of interest to you or your child, you can take in both the Armor Court and the Egyptian collection in a single trip to the second floor. (Thanks to a recent $1.25-million grant, the museum is reinstalling these popular collections.) As with any museum, alarms do go off if you venture too close to exhibits or attempt to climb enticing statues—we know firsthand.

The very best way we found to get to know the museum is through its program of Saturday classes designed for everyone from toddlers to teens. (Kids seem to own the place on Saturdays.) Art for Parent and Child (which we took twice) was one of the best museum experiences we have had together. For a taste of the classes, try Family Express, offered every third Sunday. It is a free program for parents and children that introduces art appreciation with a make-and-take project.

Other annual treasures for families are the offbeat Parade the Circle celebration in the summer, Chalk Festival in the fall, and candle-lit Holiday CircleFest in the winter. Also, the museum cafeteria, located on the lower level, is a cut above most. The courtyard, too, is a very pleasant place indeed.

MUSEUMS & HISTORY

Address:	11150 East Blvd.
Phone:	(216) 421-7340
WWW:	http://www.clemusart.com/
Season:	Year-round
Hours:	Tue, Thu–Fri 10 a.m.–5:45 p.m., Wed 10 a.m.–9:45 p.m., Sat 9 a.m.–4:45 p.m., Sun 1 p.m.–5:45 p.m.
Prices:	FREE, except for special exhibits
Direct.:	I-90 to exit 177; south on Martin Luther King, Jr. Blvd. across E. 105 St.; bear left around traffic circle; right on East Blvd.

- Strollers
- Diap. Chg.
- Groups
- Picnic
- Food Serv.
- Food Nearby
- Parking
- Pub. Trans.
- Birthdays
- Handicap. Access

Cleveland Museum of Natural History
Area: **Near East**   City: **Cleveland**   Ages: **All**   Cost: **$–$$**

The Cleveland Museum of Natural History boasts a wide array of activities, lectures, and classes. Into dinosaurs? No problem. Head to Kirtland Hall, which has complete skeletons of a Mastodon, an Allosaurus, and a Nanotyrannus, among others. Astronomy? For an additional $1.50, 30-minute-long planetarium shows are well worth the money. The cavernous Sears Hall houses multilevel exhibits of indigenous peoples from all over the world in historical surroundings. Mounted wolves and mountain lions lurk above glass-enclosed cases of masks, amulets, figurines, and pottery. At toddler level, dioramas depict hunts, different styles of shelter, and fire building. While some exhibits may seem a bit static, renovation plans promise to bring more interactivity and visual appeal in coming years. Scheduled to open in late 1997 is the Reinberger Hall of Earth and Planetary Exploration. Another updated exhibit will present what is known about geologic formations on other planets in the solar system.

Be prepared to spend some time here, because there is a lot to see for youngsters and parents alike. The regularly scheduled live animal programs are a favorite with families. Also very popular are year-round classes for ages 4–18 covering everything from astronomy to rain forest ecosystems.

A few of the museum's displays could use a face-lift, or at least better signage. If we had not visited the hands-on rain forest exhibit in the lower level Discovery Center, we would never have found the museum's prehistoric amber collection.

The museum can easily handle weekend crowds, but the same cannot be said for its modest parking lot; expect a hike if you come after 11:30 a.m. Don't forget to browse the museum store—it's a good one.

Address: 1 Wade Oval Dr.
Phone: (216) 231-4600
WWW: http://www.cmnh.org/
Season: Year-round
Hours: Mon–Sat 10 a.m.–5 p.m.; Sun noon–5 p.m.; Wed (Sept–May) 10 a.m.–10 p.m.; closed holidays
Prices: $6, $4 for ages 5–17, seniors, & students with ID; Free under age 5; Free admission Tue & Th 3-5 p.m.
Direct.: I-90 to exit 177; south on Martin Luther King, Jr. Blvd. across E. 105 St.; bear left around traffic circle; right on East Blvd.

- Strollers
- Diap. Chg.
- Groups
- Picnic
- Food Serv.
- Food Nearby
- Parking
- Pub. Trans.
- Birthdays
- Handicap. Access

Photo: Jonathan Wayne

Cleveland Police Museum
Area: **Downtown**   City: **Cleveland**   Ages: **8 & up**   Cost: **FREE**

This museum houses a growing collection of historical items pertaining to Cleveland's public safety history, specifically that of the Cleveland Police Department. Collection items include a revolver signed out to Eliot Ness, a 1920s jail cell, lots of confiscated weapons, uniform displays, and two vintage Harley Davidson motorcycles.

10 Great Things to Do...

To Celebrate Cleveland History:

◉ Tour the Western Reserve Historical Society—especially during annual Family Days. (p. 70)

◉ Watch a glassblower or cheese maker work the way settlers did at Hale Farm and Village. (p. 46)

◉ Walk the self-guided tour through Lake View Cemetery. (p. 52)

◉ Tour the greenhouses and grounds of the Rockefeller Greenhouse. (p. 62)

◉ Taste fresh, hot apple butter at Century Village. (p. 33)

◉ Visit 19th-century Cleveland at Dunham Tavern Museum, still standing at its original Euclid Ave. location. (p. 42)

◉ Dig for arrowheads at the Indian Museum of Lake County. (p. 49)

◉ Try on a dinosaur head at the McKinley Museum. (p. 55)

◉ Tour the theaters at Playhouse Square Center. (p. 153)

◉ Try square dancing at the Frostville Museum. (p. 44)

As there are no real kids' programs or hands-on activities here, this museum is better suited for elementary school children or school groups especially interested in the subject matter.

Address: Justice Center, 1300 Ontario St. (first floor, adjacent to Ontario St. entrance)
Phone: (216) 623-5055
Season: Year-round
Hours: Mon–Fri 10 a.m.–4 p.m.; guided tours by reservation only
Prices: FREE
Direct.: I-90 eastbound: Exit 171B, north on Ontario St.
I-90 westbound: take SR 2 west to E. 9 St.; left (south) on E. 9 to Lakeside Ave.; right (west) to Ontario St.; Justice Center at corner of Lakeside and Ontario.

| Strollers | • Groups | Food Serv. | • Parking | Birthdays |
| Diap. Chg. | Picnic | • Food Nearby | • Pub. Trans. | • Handicap. Access |

MUSEUMS & HISTORY

Crawford Auto-Aviation Museum (Western Reserve Hist. Soc.)
Area: **Near East**   City: **Cleveland**   Ages: **3 & up**   Cost: **$–$$**

Museum founder and former industrialist Frederick Crawford collected early automobiles because then, unlike today, no model ever looked like another. Therein lies the strength of this museum: each of the dozens of cars on display represents a distinct form of early automotive excellence.

The museum's collection features nearly 200 automobiles, aircraft, bicycles, and other vehicles. Split between two levels, this eclectic collection boasts leaders in a variety of categories, including the oldest known car in North America, the Parisian-made 1895 Panhard et Levassor. On the top floor, special emphasis is given to the automobiles produced in Northeast Ohio in the late 1800s and early 1900s, when Cleveland was a leading national automotive center. The museum displays a 1932 Peerless (the last passenger car made in Cleveland) as its centerpiece. A prototype, it is the only one of its kind and has an estimated value of $2.5 million. Two new and semi-permanent exhibits featuring White Motors and the National Air Races also occupy the upper floor. They are interactive (with computer monitors and recorded interviews) as well as memorabilia-filled, with authentic trucks and airplanes on display. "Working at White" also features interactive art for children.

Downstairs you will find most of the older cars (up to 1930), along with a full-size replica of a late 1800s Main Street. Rotating exhibits of motorcycles, roadsters, race cars, concept cars, model trains, and other transportation-related items also appear on the lower level.

For the budding car buff, detailed information is provided on each exhibit. While there are computer screens and art boards to touch, much of the Crawford Auto-Aviation Museum is an eyes-only experience. Yet to appeal to younger visitors, special events and workshops are scheduled as part of the Crawford Kids Club.

Address: 10825 East Blvd.
Phone: (216) 721-5722
WWW: http://www.wrhs.org
Season: Year-round
Hours: Daily 10 a.m.–5 p.m.
Prices: $6, $5 for seniors, $4 children ages 6–12 (Free age 5 and under); members admitted FREE
Direct.: I-90 to exit 177; south on Martin Luther King, Jr. Blvd. across E. 105 St.; bear left around traffic circle; right on East Blvd.; on left, parking in rear (follow signs).

- Strollers   ● Groups   ● Food Serv.   ● Parking   Birthdays
  Diap. Chg.   ● Picnic   ● Food Nearby   ● Pub. Trans. ● Handicap. Access

Photo by Matthew Kocsis / courtesy of Western Reserve Hist. Soc.

Cultural Center for the Arts
Area: **Farther South** City: **Canton**   Ages: **All**   Cost: **$**

The centerpiece of the Cultural Center for the Arts, the Canton Museum of Art is a small, brightly lit two-room gallery hosting various traveling shows and a small permanent exhibit. When we visited, a collection of pots, bowls, and assorted ceramics was on display. Classes are offered year-long for families and children (preschool and up) and range from clay workshops to cartooning and jewelry making.

Next door, the Canton Ballet performs in the Palace Theatre October through March. Post-production parties are regularly held for adults and children. Past performances have included *Dracula—The Ballet*, *The Nutcracker*, *Cinderella*, and the "Emerging Choreographers' Showcase."

Also performing in the facility are the Canton Symphony Orchestra (limited schedule) and the Players' Guild of Canton. Family theater productions have included *The Wonderful Wizard of Oz*, *Raggedy Ann and*

Andy, Charlie and the Chocolate Factory, and *Cinderella.* Acting classes for first-graders through adults are available and include Creative Drama, Improvisation, Scene Study, Vocal Production, and Actor's Gym.

Address: 1001 Market Ave. N
Phone: (330) 453-7666 (Canton Museum of Art); (330) 455-7220 (Canton Ballet box office); (330) 452-2094 (Canton Symphony Orchestra;, (330) 453-7617 (Players' Guild of Canton)
WWW: http://2.4.210.221.2/Canton_Museum_of_Art
Season: Year-round
Hours: Tue–Sat 10 a.m.–5 p.m., Tue–Thu evenings 7–9 p.m., Sun 1–5 p.m.
Prices: $2.50 adults, $1.25 seniors, students & children; Tue FREE
Direct.:   I-77 to Exit 107 (US 62); east on US 62; south on Market Ave. for 18 blocks.

| • Strollers | • Groups | Food Serv. | • Parking | Birthdays |
| Diap. Chg. | Picnic | • Food Nearby | • Pub. Trans. | • Handicap. Access |

Dittrick Museum of Medical History
Area: **Near East**   City: **Cleveland**   Ages: **8 & up**   Cost: **FREE**

Located in the historic Allen Medical Library building on the campus of Case Western Reserve University, the Dittrick is stocked with items and exhibits pertaining to the early practice of medicine, both locally and nationally. Small but informative, and great for kids and teens with an interest in science and medicine.

As there are no real kids' programs or hands-on activities here, this museum is better suited for elementary-school children (and up) or school groups especially interested in the subject matter.

Address: 11000 Euclid Ave.
Phone: (216) 368-3648
Season: Year-round
Hours: Mon–Fri 10 a.m.–5 p.m.; closed most holidays
Prices: FREE
Direct.:   I-90 to Exit 177; south on Martin Luther King, Jr. Blvd.; left on Euclid Ave.

| Strollers | • Groups | Food Serv. | Parking | Birthdays |
| Diap. Chg. | Picnic | • Food Nearby | • Pub. Trans. | • Handicap. Access |

Dunham Tavern Museum
Area: **Near East**   City: **Cleveland**   Ages: **5 & up**   Cost: **$**

The Dunham Tavern is the oldest building in Cuyahoga County still standing in its original location. The main structure, completed in 1824, survived Euclid Avenue's many changes—first from rough path to Cleveland's most glamorous residential street, later into a bustling commercial thoroughfare. The Tavern operated originally as a stagecoach stop on the Buffalo-Cleveland-Detroit Road and was quite a busy place. Converted to a museum in 1938, it still preserves the atmosphere of an early meeting place. The Dunham staff customizes activities for the age range and size of visiting groups.

Address: 6709 Euclid Ave.
Phone: (216) 431-1060
WWW: http://www.multiverse.com:80/tavern/
Season: Year-round
Hours: Wed & Sun 1–4 p.m. by arrangement
Prices: $2, $1 ages 6–16, no charge under age 6
Direct.: I-90 eastbound to Exit 173B (Chester Ave./US 322); right (east) on Chester; right (south) on E. 66; left (east) on Euclid Ave. (US 20).
I-90 westbound to Exit 175 (E. 55 St.); south on E. 55; left (east) on Euclid Ave. Parking on side and in the rear.

| Strollers | ● Groups | Food Serv. | ● Parking | Birthdays |
| Diap. Chg. | ● Picnic | ● Food Nearby | ● Pub. Trans. | Handicap. Access |

Fairport Marine Museum (Fairport Harbor Historical Society)
Area: **Far East**   City: **Fairport Harbor**   Ages: **6 & up**   Cost: **$**

A ship's wheel in a re-created pilot house is the best attraction here for kids. The entire exhibit is equipped with nautical instruments from the early 1900s, more than enough for a successful pretend sea voyage.

With a 60-foot spiral staircase of 69 steps, the route up to the top of the lighthouse can be challenging. However, there is a reward: the observation platform offers a splendid view of Lake Erie and the harbor. You may even want to bring a camera, especially on clear, sunny days.

Navigation instruments, marine charts, paintings of ships, tools, models, and half-hulls of lake freighters are just a few of the items in the museum's collection.

Address: 129 Second St.
Phone: (216†) 354-4825
Season: Memorial Day to mid-Sept
Hours: Wed, Sat, Sun, holidays 1–6 p.m.
Prices: $2, $1 students & seniors, Free under age 6
Direct.: SR 2 to exit for Painesville/Fairport Harbor (Richmond Rd.); north on Richmond across the Grand River to Second St. (Richmond becomes High St. after East St.); on corner of High and Second.

| Strollers | ● Groups | Food Serv. | Parking | Birthdays |
| Diap. Chg. | ● Picnic | ● Food Nearby | ● Pub. Trans. | Handicap. Access |

Frostville Museum

Area: **West**   City: **North Olmsted**   Ages: **All**   Cost: **FREE**

This collection of early-19th-century buildings is named for Elias Carrington Frost, who settled in Olmsted in 1819. Located in the Rocky River Reservation of the Cleveland Metroparks (see separate listing), the small settlement is run by the dedicated volunteers of the Olmsted Historical Society. Its displays depict early life in the Western Reserve and include a one-room cabin with a center-cooking fireplace, a furnished Victorian farmhouse display, and a general store.

This is mostly a look-not-touch group of exhibits, so families might choose to visit during one of the various annual celebrations. Summer brings Friday night square dances; Christmas is celebrated with hot cider, cookies, and decorations. (Although there are gravel walkways, be sure to wear boots in the winter months.) A general store offers period items for sale.

Address: 24101 Cedar Point Rd.
Phone: (216†) 777-0059
Season: Memorial Day–Oct; special events during week
Hours: Sun 2–5 p.m. & by special appt.; group tours available
Prices: FREE
Direct.:   I-480 to Exit 6 (SR 252); south on SR 252; left on Columbia Rd. right (east) on Cedar Point Rd. to bottom of hill; on right.

- Strollers   • Groups   Food Serv.   • Parking   Birthdays
  Diap. Chg.   • Picnic   Food Nearby   Pub. Trans.   • Handicap. Access

Great Lakes Science Center

Area: **Downtown**   City: **Cleveland**   Ages: **All**   Cost: **$$**

Encompassing 165,000 square feet with 300 interactive exhibits, the Great Lakes Science Center is this region's big daddy of interactive museums. Taking its cue from the area's ever-changing climate, environment, and industry, everything from the museum's ample windows overlooking Lake Erie to the exhibits themselves is designed to give families a better understanding of how things work in and around the Great Lakes. Weekdays and early hours continue to be the best times for visits with small children and preschoolers.

The Science Center's environmental exhibits, located on the lower level, take up one-third of the museum's space. There, families can pilot an ore boat up a scaled-down replica of the Cuyahoga River or "play" a 20-foot-long sculpture that uses vertical pipes to aurally demonstrate the size of the Great Lakes. Next door is the auditorium-like Situation Room, where 25 computer terminals are linked to each other and to a 25-foot video grid at the front of the room, on which families can play Great Lakes Jeopardy or Environmental Bingo.

Courtesy of Great Lakes Science Center

Above, at ground level, are the Biomedical and Infotech areas, where a computer-aided batting cage can assess your swing and where, thanks to digital technology, you can move your eyes, ears, and other facial features around on a computer screen. On the top level, step inside a cauldron and watch how steel is made, or lift a 2,000-pound crushed car by a single strand of kevlar. Those under 48 inches tall will want to venture to the Polymer Playhouse, where they can wind through a maze full of balls and discover stretchy, sticky, bouncy, and other types of polymers.

The six-story-tall OMNIMAX Theater, which can be visited separately without having to enter the museum, shows a series of science, natural history, and technology films, all manipulating OMNIMAX's own multi-sensation technology. A lower-level restaurant area, with ample outdoor lakeside seating and walkways, is a popular gathering place. The gift shop is a good one.

Birthday parties here are a virtual science bash. Party-goers have the run of the place (with a staff guide) and can conduct age-appropriate experiments in a private party room.

Address: 601 Erieside Ave. (North Coast Harbor)
Phone: (216) 694-2000
WWW: http://www.greatscience.com
Season: Year-round
Hours: Daily 9:30 a.m.–5:30 p.m.; OMNIMAX shows vary
Prices: $6.75, $4.50
Direct.: I-90 to SR 2 west to exit for E. 9 St.; right (north) on E. 9; left on Erieside; on right, adjacent to Rock and Roll Hall of Fame and Museum. Parking at Port Authority lots, North Point garage, E. 9 St. Garage, and Burke Lakefront Airport.

● *Strollers*   ● *Groups*   ● *Food Serv.*   *Parking*   ● *Birthdays*
● *Diap. Chg.*   ● *Picnic*   ● *Food Nearby*   ● *Pub. Trans.*   ● *Handicap. Access*

Hale Farm and Village (Western Reserve Historical Society)
Area: **Far South**   City: **Bath**   Ages: **All**   Cost: **$-$$**

This replicated village, dubbed a living history museum, allows you to imagine the everyday lives of Ohio's settlers in the mid-1800s. The buildings were moved from all over Northeast Ohio to re-create a working village. Painstaking restoration of homes, gardens, barns, and even a little one-room log schoolhouse makes it work.

Scattered throughout the village are live demonstrations by blacksmiths, glassblowers, cheesemakers, and other period craftspeople. Guides are stationed in the homes and gardens to answer questions. The setting in Cuyahoga Valley is wooded, hilly, and serene, and although the houses and demonstrations are not set up for the youngest visitors, running and touching are encouraged outside.

On a recent visit, we came prepared with a picnic lunch and settled on a hill overlooking the woods. Later we stopped for a treat at the small store and snack bar. We extended our stay to listen to an impromptu concert of folk music.

Hale Farm's special events are very popular. An annual Children's Day in mid-summer features 19th-century games and activities; a folk festival brings musicians to the site.

Address: 2686 Oak Hill Rd., P.O. Box 296
Phone: (330) 666-3711
Season: May–Oct, plus special events
Hours: Tue–Sat 10 a.m.–5 p.m.; Sun 12–5 p.m.
Prices: $9, $7.50 seniors, $5.50 ages 6–12, Free 5 and under
Direct.: I-77 to Exit143 (Richfield); right on Wheatley Rd.; right on Brecksville Rd.; left on Ira Rd.; left on Oak Hill to Hale Farm.

● Strollers   ● Groups   ● Food Serv.   ● Parking   Birthdays
● Diap. Chg.   ● Picnic   Food Nearby   Pub. Trans.   Handicap. Access

Courtesy of Hale Farm and Village

The Health Museum of Cleveland
Area: **Near East**   City: **Cleveland**   Ages: **3 & up**   Cost: **$**

If your child has been barraging you with questions about how the human ear hears, or how the heart works, or how babies are born, this is the place to go. The Health Museum of Cleveland's exhibits are matter-of-fact and loaded with detail.

Several exhibits will interest 3- or 4-year-olds, such as Touch Island and the Children's Health Fair, but this museum is best-suited for children ages 6 and up. And though the layout is logical and there are things to do and learn about, most of the exhibits are in need of modernization: the audio cones that explain how things work are at least a decade old, descriptions of how to use exhibits are cumbersome, and the computers and videotapes need several minutes to reboot or rewind. Much better are the frequently featured traveling exhibits and programs which supplement the 150 permanent exhibits.

Special programs for families are scheduled throughout the year and are worth investigating, as is a summer program for preschoolers and up. Year-round, the museum staff conducts classes exploring such subjects as sight, hearing, and smell. Also available are day camps, birthday parties, and several family and older children/teen programs designed to promote fitness and health education.

Address: 8911 Euclid Ave.
Phone: (216) 231-5010
Season: Year-round
Hours: Mon–Fri 9 a.m.–5 p.m.; Sat 10 a.m.–5 p.m.; Sun noon–5 p.m.
Prices: $4.50 adults, $3 ages 6–17, college students w/ ID, and seniors; Free age 5 & under with adult family member
Direct.: I-90 eastbound to Exit 172D (Carnegie Ave.); right (east) on Carnegie; left (north) on E. 89 St. for 1 block to Euclid; on corner of E. 89 and Euclid. I-90 westbound to Exit 175 (E. 55 St.); south on E. 55; left (east) on Euclid Ave.

● Strollers   ● Groups   Food Serv.   ● Parking   ● Birthdays
● Diap. Chg.   Picnic   ● Food Nearby   ● Pub. Trans.   ● Handicap. Access

Hoover Historical Center
Area: **Farther South** City: **North Canton**   Ages: **3 & up**   Cost: **FREE**

This small museum is among the most specialized collections in Ohio. Inside the completely restored, Victorian-era farmhouse—the boyhood home of William H. Hoover, founder of the Hoover Company—is the world's most extensive collection of antique vacuum cleaners. They range from 1800s sweepers to early electric models—some weighing nearly 100 pounds.

What makes the Hoover Historical Center an attraction for families is its schedule of annual events. They include shadow-puppet performances, a program of storytelling for children geared to ages 4–7 (held outside in the herb garden during the summer with a snack provided), and holiday festivals. Most events are free. Also worth mentioning are the elaborate herb gardens maintained by the center's Herb Society.

Address: 2225 Easton Ave. NW
Phone: (330) 499-0287
Season: Year-round
Hours: Tue–Sun 1–5 p.m.
Prices: FREE
Direct.: I-77 to Exit 111 (North Canton/Canal Fulton); east on Portage Rd. through North Canton (follow signs to Walsh College); right on Whipple St.; left on Maple St. (becomes Easton Ave.); across from Walsh College.

Strollers	● Groups	Food Serv.	● Parking	Birthdays
Diap. Chg.	● Picnic	● Food Nearby	● Pub. Trans.	● Handicap. Access

Hower House Victorian Mansion
Area: **Far South**   City: **Akron**   Ages: **School age**   Cost: **$**

That the Hower House remains a historic home is an accomplishment in itself. Instead of letting the splendid 28-room mansion become a fraternity house, Grace Hower Crawford deeded it to the University of Akron, provided she be allowed to live out her final years in it. After her death in the 1980s, the school restored the house, built in 1871 by industrialist John Henry Hower, using funds donated by two volunteer groups that worked on the renovation.

Inside and out, the home now gleams and shines just as it did in the days when Hower lived there. Wealthy and well-traveled, the Howers fitted their home lavishly. Inside, a cupboard is inlaid with mother of pearl, and chandeliers hang from the ceiling in every room. The exterior features a sloping mansard roof, soaring tower, and wrap-around porch.

For families with younger kids less keen on hands-off history, there are special events (such as storytimes) throughout the year and a Christmas display and celebration with cookies and wassail for everyone. Call for the most current schedule information.

Address: 60 Fir Hill
Phone: (330) 972-6909
Season: Feb–Dec; closed major holidays
Hours: Tours: Wed–Sat noon–3:30 p.m., Sun 1 p.m.–4 p.m.
Prices: $4 adults, $3.50 seniors, $2 students, children under 6 Free
Direct.: I-77 to exit for SR 8 in Akron; north on SR 8 to exit for Buchtel Ave.; west on Buchtel; right (north) on Fir Hill.

Strollers	● Groups	Food Serv.	● Parking	Birthdays
Diap. Chg.	Picnic	● Food Nearby	● Pub. Trans.	Handicap. Access

Indian Museum of Lake County

Area: **Far East**   City: **Painesville**   Ages: **3 & up**   Cost: **$**

What began in 1980 as the hobby of Gwen and William King and a group of Indian culture enthusiasts (the Lake County chapter of the Archaeological Society of Ohio) has thus far attracted more than 80,000 visitors. It has become a favorite of the grade-school field trip circuit: during the week it is typically filled with youngsters listening to stories and legends about Indian culture and beliefs.

The museum traces the development of Indian tribal groups who lived here between 22,000 B.C. and 1600 A.D., in addition to the history of today's Native Americans from 1800 to the present. Several hands-on activities are excellent for parents and children to work on together. Our favorite was a large wooden learning board filled with colorful pictures of Indian dwellings. The goal: match tribes with their homes.

School-age children (grades 4 and up) are invited to participate in a mini-archaeological dig. Several sandboxes—each containing bones, teeth, or arrowheads—come equipped with brushes so that children can gently brush off the sand to reveal what lies beneath. For preschoolers, there are grinding bins equipped with stones and dried corn to grind into corn flour.

Although the museum is housed in just one room, its exhibits are well laid out and extensive. Displays cover an array of artifacts from North American indigenous cultures, including ceremonial masks, baskets, beadwork, and other crafts. A reproduction of a Hopewell Shaman (an elaborately adorned medicine man) and colorful totem pole are striking—toddlers will be either fascinated or terrified. Some displays are changed annually to feature unique Native American cultures.

Tour programs can be arranged for adults and children ages 4 and up by reservation only.

Address: 391 W. Washington St.
Phone: (216†) 352-1911
Season: Year-round
Hours: Mon–Fri 10 a.m.–4 p.m., Sat–Sun 1–4 p.m.; closed holiday weekends & during Lake Erie College winter break (mid-Dec through mid-Jan)
Prices: $1.50 adults, $1 students & seniors, preschool ages Free
Direct.: I-90 to Exit 200 (SR 44); north on SR 44 first exit for SR 84; right at top of exit ramp; left on Chestnut St.; right (east) at dead end on Mentor Ave. (US 20) in Painesville for 1/2 mile.; right into the campus of Lake Erie College; adjacent to Morley Music Hall.

| • Strollers | • Groups | Food Serv. | • Parking | Birthdays |
| Diap. Chg. | Picnic | • Food Nearby | • Pub. Trans. | • Handicap. Access |

Inland Seas Maritime Museum (Great Lakes Historical Society)
Area: **Far West**   City: **Vermilion**   Ages: **All**   Cost: **$**

If you're interested in Great Lakes history, this is your place. There are paintings, artifacts (such as marine engines and tools), and detailed models of Great Lakes vessels. Vermilion, possessing one of the best natural harbors on Lake Erie, once competed with Cleveland for maritime traffic. Now, visitors can watch that traffic pass by from the museum's fully equipped freighter pilot house overlooking the lakefront.

The Inland Seas Maritime Museum was created in 1953 and housed in the converted Commodore Wakefield Mansion. Acquisitions increased and, in 1968, a modern two-story section was added. The museum now boasts one of the largest collections of marine engines in the United States, including a 14-foot-high harbor tug steam engine built in 1913. Other good stuff: the lighthouse exhibit and a scale model of the 729-foot *Edmund Fitzgerald*, the ill-fated freighter that went down in Lake Superior in 1975. An adult-child boat-building program results in a seaworthy boat built from scratch over a weekend.

Address:	480 Main St.
Phone:	(216†) 967-3467; (800) 893-1485
Season:	Year-round
Hours:	Daily 10 a.m.–5 p.m.
Prices:	$5 adults, $4 seniors, $3 ages 6–16, Free ages 5 & under
Direct.:	SR 2 west to exit for SR 60/Vermilion; north on SR 60 (becomes Main St. in Vermilion); follow to end; on left.

- Strollers
  - Diap. Chg.
- Groups
- Picnic
- Food Serv.
- Food Nearby
- Parking
  - Pub. Trans.
- Birthdays
- Handicap. Access

Inventure Place & National Inventors Hall of Fame
Area: **Far South**   City: **Akron**   Ages: **All**   Cost: **$$**

Inventure Place is one of Ohio's premier hands-on institutions. Everything from its slick exhibits to its first-rate architecture has raised the quality of family museum-going in this state to new heights. The mission of the $38-million museum is to get children to "play" science the way they would play games or sports. It has succeeded.

The museum design funnels traffic in two directions: up to the National Inventors Hall of Fame and down to the main exhibit area located below street level. Once below, kids will immediately be drawn to a frame holding a series of simple plumbing tubes and stainless steel detours that, if connected properly, will allow gravity to keep a golf ball in motion. (Off to the right is a rest area for adults, furnished with comfortable chairs and an eclectic collection of coffee-table books.) Next is a series of exhibits devoted to fiber optics, magnetics, and lasers.

The genius of the place is that they have truly made science fun. Our

6-year-old spent 20 minutes alone repositioning little mirrors refracting beams of red light through a steamy mist. This of course prompted a series of questions about lasers, lights, and beams that unfortunately could not be answered. If there is a weakness here, it is the lack of explanation (an element designed "to spur creativity"). If you were clueless on the way in as to how things such as a magnetic resonance scanner work, you will exit in almost as much ignorance. (A couple of free-standing personal computers do offer some help.) Other exhibit highlights include a workshop area where kids can dissect old electronic castaways such as typewriters and computers or assemble new creations using any one of dozens of parts from the material-rich bins.

The National Inventors Hall of Fame occupies several levels overlooking the main exhibit space. Compared to the action in the exhibition area, the Hall is rather sleepy and low tech, with pictures of inductees hanging on the walls. There are several interesting video displays, including one on how a market was created for the Polaroid camera, but these are too sparse.

The small green signs directing you to Inventure Place are too sparsely spaced around town to offer much help. Aim for the University of Akron and look for the curved stainless-steel wall.

Address: 221 S. Broadway
Phone: (330) 762-4463; (800) 968-IDEA
WWW: http://www.invent.org/
Season: Year-round
Hours: Mar 24–Labor Day: Mon–Sat 9 a.m.–5 p.m., Sun noon–5 p.m. After Labor Day
               Wed–Sat 9 a.m.–5 p.m., Sun noon–5 p.m.
Prices: $7.50 adults, $6 seniors and ages 3-8, under 3 Free; group rate $5.50
Direct.:   I-76/I-77 to exit for Main St./Broadway Ave.; north on Broadway 1.5 miles; on
               right (east) side; parking just past the building.

- Strollers   ● Groups   ● Food Serv.   Parking   ● Birthdays
- Diap. Chg.   Picnic   ● Food Nearby   ● Pub. Trans.   ● Handicap. Access

Photo: Bruce Ford / Courtesy of City of Akron

MUSEUMS &
HISTORY

Lake County History Center
Area: **Far East**   City: **Kirtland Hills**   Ages: **5 & up**   Cost: **FREE–$**

From September to November and again from April to June, children can be transported back in time with the "Pioneer School" program, where staff members decked out in pioneer garb let kids experience everything from candle making to colonial-style lunch preparation. No microwaves here; kids must make, then bake, their own johnnycakes, starting by hand-grinding the corn. This program offers maximum hands-on experience.

Non-school groups and visitors of all ages get some of the same experiences by visiting the main museum and its galleries, two Indian cabins, log cabins, and a one-room schoolhouse in the nine-building living history compound. Antique music boxes and toys are to be added to the museum's collection in 1997.

Christmas on the Western Reserve, with the staff aided by high school volunteers, offers a day of crafts and cookies for ages 5–12. During the summer (late July), look for the Little Mountain Folk Festival, which features craft demonstrations, music, and living history exhibits and performances. All summer long, 1860s-style Base Ball is played, and in September hundreds of Civil War reenactors gather for the largest Civil War encampment and battle reenactment in Northeast Ohio.

Address: 8610 King Memorial Rd.
Phone: (216†) 255-8979
Season: Year-round
Hours: Tue–Fri 10 a.m.–5 p.m.; Sat–Sun 1–5 p.m. (closed weekends Jan–Mar)
Prices: Donation requested for museum tour; nominal fee for youth, preschool programs
Direct.:   I-90 to Exit 193 (SR 306); north on SR 306 for 2 blocks; east on SR 84 2.5 miles; south on Little Mountain Rd.; follow signs.

- ● Strollers   ● Groups   Food Serv.   ● Parking   Birthdays
- ● Diap. Chg.   ● Picnic   ● Food Nearby   Pub. Trans.   ● Handicap. Access

Lake View Cemetery
Area: **East**   City: **Cleveland**   Ages: **3 & up**   Cost: **FREE–$**

Many famous people are buried in Lake View Cemetery, from President James Garfield to sports figures to Cleveland mayors and business tycoons (including John D. Rockefeller). It is also a 285-acre arboretum. While you can see much on your own, a guided tour here runs from 45 minutes to an hour and includes a walk through the landscape, the Gothic and Romanesque-style Garfield Monument, and Wade Chapel, which features exceptional glass tilework by Louis Tiffany.

Children may be interested in the ancient trees (most are marked by botanical tags), the statues and monuments, and a quarry located on the grounds. There is also a good view of Lake Erie and the downtown skyline—especially after a climb up the towering Garfield Monument.

Rubbings of gravestones are allowed with adult supervision; the cemetery provides the supplies. Reservations are advised for everyone and are necessary for groups, which can include 10 to 30 people.

MUSEUMS & HISTORY

Address:	12316 Euclid Ave.
Phone:	(216) 421-2665
Season:	Apr 1–Nov 19
Hours:	Daily 7:30 a.m.–5 p.m.
Prices:	Donation requested
Direct.:	I-90 to Exit 173B (Chester Ave./US 322); east on Chester to Euclid Ave. in University Circle; left (east) on Euclid Ave. (US 20) to main entrance on right (after RTA tracks). Admin. office on right.
	From east suburbs, follow Mayfield Rd. (US 322) to Kenilworth Rd. entrance.

Strollers	● Groups	Food Serv.	● Parking	Birthdays
Diap. Chg.	Picnic	● Food Nearby	● Pub. Trans.	● Handicap. Access

Photo: Jonathan Wayne

Lawnfield, James A. Garfield National Historic Site and Visitor Center (Western Reserve Historical Society)

Area: **Far East**   City: **Mentor**   Ages: **5 & up**   Cost: **$**

The spirit of James A. Garfield lives on in Lawnfield, home of the former president. No, the house is not haunted; a real live member of the family works here. Garfield's great-grandson, James R. Garfield, now in his 70s, is a groundskeeper who will talk about the history here with anyone who asks. Currently, the entire mansion is closed as it undergoes an extensive restoration. It is scheduled to reopen in late 1998. The carriage house museum/visitor center remains open.

This one-story farmhouse was built in 1832 and expanded in the 1870s and 1880s. It was bought by the future 20th president of the United States in 1876; while campaigning in 1880, he used the front porch for speech making. Each of 12 rooms is dressed in late 19th-century style; together they set the stage for Victorian-era make-believe. The library is a favorite spot, with walls of books from Garfield's own collection. The carriage house is complete with five period carriages. (Children often ask whether the house has secret passages; the answer is no.) The newly added museum/visitor center, built inside the 1893 carriage house on the property, features historic exhibits and other audio/visual information about President Garfield and the period. Audio components allow visitors to listen to Garfield's speech to the 1880 Republican convention or hear his thoughts on slavery.

Address:	8095 Mentor Ave.
Phone:	(216†) 255-8722
Season:	Year-round
Hours:	Tue–Sat 10 a.m.–5 p.m.; Sun noon–5 p.m.
Prices:	$4.00, $2.50 ages 6–12, no charge under age 6
Direct.:	I-90 to Exit 193 (SR 306, Mentor-Kirtland Rd.); north on SR 306 for 2 miles; right (east) on US 20 (Mentor Ave.) for 2 miles; on left (north) side.

● Strollers	● Groups	Food Serv.	● Parking	Birthdays
● Diap. Chg.	● Picnic	● Food Nearby	● Pub. Trans.	● Handicap. Access

Mad River & NKP Railroad Society Museum
Area: **Farther West**   City: **Bellevue**   Ages: **All**   Cost: **$**

As part of a bicentennial project, the Mad River railroad depot reopened in 1976 and has since become the last stop for many of the trains that once passed through. In all, there are 35 vintage rail cars and engines, a 19th-century rural American depot, a watchman's tower, and, of course, a gift shop.

What kinds of cars are we talking about? There are diesel engines, refrigerated produce cars, freight, dining, and mail cars, troop transports, and the nation's first domed observation car.

The museum collection includes not only several train cars and a caboose where conductors lived, but also uniforms, timetables, lanterns, china, and locks. Also, there is a troop sleeper filled with wartime memorabilia.

Address:	233 York St.
Phone:	(419) 483-2222
Season:	Memorial Day–Labor Day, weekends in May, Sep & Oct
Hours:	Daily 1–5 p.m.
Prices:	Admission charged

Direct.:   Ohio Turnpike (I-80/I-90) to Exit 6A (SR 4); south on SR 4; right (west) on SR
113; in Bellevue, SR 113 becomes E. Main St.; left on Kilbourne, then left (south)
on York St.

● Strollers	● Groups	Food Serv.	● Parking	Birthdays
● Diap. Chg.	● Picnic	● Food Nearby	Pub. Trans.	● Handicap. Access

MUSEUMS &
HISTORY

McKinley Museum of History, Science, & Industry
Area: **Farther South**   City: **Canton**   Ages: **3 & up**   Cost: **FREE–$$**

Since the addition of Discover World, the McKinley Museum has
become a winner for families and well worth a special trip.

The original part of the museum is devoted to re-creating the late-
Victorian era of President William McKinley. Upstairs, the Museum of
History includes several replicated early-American rooms along with a
Street of Shops lined with life-size stores.

Your kids, however, will want to head straight to the basement. (You
should, too, if your time is limited to an hour or so.) First stop: Natural
History Island, a land of fossils and skeletons guarded by a roaring, life-
size Allosaurus named Alice. (Alice is programmed to stop every three
minutes, to allow younger kids to pass.) A cave-like burrow allows you
to climb up and try on the skeleton head of a Tyrannosaurus Rex. At
Ecology Island a massive oak tree, trickling water, and bird sounds set
the mood. A series of ponds equipped with inverted periscopes allow
even the smallest of visitors to glimpse the underwater life. We spent the
most time at Spacestation Earth, tinkering with the various lasers, mag-
nets, and pumps.

Before you visit, call to check on special activities. There are regu-
larly scheduled sound shows, electric shows, and sessions with live ani-
mals, as well as a make-and-take project series for ages 5 and up.

In the adjacent Hoover-Prive Planetarium, sky productions change
regularly. (Children under 5 are not permitted in the planetarium.) The
towering National Memorial provides a good climb for all ages—a great
way to work out the kinks from a car ride.

Address: 800 McKinley Monument Dr. NW
Phone: (330) 455-7043
Season: Year-round
Hours: Mon–Sat 9 a.m.–5 p.m., Sun noon–5 p.m.; Summer hours (mid-Jun–Labor
Day): Mon–Sat 9 a.m.–6 p.m, Sun noon–6 p.m.
Prices: Museum: $6, $5 seniors, $4 ages 3–18, no charge under age 3; National
Memorial: FREE
Direct.:   I-77 to Exit 106; left at first light off highway, stay in far right lane; right at
Monument Park (through yellow gates); follow road to end; right down lane to
monument.

● Strollers	● Groups	● Food Serv.	● Parking	● Birthdays
● Diap. Chg.	● Picnic	● Food Nearby	Pub. Trans.	● Handicap. Access

Merry-Go-Round Museum
Area: **Farther West**   City: **Sandusky**   Ages: **3 & up**   Cost: **$**

Carved carousel animals are now an endangered species: of the more than 7,000 merry-go-rounds built, only 200 are still in existence. Sandusky's Merry-Go-Round Museum, located in a former post office, is home to the collection of carved animals, tools, and workbenches of the Gustav Dentzel Carousell Builder shop, re-created here from the 1800s Philadelphia original. Visitors will also find traveling exhibits on display from other museums around the world, such as a recent exhibit from the National Folk Art Museum in Paris.

While the carvings themselves may not entice all youngsters, a tour includes a look at a carousel carver at work and a ride on a fully restored Allen Herschell carousel.

Reservations are not required. Tour groups qualify for special rates if prior arrangements are made.

Address: W. Washington & Jackson Sts.
Phone: (419) 626-6111
Season: Year-round
Hours: Wed–Sat 11 a.m.–5 p.m.; Sun noon–5 p.m.; Mon 11 a.m.–5 p.m. (summer months only)
Prices: $4 adults, $3 seniors, $2 ages 4–14, no charge under age 3
Direct.: SR 2 to exit for SR 101; north on SR 101 into Sandusky; follow signs.

● *Strollers*   ● *Groups*   *Food Serv.*   ● *Parking*   *Birthdays*
   Diap. Chg.   *Picnic*   ● *Food Nearby*   *Pub. Trans.*   ● *Handicap. Access*

NASA-Lewis Research Center Visitor Center
Area: **Near West**   City: **Cleveland**   Ages: **3 & up**   Cost: **FREE**

Nearly 8,000 square feet of this huge NASA complex are devoted to educating the public about space exploration, propulsion, aeronautics, and research. There is also a nifty collection of space stuff, including the Apollo Skylab 3 capsule, a moon rock, and a space station model.

The Visitor Center is at its best when it sticks to the nuts and bolts of space technology, such as how a jet engine functions, or what the various layers of an Apollo space suit are, or how metal reacts to heat and stress in space travel. But the interactive exhibits are less effective. When we went, no one could get the video disc machines to work for either the Apollo capsule or the LandSAT displays, and equipment for an audio presentation about James Lovell's Apollo 8 suit was apparently broken. Hopefully repairs will have been completed in time for future visits.

Still, the staff here shines. A short presentation about space travel was very worthwhile. These folks understand how things work and can convey that understanding to youngsters. The presentation was followed by a video, "Astrosmiles," which consisted of 15 minutes of Space

Shuttle gravity jokes and was a big hit with the kids. For older visitors (ages 16 and up), there is a guided tour of the test facilities on Wednesdays and one Saturday each month. Call ahead for exact date and time.

Also, make sure you bring your driver's license; it is asked for at the main gate as a security precaution.

MUSEUMS & HISTORY

Address: 21000 Brookpark Rd.
Phone: (216) 433-2001
WWW: http://www.lerc.nasa.gov/
Season: Year-round
Hours: Mon, Wed–Fri 9 a.m.–4 p.m.; Tue 9 a.m.–8 p.m.; Sat 10 a.m.–3 p.m.; Sun 1–5 p.m.
Prices: FREE
Direct.: I-480 to Exit 9 for Grayton Rd.; south on Grayton to Brookpark Rd. (SR 17); right (west) on Brookpark; right on NASA access road just west of Old Grayton Rd., under bridge to main gate.
From Brookpark Rd. eastbound, use NASA entrance just east of Brookpark Rd. bridge over Rocky River Reservation.

| Strollers | ● Groups | Food Serv. | ● Parking | Birthdays |
| Diap. Chg. | Picnic | ● Food Nearby | Pub. Trans. | ● Handicap. Access |

Oldest Stone House Museum (Lakewood Historical Society)
Area: **West**   City: **Lakewood**   Ages: **3 & up**   Cost: **FREE**

The Oldest Stone House, built in 1838, illustrates life in pioneer days through displays and tours. Children can experience the pioneer lifestyle directly in the Ohio Heritage classes held each June. Offered in conjunction with the Lakewood Recreation Department, this week-long course (morning or afternoon sessions) gets children involved with pioneer crafts, games, activities, and chores. Brownie Teas, for Brownie troops, encourage girls ages 7–10 to bring their favorite stuffed or plastic friend to tea parties to sip "Stone House" tea from old china teacups and learn about the history of dolls.

Address: 14710 Lake Ave.
Phone: (216) 221-7343
Season: Closed Dec & Jan
Hours: Wed 1 p.m.–4 p.m., Sun 2–5 p.m.
Prices: FREE
Direct.: I-90 to Exit 165 for Warren Rd.; north on Warren to Clifton Blvd.; right (east) on Clifton for 2 blocks; left (north) on Belle Ave. for 1 block; right (west) on Lake Ave.; on right (north) side.

| Strollers | ● Groups | Food Serv. | ● Parking | Birthdays |
| Diap. Chg. | ● Picnic | Food Nearby | ● Pub. Trans. | Handicap. Access |

Plidco Pipe Line Museum
Area: **Near West**   City: **Cleveland**   Ages: **All ages**   Cost: **FREE**

The Plidco Pipe Line Museum, stocked with pipelines from different eras, provides a perspective on Cleveland's industrial past. Exhibits include pipe samples as old as the Roman Empire and as recent as the Alaskan oil pipeline. (There are no real kids' programs or hands-on activities here, so this museum is better suited for elementary-school children or school groups especially interested in the subject matter.)

Address: 1841 Columbus Rd. (east bank of the Flats)
Phone: (216) 871-5700
Season: Year-round
Hours: Mon–Fri, visiting hours by appt.
Prices: FREE
Direct.: I-90 eastbound to Exit 170 (W. 25 St.); north on W. 25; right (east) on Bridge Ave. (merges with Franklin Ave.); left on Columbus Rd.; on right after lift bridge.
I-90 westbound to Exit 171C (W. 14 St.); left (west) from offramp on Abbey Rd.; right (north) on Columbus Rd.; on right after lift bridge.

Strollers	● Groups	Food Serv.	● Parking	Birthdays
Diap. Chg.	Picnic	Food Nearby	Pub. Trans.	Handicap. Access

Professional Football Hall of Fame
Area: **Farther South**   City: **Canton**   Ages: **All**   Cost: **$-$$$**

The Hall is first and foremost a shrine to the greatest players of the gridiron. Indeed, there are enough bronze busts, shriveled pads, faded shoes, and dirty jerseys to numb even the heartiest fan. But after attendance tapered in the early 1990s, management huddled and emerged with a $9.1-million renovation that put motion back in the backfield and added 4,500 square feet of new exhibit space.

Most prominent in the expansion is "Game Day Stadium," a turntable theater film that puts visitors in the locker room as the Kansas City Chiefs and Pittsburgh Steelers prepare for a game at Arrowhead Stadium. As the teams leave the locker room, the theater floor turns 180 degrees to face a darkened wall, and the sound of cleats is heard clattering on the runway toward the field. Highlights of several other teams are shown, ending with clips from a recent Super Bowl. Three TV monitors play locker room celebrations as you walk out. Fans will appreciate the fact that NFL Films put together the entire sequence. (For the uninitiated, these are the guys who made football highlight films into struggles of epic proportions complete with pulse-quickening music, on-field sound effects, and slow-motion recaps of on-field brilliance.) The experience lasts 30 minutes.

The museum also added a research center, which is not open to the public for browsing. However, if you or your school-age child have a specific player or topic you want to investigate, make an appointment upon entering.

If you prefer an interactive approach, head to the lower level of the new addition. There, plays from the 24 Super Bowls are cued up on video screens. An announcer sets up each play; visitors guess, via a computer keyboard, what play, for example, then-49ers Quarterback Joe Montana decided to call during the last 2 minutes of Super Bowl XXIII. Also located in the same area is a multiple-choice game of football trivia.

MUSEUMS & HISTORY

Address: 2121 George Halas Dr. NW
Phone: (330) 456-8207
WWW: http://www.canton-ohio.com/hof/
Season: Year-round
Hours: Memorial Day–Labor Day daily 9 a.m.–8 a.m.; remainder of the year daily
9 a.m.-5 p.m.
Prices: $9 adults, seniors $6, ages 6-14 $4, families $22
Direct.: I-77 to Exit 107A; follow signs.

- Strollers   • Groups   • Food Serv.   • Parking   Birthdays
- Diap. Chg.   Picnic   • Food Nearby   Pub. Trans.   • Handicap. Access

Rainbow Children's Museum (and TRW Learning Center)
Area: **Near East**   City: **Cleveland**   Ages: **1-1/2–10**   Cost: **$**

The Rainbow Children's Museum (formerly the Cleveland Children's Museum) was the pioneer touch-look-ask museum in the area. Everything is designed to be taken apart, rebuilt, and crawled over, under, and on. At every turn kids can explore, learn, and have fun. Museum volunteers staff nearly every exhibit to offer assistance.

On the lower level, the long-running Over and Under Bridges exhibit boasts everything from small-scale bridges that kids can run across to a huge pit of blocks where they can design and build their own.

There is a separate area for toddlers for quiet play, but the museum can get crowded on weekends and school days when there are large groups. So for the younger ones, try Tuesday mornings, when the museum is open only to preschoolers. Weekday afternoons also tend to be more relaxed. Also, a new Tot Spot is a safe, carpeted area filled with Little Tikes equipment geared to the preschool set.

The museum's special events are interactive celebrations with singing, dancing, storytelling, toy making, bead stringing . . . the list goes on. Check out the seasonal calendar for special programs.

The museum store at the main entrance is tough to miss. It is stocked with unusual toys, books, and games.

Address: 10730 Euclid Ave.
Phone: (216) 791-KIDS; office: (216) 791-7114
WWW: http://www.ohioonline.net/kids

Season: Year-round

Hours: Summer: Mon–Fri 11 a.m.–5 p.m.; school year: Tue–Fri 1 p.m.–5 p.m.; Sat (year-round) 10 a.m.–5 p.m.; Sun (year-round) 1–5 p.m.; closed Mon during school year. Call for special holiday hours. Preschool Primetime: Tue 9 a.m.–noon.

Prices: $5 adults, $4.50 seniors, $4 children ages 2–15, no charge under age 2; $1 every 2nd Wed of month 5–8 p.m. only

Direct.: I-90 to Exit 177; south on Martin Luther King, Jr. Blvd.; right (south) on E. 105 St.; left (east) on Euclid Ave. across E. 107 St.; right into parking lot.

- Strollers
- Diap. Chg.
- Groups
- Picnic
- Food Serv.
- Food Nearby
- Parking
- Pub. Trans.
- Birthdays
- Handicap. Access

Courtesy of Rainbow Childrens Museum

Rock and Roll Hall of Fame and Museum
Area: **Downtown**   City: **Cleveland**   Ages: **School-age & up**   Cost: **$$$**

    I. M. Pei's pyramid-shaped glass-faced Rock Hall rises up from Lake Erie, dramatically reshaping the city's skyline. Inside, much of the action is below street level in the Ahmet M. Ertegun Exhibition Hall. There you are greeted by black-and-white photos of rock's early influences. Just beyond is a section called "The Beat Goes On" where you can tap computer screens to call up song snippets and film clips and follow a musical family tree to see, for example, that Fats Domino was influenced by Amos Milburn and that Muddy Waters motivated Jimi Hendrix.

    There are plenty of rock accessories to gaze at—the Temptations' blue tuxedos, Alice Cooper's boots, Madonna's bustier, a piece of fuselage from the plane in which Otis Redding died, and Jim Morrison's Cub

10 Great Things to Do...

Nominated by Cleveland Parent Readers

- ⦿ Explore the Cleveland Museum of Art through the Young People's classes or Family Express. (p. 36)

- ⦿ Visit the Memphis Kiddie Park for a first-time roller-coaster ride. (p. 24)

- ⦿ Have an outdoor breakfast at a Metroparks picnic pavilion. (p. 84)

- ⦿ Practice manners and sip tea at the Ritz-Carlton Hotel.

- ⦿ Go early and participate in the Parade the Circle celebration. (p. 36)

- ⦿ Climb mazes and play pirates at Sea World. (p. 26)

- ⦿ Ride the wild rides and roller coasters at Cedar Point or Geauga Lake. (p. 16, 20)

- ⦿ Sample ethnic foods at one of the city's many summer/fall neighborhood festivals. (See "Favorite Family Events," (p. 223)

- ⦿ Spend an afternoon at one of the area's orchards for apple picking.

- ⦿ Participate in the hands-on offerings at one of the area's family festivals —KidsFest, Art in the Park, Cain Park. (p. 138)

Scout shirt, to mention only a few. There is no shortage of guitars and shoes.

And you are never far from the music. Another bank of interactive computer screens features performers discussing their lives and music. "What'd I Say?" dissects how several songs were made through interviews with performers, producers, and songwriters.

Woven into this mix are several movie-like exhibits, one of which explains how songs were inspired. Another room boasts two walls of TV monitors, one displaying modern American history, the other music and musicians of the times. It is simultaneously disturbing and entertaining.

At the narrowed top of the building sits the actual Hall of Fame, a darkened chapel-like place where the only light comes from the ghostly black-and-white images of rock's most venerable artists that fade in and out on small monitors.

While lots of families were there on our visit, we were hard-pressed to find a reason to bring our 6-year-old along—there is little to touch or do. As for even littler kids, leave them at home; they just won't get it. Upstairs, the cafe serves spotty fare, but its view of Lake Erie is great, no matter what the season.

This place is new, so its rhythm isn't well established yet. Daily attendance varies from 1,000 to 9,000; the average stay is about three hours. There are three nearby parking lots: one directly to the north of the museum on E. 9 St.; one south, also on E. 9; and one at the Cleveland-Cuyahoga Port Authority (plan on spending about $5). For really brutal days, the Port Authority has valet service for $8.

Address:	1 Key Plaza (North Coast Harbor, corner of E. 9 St. & Erieside Ave.)
Phone:	(216) 781-7625; (800) BUCKEYE
WWW:	http://www.rockhall.com/index.html
Season:	Year-round
Hours:	Daily 10 a.m.–5:30 p.m., Wed 10 a.m.–9 p.m.; summer hours (Memorial Day–Labor Day) Wed–Sat 10 a.m.–9 p.m.
Prices:	$12.95 adults, $9.50 seniors (55+) and children ages 4–11
Direct.:	I-90 to SR 2 west to exit for E. 9 St.; right (north) on E. 9; parking at Port Authority lots, North Point garage, E. 9 St. Garage, and Burke Lakefront Airport.

● Strollers	● Groups	● Food Serv.	● Parking	● Birthdays
Diap. Chg.	Picnic	● Food Nearby	● Pub. Trans.	● Handicap. Access

Rockefeller Park Greenhouse
Area: **Near East**   City: **Cleveland**   Ages: **All**   Cost: **FREE**

Rockefeller Park Greenhouse is owned and operated by the City of Cleveland. The greenhouses were completed in 1905 on land donated by John D. Rockefeller. There are extensive indoor and outdoor collections of flowers and plants that are well maintained and attractively displayed. Detailed fountains and sculptures lend a sense of history.

The outdoor grounds provide ample running room, plus a path through a Japanese garden that includes a small bridge—always a hit with the toddler and preschool set. (There are also several wishing ponds—bring pennies.) In addition to the seasonal plantings, there is the Betty Ott Talking Garden for the Blind, which offers walk-by-activated audio explanations of the visual displays in the garden.

Inside, the greenhouse displays ferns, cacti, orchids, and tropical plants, as well as changing exhibits. All are easy to see—some are also easy to touch, though not by design. These hothouses are a great place to escape a raw winter day for an hour or so.

Each year, the Friends of the Greenhouse schedule a variety of special events, including an annual June Garden Party and plant sale and a Christmas-preview poinsettia party.

Address: 750 E. 88 St.
Phone: (216) 664-3103
Season: Year-round
Hours: Daily 10 a.m.–4 p.m.
Prices: FREE
Direct.: I-90 to Exit 177; south on Martin Luther King, Jr. Blvd. to 1st traffic light; left on E. 88; look for Greenhouse sign.

| Strollers | ● Groups | Food Serv. | ● Parking | Birthdays |
| ● Diap. Chg. | ● Picnic | ● Food Nearby | ● Pub. Trans. | ● Handicap. Access |

Roscoe Village Foundation
Area: **Farther South**   City: **Coshocton**   Ages: **3 & up**   Cost: **FREE–$$**

Roscoe was once a thriving commercial center along the Ohio and Erie Canal (which was built to connect the Ohio River with Lake Erie). The village fell on hard times after the canal closed in 1913. An extensive restoration, completed in 1968, allows visitors to experience life in the early canal days, circa 1830. Living History buildings include a printshop, a blacksmith shop, and a schoolhouse. The Living History Tour offers demonstrations of broom-, toy-, and barrel-making, and other period crafts. The tour includes hands-on activities for kids.

A visitor center includes a theater with a 15-minute slide show about canal life in the 1830s. The exhibit hall below has a room full of dioramas—miniatures depicting details of early American life.

The biggest hit for kids is the canal boat *Monticello III*, which provides rides from Memorial Day through Labor Day. This replica canal boat, drawn by horses, takes you up the canal and back on a 45-minute tour. Reservations are not required, and there is no group size minimum. Horse-drawn trolleys also operate during the summer months.

Special events typically focus on music, food, and crafts of early Americans.

Address:	381 Hill St.
Phone:	(800) 877-1830; (614) 622-9310
Season:	Year-round; special events Feb–Dec
Hours:	Sun–Thu 10 a.m.–6 p.m., Fri–Sat 10 a.m.–8 p.m.; Living History Tour 10 a.m.–3:30 p.m.
Prices:	Village admission: Free; tour: $7.95 adults, $3.95 children ages 5–12
Direct.:	I-77 to Exit 65 (US 36 west/Newcomerstown), 20 miles to Coshocton; left on County Road 495 for 1/4 mile to Roscoe Village entrance.

● Strollers   ● Groups   ● Food Serv.   ● Parking   Birthdays
   Diap. Chg.   ● Picnic   ● Food Nearby   ● Pub. Trans.   ● Handicap. Access

Rose Hill Museum (Bay Village Historical Society)
Area: **West**   City: **Bay Village**   Ages: **All ages**   Cost: **FREE**

Near the shore of Lake Erie, Rose Hill preserves the history of the Cahoon Family homestead and farm from the late 1800s.

Address:	27715 Lake Rd.
Phone:	(216†) 871-7338
Season:	Mar–Dec; groups should call ahead for appointments
Hours:	Sun 2 p.m. to 4:40 p.m. (call ahead to confirm)
Prices:	FREE
Direct.:	I-90 to Exit 159 (Columbia Rd./SR 252); north on SR 252; left (west) on Lake Rd.; on the south side, on the grounds of the Cleveland Metroparks Huntington Reservation.

   Strollers   ● Groups   Food Serv.   ● Parking   Birthdays
   Diap. Chg.   ● Picnic   Food Nearby   Pub. Trans.   ● Handicap. Access

St. Helena III and Canal Fulton Heritage Society
Area: **Farther South**   City: **Canal Fulton**   Ages: **Preschool & up**   Cost: **$-$$**

When roads were little more than paths of muddy potholes and the nation's rail system was still on the drawing board, canal riverboats shuttled goods and people throughout much of the eastern half of the United States.

Thanks to the Canal Fulton Heritage Society, visitors can sit aboard the *St. Helena III* (a replica of a typical flat-bottomed canal boat circa 1860) and take a lazy ride up one of the few sections of the Ohio and Erie Canal that hasn't been filled in the past 150 years.

Designed to haul barrels of corn and other goods to points east, the *St. Helena III* can easily fit a few dozen people, who ride the canal the same way passengers of the 1800s did—pulled by hefty Belgian horses that walk alongside the canal. At the laconic speed of two miles per hour, the world passes lazily by the *St. Helena III* (*St. Helena II* sits warped and worn-out near the parking lot entrance). On one side of the canal is a wall of trees; on the other, the backs of Canal-Fultonite homes. The whole trip takes about 45 minutes. A pair of pubescent Huck Finn clones man the boat and recount the rise and fall of Ohio's canal industry. While it is safe to walk or run around, parents of crawlers should remember that this is a boat and make sure their progeny don't fall overboard.

MUSEUMS & HISTORY

Address:	103 Tuscarawas St. (SR 93)
Phone:	(330) 854-3808 or (800) HELENA-3
Season:	May–Oct
Hours:	Jun–Aug daily 1–3 p.m., May & Oct weekends 1–3 p.m. (boat rides leave hourly); museum open 1–4 p.m.
Prices:	$5 adults, $4 seniors, $3 children ages 4–12
Direct.:	I-77 to Exit 111 (North Canton/Canal Fulton); right on Portage Rd. into Canal Fulton; adjacent to intersection of Portage Rd. and SR 93.

Strollers	• Groups	Food Serv.	• Parking	Birthdays
Diap. Chg.	• Picnic	• Food Nearby	Pub. Trans.	Handicap. Access

Sauder Farm and Craft Village
Area: **Farther West**   City: **Archbold**   Ages: **3 & up**   Cost: **$–$$**

Erie Sauder, who still lives in the area, founded this living history village. It is hands-on history at its best. Special seasonal programs highlight life in the 1860s and allow visitors to take part in typical chores, such as hand-washing clothes on a scrub-board and spinning wool. Other activities include stilt walking and candle making (these seem like more fun). There are many animals, ranging from horses and cows to peacocks and oxen, in the homestead area.

Check out their schedule in advance; many special celebrations take place throughout the year, including the Quilt Show in April, Butchering Day, a Woodcarving Fair, Summer on the Farm, and the Children's Fall Festival (a family favorite). You can spend three hours or more touring the village and watching craft demonstrations. No reservations are required.

Address:	22611 SR 2
Phone:	(800) 590-9755; (216†) 446-2541
WWW:	http://www.a1.com/sauder
Season:	Mid-Apr–Oct
Hours:	Mon–Sat 10:00 a.m.–5 p.m.; Sun 1:00–5 p.m.
Prices:	$9 adults, $8.50 seniors, $4.50 students 6–16, no charge under age 5
Direct.:	Ohio Turnpike (I-80/I-90) to Exit 3 (Wauseon); eft (south) on SR 108 to first stoplight; right (west) on US 20-Alt.; left (south) on SR 66 for 2 miles; left (east) on SR 2 for 1/4 miles; on right (south) side.

• Strollers	• Groups	• Food Serv.	• Parking	Birthdays
• Diap. Chg.	• Picnic	• Food Nearby	Pub. Trans.	• Handicap. Access

MUSEUMS & HISTORY

Shaker Historical Society Museum

Area: **East**   City: **Shaker Hts.**   Ages: **5 & up**   Cost: **FREE**

Many local schools teach Shaker history in the third grade, so the Shaker Historical Society Museum will likely appeal to this age group. The museum building is a stately old house that is actually not of Shaker heritage (it was built as part of the Van Sweringen brothers' original "Garden Community" of Shaker Heights), but curators say the design provides a provocative contrast to the Shaker ideal of simplicity and stimulates conversation about what is "real Shaker." Nearby, between North Park and South Park boulevards, some vestiges remain of the North Union Shaker community that prospered here from 1822 to 1889. The house stands on the site of an original Shaker apple orchard, opposite Shaker Horseshoe Lake (Upper Shaker Lake).

Inside there are displays of Shaker furniture, artifacts, and memorabilia. There is not much in the way of hands-on exhibits, so children under age 4 may get a little squirmy. There *is* much in the way of Shaker inventions: the modern flat broom, tilter chairs, clothespins, and seed packets. On the landing there are dioramas of Shaker life, complete with miniature wooden people. The gift shop is stocked with stencils, herbs, candles, books, music, and miniature furniture—all of Shaker design.

Keep an eye out for the apple festival scheduled each October.

Address: 16740 S. Park Blvd.
Phone: (216) 921-1201
WWW: http://www.cwru.edu/orgs/shakhist/shaker.htm
Season: Year-round
Hours: Tue–Fri 2–5 p.m.; Sun 2–5 p.m.
Prices: FREE; charge for group tours
Direct.:   I-271 to Exit 29 (Chagrin Blvd.); west on Chagrin; north on Lee Rd.; right (east) on S. Park Blvd.; 4th driveway on right (south) side of street, opposite Shaker Horseshoe Lake (Upper Shaker Lake).

• *Strollers*	• *Groups*	*Food Serv.*	• *Parking*	*Birthdays*
Diap. Chg.	*Picnic*	• *Food Nearby*	• *Pub. Trans.*	*Handicap. Access*

Spring Hill

Area: **Farther South**   City: **Massillon**   Ages: **School-age**   Cost: **$**

Built in the 1820s, the Spring Hill Historic Home (and station on the Underground Railroad) is filled with interesting items like a bee room, a secret stairway, wig and false teeth drawers, a playroom, and a basement kitchen with a cooking fireplace, one of the oldest in Ohio. A tour of the grounds includes the springhouse, smokehouse, woolhouse, and milkhouse. Trails wind through gardens and woods.

Annual special events include an Easter egg hunt, children's fun and games day, Fall Fest, and a Christmas party.

Address: 1401 Spring Hill Lane NE
Phone: (330) 833-6749
Season: Apr–Oct
Hours: Wed, Thurs & Sun 1–4 p.m. (Jun-Aug)
Prices: $3 Adults, $1 ages 6–17, under 6 Free
Direct.: I-77 south to exit for SR 241; south on SR 241 to 2nd light in Massillon (Lake Ave. NE); left on Spring Hill Lane NE (continuation of Lake Ave. NE); at top of hill.

• Strollers	• Groups	• Food Serv.	• Parking	Birthdays
Diap. Chg.	• Picnic	• Food Nearby	Pub. Trans.	Handicap. Access

MUSEUMS & HISTORY

Stan Hywet Hall and Gardens
Area: **Far South**   City: **Akron**   Ages: **All**   Cost: **$$**

There are several nifty *little* things in this 65-room Tudor mansion—the library bookcase that opens into a secret passageway and telephones tucked behind carved wood panels—but just about everything else here is big.

Built in 1915 on a 3,000-acre bluff, Stan Hywet Hall and its adjacent gardens now take up 70 acres. A mansion with formal gardens, grape arbor, greenhouse, lagoon, and parade of white birch trees needs that much space. Everything about Frank and Gertrude Seiberling's house makes a grand statement, from the three-story-tall ceilings in the great room to the 16th-century tapestries and European antiques that Seiberling, co-founder of the Goodyear Tire and Rubber Co., imported to re-create the feel of the 1700s.

Depending on your guide, the tour can be an entertaining peep show into the lives of one of Ohio's most famous industrialists, replete with tidbits such as why the stone on the hallway floor is worn in spots (Gertrude wanted the place to look broken in). Guides take a dim view of younger children who want to handle the silverware and wander past the ropes. On-site attractions also include seasonal flower displays and special events, such as the Decorated Egg Show, Shakespeare at Stan Hywet, Arts and Crafts Fair, Miniature Faire, and Christmas Then and Now, which features a 14-foot Christmas tree in the Great Hall.

Address: 714 N. Portage Path
Phone: (330) 836-5533
Season: Year-round
Hours: Jan–Mar 31: Tue-Sat 10 a.m.–4:30 p.m., Sun 1–4 p.m.; open seven days a week after Apr 1; Museum Shop open Tue–Sat 10 a.m.–5 p.m., Sun noon–5 p.m. (closed Mon)
Prices: $7 adults, $6.50 seniors, $3.50 children 6–12, under 6 Free (gardens & grounds can be toured separately at a reduced charge)
Direct.: I-77 to Exit 138 (Ghent Rd.); right (south) on Ghent Rd.; left (east) on Smith Rd. to dead end; right (south) on Merriman; right (south) on North Portage Path.

Strollers	• Groups	Food Serv.	• Parking	Birthdays
Diap. Chg.	• Picnic	• Food Nearby	• Pub. Trans.	• Handicap. Access

Steamship William G. Mather Museum (Harbor Heritage Soc.)
Area: **Downtown**   City: **Cleveland**   Ages: **3 & up**   Cost: **$**

The *Steamship William G. Mather* is the former flagship of the Cleveland Cliffs Iron Company's line of freighters. When christened in 1925, it was the grand lady of the Great Lakes, a behemoth craft that combined cavernous cargo holds (capable of holding 13,300 tons of iron ore) with elegant oak-paneled guest dining rooms and cozy staterooms.

The tour begins through a cut-away cargo hold and winds through small crew bunk rooms, across the top of the ship, into the state rooms and engine room, and back across the top to the pilot house. The dining room has been painstakingly restored, as have other parts of the *Mather*.

Staff members are second to none when it comes to knowledge of the freighter; many worked aboard this 618-foot-long ship or similar vessels that hauled loads of ore from northern Minnesota to the steel mills of Cleveland and other Great Lakes ports. Take advantage of their willingness to give you a tour. If you still want to know more at the end, a short film runs throughout the day.

The vessel tour requires climbing several sets of steep steps. Strollers and child-carrying backpacks are not allowed. Although the guardrails have been significantly reinforced and augmented, parents of toddlers and small children will want to hang on to their offspring when walking atop the ship.

Address: 1001 E. 9 St. (E. 9 St. Pier in North Coast Harbor)
Phone: (216) 574-6262
WWW: http://little.nhlink.net:80/wgm/wgmhome.html
Season: May–Oct
Hours: Memorial–Labor Day: Mon–Sat 10 a.m.–5 p.m., Sun noon–5 p.m.; Fri–Sun in May, Sept, and Oct
Prices: $5 adults, $4 seniors, $3 children ages 5–12, Free children under 5
Direct.: I-90 to SR 2 west to exit for E. 9 St.; right (north) on E. 9; parking at Port Authority lots, North Point garage, E. 9 St. Garage, and Burke Lakefront Airport.

| *Strollers* | ● *Groups* | *Food Serv.* | ● *Parking* | ● *Birthdays* |
| *Diap. Chg.* | *Picnic* | ● *Food Nearby* | ● *Pub. Trans.* | *Handicap. Access* |

Temple Museum of Religious Art, The
Area: **Near East**   City: **Cleveland**   Ages: **All ages**   Cost: **FREE**

Founded in 1950 and a member of the Council of American Jewish Museums, The Temple Museum is the fourth-oldest museum of Judaica in the United States and houses one of the most prominent and comprehensive collections of religious and Judaic art.

As there are no real kids' programs or hands-on activities here, this museum is better suited for elementary-school children or school groups especially interested in the subject matter.

MUSEUMS & HISTORY

Address: 1855 Ansel Rd.
Phone: (216) 791-7755
Season: Year-round
Hours: Mon–Fri 9 a.m.–4 p.m.; tours by appt. (please call ahead)
Prices: FREE
Direct.: I-90 to Exit 177; south on Martin Luther King, Jr. Blvd.; left (south) on E. 105 St.;
immediate right on Mt. Sinai Dr.; left on Ansel Rd.

Strollers	• Groups	Food Serv.	• Parking	Birthdays
Diap. Chg.	Picnic	• Food Nearby	• Pub. Trans.	Handicap. Access

MUSEUMS & HISTORY

Trolleyville USA
Area: **West**   City: **Olmsted Township**   Ages: **All**   Cost: **$**

Cleveland was once lined with many miles of trolley tracks, a fact you can explore thoroughly at Trolleyville USA. The museum, begun in 1954, is really named after its founder and is officially titled the Gerald E. Brookins Museum of Electric Railways, Inc., but everyone calls it Trolleyville. Its collection displays more than 34 pieces of historic electric railway equipment, such as interurbans and streetcars—many of which can be ridden—that are hooked up and hauled through a neighboring trailer park. Yes, trailer park. Midway, the convoy of trains stops at a railway depot and gift shop before venturing home.

Kids will be interested in the winter holiday celebrations here. At Christmastime, the place is filled with lights; the cars are running (most are heated), and free cider and goody bags are provided. Santa is often stationed at the depot on weekends.

Address: 7100 Columbia Rd.
Phone: (216†) 235-4725
Season: May–Dec
Hours: Wed, Fri 10 a.m.–3 p.m., Sat–Sun and holidays noon–5 p.m.; groups by appt.
only
Prices: $4 adults, $2 children, no charge under age 2
Direct.: I-480 to Exit 6 (SR 252); south on SR 252 (becomes Columbia Rd.); on right past
John Rd., behind Columbia Shopping Center.

• Strollers	• Groups	Food Serv.	• Parking	• Birthdays
Diap. Chg.	• Picnic	• Food Nearby	• Pub. Trans.	Handicap. Access

USS COD
Area: **Downtown**   City: **Cleveland**   Ages: **All**   Cost: **$**

Commissioned in 1943 and a veteran of action in the South Pacific, the *USS COD* is the only surviving submarine in original World War II condition. That means if you want to visit this landmark (it is listed in the National Register of Historic Ships), you had better be able to climb ladders and squeeze through the same hatches that a crew of 155 navy seamen had to negotiate over 50 years ago.

Inside, you have the run of the place, with the exception of the conning tower, the head (it took seven steps to flush the toilet), and the mess. But don't try to backtrack, because traffic flows only from the rear torpedo room to the forward torpedo room, where you climb another ladder to get out.

There are no hands-on exhibits. Atop the *COD* sits a five-inch gun that can no longer fire but can still be turned and adjusted. Nearby on the grounds, the periscope is set up for viewing. Signs and lighting are decent but not exceptional. But for the feel of life on a sub, this is the place. If you have questions, ask one of the old salts who man the gate.

Address:	1089 E. 9 St.
Phone:	(216) 566-8770
Season:	May–Sep
Hours:	Daily 10 a.m.–5 p.m.
Prices:	$4, $2 students, Free under age 5
Direct.:	I-90 to Exit 174B for SR 2; west on SR 2 to exit for E. 9 St.; right (north) on E. 9, right on N. Marginal Rd. towards Burke Lakefront Airport; *USS COD* on left.

Strollers	● Groups	Food Serv.	● Parking	Birthdays
Diap. Chg.	● Picnic	● Food Nearby	● Pub. Trans.	Handicap. Access

Western Reserve Historical Society

Area: **Near East**   City: **Cleveland**   Ages: **5 & up**   Cost: **$$**

The Western Reserve Historical Society, housed in two connecting early-20th-century mansions, is a microcosm of early Cleveland's greatness. The Hay-McKinney Mansion is intact as a mansion and is decorated to reflect turn-of-the-century decor. Every year the house is trimmed for the holidays with decorations appropriate for the period, chronicling the traditions brought to Cleveland by its many diverse immigrants.

The Bingham-Hanna Mansion has been converted into gallery space, and while visitors can still enjoy the beauty of the structure and its ornate ceilings, only the dining room and breakfast nook remain in their original condition. This part of the museum contains rotating history exhibits on an array of diverse Northeast Ohio topics, which in recent years have included baseball history, African-American churches, Cleveland music history, and leisure-time history, to name a few. The History Museum also houses the Chisholm-Halle Costume Wing. Its rotating exhibitions feature historic design styles and illustrate how one's choice of clothing can be as telling as a personal diary.

While adults may easily get caught up in the elegant interiors of the Hay-McKinney and Bingham-Hanna mansions, to make the most of a family visit here make sure you ask—or more likely accept an offer from—a staff member for a tour. The staff's wealth of knowledge goes well beyond the posted information plaques. And by all means get a map at the admissions desk (located directly in front if you enter from East Blvd., or the third building to your left if you use the parking lot and enter through Reinberger Gallery.)

The museum has made attempts to be child-friendly: exhibits contain interactive components from puzzles to computers. Children's programming is scheduled monthly, and there is a new Education Center at the bottom of the Hay Mansion that is open to school tours and visitors (check in advance with the Education Department).

An annual Family Day celebration (the weekend after Thanksgiving) includes craft demonstrations, entertainment, and special events designed around a different theme each year.

Also part of the Historical Society are the Frederick C. Crawford Auto-Aviation Collection (see separate listing) and the Library of the Western Reserve Historical Society, which specializes in history and genealogy—just the place to chart your family tree.

Address: 10825 East Blvd.
Phone: (216) 721-5722
WWW: http://www.wrhs.org
Season: Year-round
Hours: Mon–Sat 10 a.m.–5 p.m., Sun noon–5 p.m.; library: Tue–Sat 9 a.m.–5 p.m., and Wed until 9 p.m.
Prices: $6 adults, $5 seniors, $4 ages 6-12; Free under 6
Direct.: I-90 to Exit 177; south on Martin Luther King, Jr. Blvd.; cross E. 105 St. and stay left around traffic circle; right on East Blvd.; on left, parking in rear.

● Strollers   ● Groups   ● Food Serv.   ● Parking   Birthdays
  Diap. Chg.   ● Picnic   Food Nearby   ● Pub. Trans.   ● Handicap. Access

Courtesy of Western Reserve Historical Society

Nature & Outdoors

Kids learn best from hands-on experiences, and nature makes a great teacher. That's why a trip to a nearby park for a hike or swim or nature class can be so satisfying. Other activities are almost unlimited, including kiting, birding, biking, cross-country skiing, sledding, tubing, environmental programs, volunteer conservation work, and more.

We're surrounded by parklands. The Cleveland Metroparks alone cover 19,000 acres around the city; the Cuyahoga Valley National Recreation Area covers another 33,000 acres. There are also several state parks, including nearby Lakefront State Parks, and the county park systems of Geauga, Lake, and Lorain counties.

As with other activities, keep in mind your children's ages and abilities when choosing a park to visit. It's also a good idea to leave home well stocked with supplies; some parks are relatively remote and have limited facilities. And, remember to bring and wear appropriate clothes—children need protection from the elements.

If you're looking for some ground to explore, what follows is a list of parks, nature centers, and nature-oriented programs for children, most of which offer guided walks, group outings, and demonstrations, in addition to plenty of opportunities for outdoor discovery.

Akron Zoological Park

Area: **Far South**	City: **Akron**	Ages: **All**	Cost: **$**

This zoo has the feel of many smaller, older urban zoos. Though five minutes from downtown, it has lots of tall trees to filter sunlight, adding to the feeling that you are taking a pleasant walk in the park. One-dollar pony rides, strollers at every turn, and plenty of park benches (made from recycled plastic refuse) help to reinforce the feeling.

While its selection of animals is not huge, few other zoos allow visitors to get as close to animals as this. When the eight macaws start squawking, the entire zoo reverberates. Visitors also can ask zookeepers questions via an intercom kiosk in front of the kitchen and well-stocked operating room.

Annual special events include Boo at the Zoo trick-or-treating in October and a Holiday Lights Celebration in December.

▲

Address: 500 Edgewood Ave.
Phone: (330) 375-2525
WWW: http://www.lrun.com
Season: Apr–Oct
Hours: Mon–Sat 10 a.m.–5 p.m., Sun & holidays 10 a.m.–6 p.m.
Prices: $5 adults, $4 seniors, $4 ages 2–14, under 2 Free
Direct.: I-77 to exit for Copley Rd.; left (east) on Copley 2.4 miles; right on Edgewood Ave.; main gate is 200 feet from Copley Rd.

- *Strollers*
- *Diap. Chg.*
- *Groups*
- *Picnic*
- *Food Serv.*
- *Food Nearby*
- *Parking*
- *Pub. Trans.*
- *Birthdays*
- *Handicap. Access*

NATURE & OUTDOORS

Bedford Reservation (Cleveland Metroparks)
Area: **Southeast**   City: **Bedford, Bedford Hts., Oakwood, Valley View, Walton Hills**
Ages: **All**   Cost: **FREE**

This 2,109-acre reservation has several all-purpose trails (including Tinker's Creek Gorge Scenic Overlook and Bridal Veil Falls), cross-country ski trails, Shawnee Hills Golf Course, ball fields, designated sledding hills, and six picnic areas.

Address: Gorge Pkwy.
Phone: (216) 351-6300
Season: Year-round
Hours: Daily 6 a.m.–11 p.m.
Prices: FREE
Direct.: I-77 south to Exit 153 (Valley Pkwy.); east on Valley Pkwy. (becomes Alexander Rd.); north on Egbert Rd.; several marked entrances on left.

- *Strollers*
- *Diap. Chg.*
- *Groups*
- *Picnic*
- Food Serv.
- *Food Nearby*
- Parking
- *Pub. Trans.*
- Birthdays
- *Handicap. Access*

Bessie Benner Metzenbaum Park (Geauga Park District)
Area: **Far East**   City: **Chester Twp.**   Ages: **All**   Cost: **FREE**

This 65-acre park has picnicking, hiking, and a mile of paved trails.

Address: 7940 Cedar Rd.
Phone: (216†) 285-2222, (216†) 564-7131
Season: Year-round
Hours: Daily, 6 a.m.–11 p.m.
Prices: FREE
Direct.: I-271 to Exit 34 (US 322/Mayfield Rd.); east on US 322 for approx. 5 miles; right (south) on Caves Rd.; left (east) on Cedar Rd.; on left (north) side.

- *Strollers*
- *Diap. Chg.*
- *Groups*
- *Picnic*
- Food Serv.
- Food Nearby
- Parking
- Pub. Trans.
- Birthdays
- *Handicap. Access*

Big Creek Park & Meyer Nature Center (Geauga Park Dist.)
Area: **Far East**   City: **Chardon**   Ages: **All**   Cost: **FREE–$$$**

The Donald W. Meyer Center, headquarters for the Geauga Park District, is the only nature center in Geauga County. It offers nature-oriented exhibits and classes, and wildlife programs such as Timbertots, which introduces children ages 3–5 and parents to birdwatching, animals, and hiking. This is the place to pick up trail maps for the entire Geauga Park District.

The 642-acre reservation includes 6-1/2 miles of well-marked trails, fishing in ponds, cross-country ski trails, and a playground.

NATURE & OUTDOORS

Address:	9160 Robinson Rd.
Phone:	(216†) 285-2222, (216†) 564-7131, (216†) 834-1856
Season:	Year-round
Hours:	Park: 6 a.m.–11 p.m.; Center: Mon–Fri 8:30 a.m.–5 p.m.; Sat–Sun 10 a.m.–6 p.m.
Prices:	FREE, fee for some classes
Direct.:	I-90 to Exit 200 (SR 44); south on SR 44 for 3 miles; left (east) on Clark Rd.; right (south) on Robinson Rd.
	US 422 to SR 44 north through Chardon; follow North St./Ravenna Rd. out of square for 1-1/4 miles; right (east) on Woodin Rd. for 1 mile; left (north) on Robinson Rd. for 1-1/2 miles; on left.

- ● Strollers   Groups   Food Serv.   Parking   Birthdays
- ● Diap. Chg.   Picnic   Food Nearby   Pub. Trans.   ● Handicap. Acce

Courtesy of Geauga Park District

Big Creek Reservation (Cleveland Metroparks)
Area: **West**   City: **Parma Hts., Middleburg Hts.**   Ages: **All**   Cost: **FREE**

All-purpose trails (including cross-country ski trails), three picnic areas with grills and shelters, ball fields, sledding at Memphis Picnic

Area (lighted at night) and Snow Road Picnic Area, and Lake Isaac Waterfowl Sanctuary.

Address: Big Creek Pkwy. (Between Brookpark Rd. and Valley Pkwy., parallel to Pearl Rd.)
Phone: (216) 351-6300
Season: Year-long
Hours: Daily 6 a.m.–11 p.m.
Prices: FREE
Direct.: I-71 to exit for Bagley Rd.; left (east) on Bagley for 3/4 mile to Big Creek Pkwy.

- Strollers
- Diap. Chg.
- Groups
- Picnic
  Food Serv.
- Food Nearby
  Parking
- Pub. Trans.
  Birthdays
- Handicap. Access

NATURE & OUTDOORS

Black River Reservation (Lorain County Metroparks)
Area: **Far West**   City: **Elyria, Lorain**   Ages: **All**   Cost: **FREE–$**

Hiking trails, picnic areas with shelters, and a playground are located on 900 acres along the Black River. A 3.5-mile asphalt hike/bike trail winds through open fields and wooded areas; guided hikes are offered by Metroparks staff.

Address: Two entrances: Ford Rd. in Elyria; E. 31 St. and Norfolk Ave. in Lorain.
Phone: (216†) 458-5121; (800) LCM-PARK
Season: Year-round
Hours: Daily 8 a.m.–dusk
Prices: FREE
Direct.: I-90 to Exit 148 (Sheffield/SR 254); west on SR 254 (Detroit Rd.) for 1 mile; right (north) on E. River Rd.; left (west) on E. 31 St. over Black River to entrance, marked Day's Dam, on left.

- Strollers
- Diap. Chg.
- Groups
- Picnic
  Food Serv.
- Food Nearby
- Parking
  Pub. Trans.
  Birthdays
- Handicap. Access

Bradley Woods Reservation (Cleveland Metroparks)
Area: **West**   City: **North Olmsted, Westlake**   Ages: **All**   Cost: **FREE**

Hiking trails, cross-country ski trails, waterfowl and wildlife areas with fishing and ice fishing (Bunns Lake), picnic area, small playground.

Address: Bradley Rd. (S. of Center Ridge Rd.)
Phone: (216) 351-6300
Season: Year-round
Hours: Daily 6 a.m.–11 p.m.
Prices: FREE
Direct.: I-90 to Exit 156 (Crocker/Basset Rd.); south on Crocker; right (west) on Detroit (SR 254); left (south) on Bradley past Center Ridge Rd.
I-480 to exit for Lorain Rd. (SR 10); east on Lorain; left on Barton Rd.; right on Bradley Rd.

- Strollers
- Diap. Chg.
- Groups
- Picnic
  Food Serv.
- Food Nearby
- Parking
- Pub. Trans.
  Birthdays
- Handicap. Access

10 Great Things to Do...

With Very Young Children:

- ◉ Milk a cow or hold a baby chick at Lake Farmpark. (p. 108)

- ◉ Listen to instruments at a Cleveland Orchestra Musical Rainbows Concert. (p. 153)

- ◉ Explore the Cleveland Museum of Art in their Art with Parent & Child class. (p. 36)

- ◉ Ask to pet the snakes at the Lake Erie Nature and Science Center. (p. 108)

- ◉ Sign up for a parent and toddler preschool dance class at the Fairmount Fine Arts Center. (p. 147)

- ◉ Listen to a story and make a craft at Lakewood Library's Weekend Wonders. (p. 216)

- ◉ Float boats or build bridges at the Rainbow Children's Museum on Tuesday morning. (p. 59)

- ◉ Make and fly a windsock while listening to music at the annual Cuyahoga Valley National Recreation Area folk festival. (p. 87)

- ◉ Take a nature scavenger hunt at Holden Arboretum. (p. 104)

- ◉ Visit the Memphis Kiddie Park for a first-time roller coaster ride. (p. 24)

Brecksville Nature Center (Cleveland Metroparks)

Area: **South**   City: **Brecksville**   Ages: **All**   Cost: **FREE–$**

Inside the Brecksville Nature Center is a Children's Corner featuring hands-on activities with shells, fossils, hives, and nests. While there are no live animals here, a stuffed red fox and quail exhibit allow kids to "search" for other animals hiding in the area.

Animal Crackers, a monthly program for ages 3–5, involves a nature hike and craft activity. During the summer months there are other naturalist programs involving hikes and crafts for school-age children. Pre-registration required; check the *Emerald Necklace* monthly newsletter for details.

The Brecksville Nature Center was opened in 1939 as part of a Works Progress Administration project and is now a part of the Cleveland Metroparks Brecksville Reservation (see separate listing).

Address: Chippewa Creek Dr., off SR 82
Phone: (216†) 526-1012
Season: Year-round
Hours: Daily 9:30 a.m.–5 p.m. except Thanksgiving, Christmas, New Year's Day
Prices: FREE; fees for some special programs
Direct.: I-77 to Exit 149 (SR 82/Chippewa Rd.); east on SR 82 past Brecksville Rd. (SR 21); right on Chippewa Creek Dr.; follow signs.

- Strollers   • Groups   Food Serv.   • Parking   Birthdays
- Diap. Chg.   • Picnic   • Food Nearby   • Pub. Trans.   • Handicap. Access

Brecksville Reservation (Cleveland Metroparks)

Area: **South**   City: **Brecksville**   Ages: **All**   Cost: **FREE**

This is a great place for younger hikers. Trails (which include the Chippewa Creek Gorge Scenic Overlook) are well marked, and with map in hand it is easy to create your own short loop because the paths intersect often.

Brecksville Reservation's 3,392 acres include ball fields, sledding, eight picnic areas, Sleepy Hollow Public Golf Course, Brecksville Stables, and the Brecksville Nature Center (see separate listings for stables and nature center).

Address: Chippewa Creek Dr. & Valley Pkwy.
Phone: (216) 351-6300; nature center: (216†) 526-1012
Season: Year-round
Hours: Daily 6 a.m.–11 p.m.
Prices: FREE
Direct.: I-77 to Exit 149 (SR 82 /Chippewa Rd.); east on SR 82 past Brecksville Rd. (SR 21) to entrance on right. *Or*, south on Brecksville Rd. to Valley Pkwy. entrance on left.

- Strollers   • Groups   Food Serv.   • Parking   Birthdays
- Diap. Chg.   • Picnic   • Food Nearby   Pub. Trans.   • Handicap. Access

NATURE &
OUTDOORS

Brookside Reservation (Cleveland Metroparks)
Area: **Near West**   City: **Cleveland**   Ages: **All**   Cost: **FREE**

Brookside Reservation was one of the city of Cleveland's oldest parks before it was acquired by Cleveland Metroparks in 1993. Within its 143 acres are football, baseball, and soccer fields; the Meadow Ridge picnic area; and an all-purpose trail that connects Brookside Reservation to the Cleveland Metroparks Zoo. Cross-country skiing is permitted when conditions are favorable.

Address: Ridge Rd.
Phone: (216) 351-6300
Season: Year-round
Hours: 6 a.m.–11 p.m.
Prices: FREE
Direct.:   I-71 to Exit 245 (W. 25 St.); south on W. 25 (becomes Pearl Rd.); right (west) on Memphis Ave.; right (north) on Ridge to entrance.

Strollers	● *Groups*	*Food Serv.*	● *Parking*	*Birthdays*	
Diap. Chg.	● *Picnic*	● *Food Nearby*	● *Pub. Trans.*	● *Handicap. Access*	

NATURE & OUTDOORS

Burnett's Pet Farm
Area: **West**   City: **Olmsted Township**   Ages: **All**   Cost: **$–$$**

Owner and operator Dr. Jim Burnett, a former teacher, designed this pet farm as a hands-on place to learn about animals. Children can pet bunnies, chicks, and ducks and see a variety of other animals. The tour includes a look at life on a working farm with traditional farm animals (goats, sheep, and horses); it also offers a look at emus, bearcats, prairie dogs, South American opossums, monkeys, and other exotic species. The pet farm includes a small vineyard and herb and flower gardens—with a gazebo, pond, and bridge—that children can wander through. Reservations are preferred.

Address: 6940 Columbia Rd.
Phone: (216†) 235-4050
Season: Mid-Apr–Oct
Hours: Daily (except Mon) 10–11 a.m.; 2–3 p.m. by appt.
Prices: $5, $4 students, no charge for infants, group discounts for 25 or more
Direct.:   I-480 to Exit 6 (SR 252); south on Columbia Rd. (SR 252) for 1 mile.
                I-71 to Exit 235 (Bagley Rd.); west on Bagley to Columbia Rd. (SR 252); north on Columbia for1 mile.

● *Strollers*	● *Groups*	*Food Serv.*	● *Parking*	● *Birthdays*	
● *Diap. Chg.*	● *Picnic*	● *Food Nearby*	● *Pub. Trans.*	● *Handicap. Access*	

Caley National Wildlife Woods (Lorain County Metroparks)
Area: **Far West**   City: **Pittsfield Twp.**   Ages: **All**   Cost: **FREE**

This mostly undeveloped reservation features hiking trails and fishing on an eight-acre lake. Guided hikes for those seeking an opportunity to view migrating waterfowl are offered here, as they are throughout the Lorain County Metroparks.

Address: West Rd. (southeast of Oberlin)
Phone: (800) LCM-PARK; (216†) 458-5121
Season: Year-round
Hours: Daily 8 a.m.–dusk
Prices: FREE
Direct.: I-480 to end (becomes SR 10/US 20); west on SR 10/US 20 to exit for Oberlin/SR 58; south on SR 58 to Whitney Rd.; left (east) on Whitney to West Rd. I-71 to Exit 226 (SR 303); west on SR 303 to West Rd.; left (south) on West Rd.

| Strollers | Groups | Food Serv. | • Parking | Birthdays |
| Diap. Chg. | Picnic | Food Nearby | Pub. Trans. | Handicap. Access |

Canal Visitor Center (Cuyahoga Valley National Recreation Area)
Area: **South**   City: **Valley View**   Ages: **All**   Cost: **FREE–$$$**

The Canal Visitor Center building was at various times a private home, a general store, a tavern, a hotel, and a dance hall. It prospered from its location when the canal was open and passengers waited to pass through the nearby lock. These days, it is home to the National Park Service's ranger office and a few permanent exhibits on canal history and the settlement of the Cuyahoga Valley. It is also a great place to find out about the features of the Cuyahoga Valley National Recreational Area.

Year-round, there are special programs here for children ages 4 and up. Preschoolers in the Park, for ages 4–6 (with a parent), includes a short hike, talk, and an activity with a nature theme.

Address: Canal Rd. at Hillside Rd.
Phone: (800) 445-9667; (216) 524-1497
Season: Year-round
Hours: Daily 8 a.m.–5 p.m.; closed Thanksgiving, Christmas, New Year's Day
Prices: FREE; fee for special events
Direct.: I-77 to Exit 155 for Rockside Rd.; east on Rockside to Canal Rd.; right (south) on Canal Rd. for 2 miles.

| • Strollers | • Groups | Food Serv. | • Parking | Birthdays |
| Diap. Chg. | • Picnic | • Food Nearby | Pub. Trans. | • Handicap. Access |

NATURE & OUTDOORS

Courtesy of Cuyahoga Valley National Recreation Area

NATURE & OUTDOORS

Carlisle Reservation & Visitors Ctr. (Lorain County Metroparks)
Area: **Far West**   City: **Lagrange**   Ages: **All**   Cost: **FREE–$**

A variety of hikes, special events, and family programs for all ages are hosted throughout the year at the Carlisle Visitors Center, which houses the administrative offices of the park district. Programs for preschoolers and parents are offered monthly and include a short hike, crafts, and a discussion. Other attractions include the Wildlife Observation Area and Children's Nature Space.

Also on the grounds are all-purpose trails (including horse trails), picnic areas with shelters, fishing ponds, baseball fields, the 18-hole Forest Hills Golf Center, and a show ring at the Equestrian Center.

Address: 12882 Diagonal Rd.
Phone: (216†) 458-5121; (800) LCM-PARK
Season: Year-round
Hours: Daily 8 a.m.–4:30 p.m.; Thu 8 a.m.–9 p.m.
Prices: FREE; fees for some classes & special events
Direct.: I-480 west to end—it becomes SR 10/US 20; west on SR 10/US 20; south on SR 301 for 1/2 mile; right (south) on Nickel Plate-Diagonal Rd. (SR 27) for about 1.5 miles to the Visitors Center entrance, on right.

● Strollers   ● Groups   Food Serv.   ● Parking   Birthdays
● Diap. Chg.   Picnic   ● Food Nearby   Pub. Trans.   ● Handicap. Access

Cascade Valley Metro Park (Metro Parks Serving Summit County)
Area: **Far South**   City: **Akron**   Ages: **All**   Cost: **FREE**

This reservation's Chuckery Trail is 3.6 miles of steep hiking and skiing terrain. The 1.2-mile Oxbow Trail and 3.2-mile Highbridge Trail connect to Gorge Metro Park (see separate listing).

▲

Address: 837 and 1061 Cuyahoga St. (Chuckery Area and Oxbow Area)
Phone: (330) 867-5511
Season: Year-round
Hours: Dawn–dusk
Prices: FREE
Direct.:   SR 8 to exit for Tallmadge Rd.; west on Tallmadge; right (north) on Cuyahoga St.;
                entrances marked (between Uhler & Sackett Aves.).

Strollers		Groups	Food Serv.	• Parking	Birthdays
Diap. Chg.	•	Picnic	• Food Nearby	Pub. Trans.	Handicap. Access

Chagrin River Park (Lake Metroparks)
Area: **East**   City: **Willoughby, Eastlake**   Ages: **All**   Cost: **FREE–$$**

This 101-acre park has an all-purpose trail, ball fields, and a picnic area with shelters and grills, sledding hills, playground, and fishing.

Address: Reeves Rd., near Lost Nation Rd. & SR 2 (W. of SR 306)
Phone: (216†) 256-PARK
WWW: http://www.harborcom.net/parks/parkinfo.html
Season: Year-round
Hours: Daily, daylight–dusk
Prices: FREE; some programs have fees
Direct.:   SR 2 to exit for Lost Nation Rd.; north on Lost Nation; left (west) on Reeves Rd.

Strollers	• Groups	Food Serv.	• Parking	Birthdays
Diap. Chg.	• Picnic	• Food Nearby	Pub. Trans.	• Handicap. Access

Chapin Forest Reservation and
Pine Lodge Ski Center (Lake Metroparks)
Area: **Far East**   City: **Kirtland**   Ages: **All**   Cost: **FREE–$$**

This 390-acre reservation includes hiking trails, ball and game fields, a playground, a designated sledding area, and picnic areas with shelters and fire pits.

At Pine Lodge, classes are scheduled year-round for ages 3–adult. These typically include a story, craft, and hike. In winter, cross-country ski and snowshoe rentals are available, and the well-groomed trails are perfect for families and beginners. The Lodge is perfect for warming up—the fire is always lit, with hot chocolate brewing.

Address: 10373 Hobart Rd.
Phone: (216†) 256-PARK; ski center: (216†) 256-3810; hotline: (216†) 256-2255
WWW: http://www.harborcom.net/parks/parkinfo.html
Season: Year-round
Hours: Daily, daylight–dusk. Pine Lodge: Mon–Thu 11 a.m.–6 p.m., Fri 11 a.m.–8 p.m.,
                Sat–Sun 9 a.m.–6 p.m.
Prices: FREE, fee for classes

Direct.:   I-90 to Exit 193 (SR 306); south on SR 306 for 3.5 miles; right (west) on Chardon Rd. (US 6) for 1 mile; right on Hobart Rd. for 1/2 mile; on right.

| • Strollers | • Groups | • Food Serv. | • Parking | Birthdays |
| • Diap. Chg. | Picnic | Food Nearby | Pub. Trans. | • Handicap. Access |

Charlemont Reservation (Lorain County Metroparks)
Area: **Far West**   City: **Wellington**   Ages: **All**   Cost: **FREE**

This reservation provides 540 acres of undeveloped natural wildlife habitat. For rugged hikes only—it has no trails. It is open for hunting during rabbit and pheasant seasons.

Address: New London-Eastern Rd. (S. of Wellington)
Phone: (216†) 458-5121; (800) LCM-PARK
Season: Year-round
Hours: Daily 8 a.m.–dusk
Prices: FREE
Direct.:   I-480 west to end (becomes SR 10/US 20); west on SR 10/US 20 to exit for SR 58; south on SR 58 past Findley State Park; right (west) on New London-Eastern Rd.; entrance past Baker Rd.

| Strollers | Groups | Food Serv. | • Parking | Birthdays |
| Diap. Chg. | Picnic | Food Nearby | Pub. Trans. | Handicap. Access |

Children's Schoolhouse Nature Park (Lake Metroparks)
Area: **Far East**   City: **Kirtland Hills**   Ages: **2–10**   Cost: **FREE–$$**

With short, well-marked hiking trails, hands-on exhibits, and small classrooms housed in a 100-year-old school, this nature center is ideal for young naturalists. The Discovery Room is full of "please touch" activities, including a Microscope Zoo (with more than 20 easy-to-use power scopes showing slides of pond water, fur, and more) and 14 Discovery Boxes from which kids can remove and examine different materials (furs, skulls, feathers). A wildlife observation room, equipped with glass walls and microphones, lets kids listen to and see birds up close. Live snakes, salamanders, and box turtles live in a 52-gallon stream aquarium.

The Look and See program, for 2- and 3-year-olds with adult, includes a short hike, craft, and snack. Magic Moments, for ages 4–5 with adult, includes a short hike, crafts, discussion, and snack. Trailside Tales, for ages 3–5 with adult, includes a story, craft, and snack with an optional hike or outdoor activity. Natural Wonders, for ages 6–7, features a craft, story or puppets, song, game or other activity, and a hike. Discovery Walks, for ages 6–10, and special programs for older school-age children combine outdoor scavenging with hiking and nature lessons. Short-term summer camps for school-age children focus on nature activities.

NATURE &
OUTDOORS

▲

Address: 9045 Baldwin Rd.
Phone: (216†) 256-3808; (216†) 256-3809
WWW: http://www.harborcom.net/parks/parkinfo.html
Season: Year-round
Hours: Scheduled classes or by appt.
Prices: Fee for classes
Direct.: I-90 to Exit 193 (SR 306); south on SR 306 for 1 mile; left (east) on Kirtland-Chardon Rd. for 2.5 miles; left (north) on Booth Rd. to Baldwin Rd.; entrance on north side of intersection.

● Strollers   ● Groups   Food Serv.   ● Parking   Birthdays
  Diap. Chg.   Picnic   Food Nearby   Pub. Trans.   ● Handicap. Access

NATURE & OUTDOORS

Cleveland Metroparks
Area: **Various**   City: **Cleveland**   Ages: **All**   Cost: **FREE–$**

The Cleveland Metroparks system was established in 1917 to ensure public access to open spaces and conserve the many natural valleys of this area. Dubbed the "Emerald Necklace" because its 14 reservations of green space encircle the city, it presently includes more than 19,000 acres.

A map of the Cleveland Metroparks is available at any nature center, at the administrative offices, or by mail. For updated lists of Metroparks events and activities, ask to be added to the mailing list for the monthly *Emerald Necklace* newsletter.

General phone numbers:
Ranger headquarters: 9301 Pearl Rd., Strongsville, (440) 243-7860
Swimming: (216) 351-6300
Winter recreation info line: (216) 351-6300
Cross-Country Ski Ctr. (216) 283-8500 (Mon–Fri), (440) 946-7669 (Sat–Sun)
Permits, picnic area reservations: (216) 351-6300

The following Cleveland Metroparks facilities are described separately in this book:

Reservations:
Rocky River Reservation
Bradley Woods Reservation
Bedford Reservation
Big Creek Reservation
Brecksville Reservation
Cleveland Metroparks Zoo
Euclid Creek Reservation
Garfield Park Reservation
Huntington Reservation

Mill Stream Run Reservation
North Chagrin Reservation
South Chagrin Reservation

Nature Centers:
Brecksville Nature Center
Garfield Park Nature Center
Lake Erie Nature & Science Ctr.
Rocky River Nature Center
North Chagrin Nature Center

Address: 4101 Fulton Pkwy. (Admin. offices)
Phone: (216) 351-6300
WWW: http://www.clemetparks.com
Season: Year-round
Hours: Vary throughout park district
Prices: FREE admission to parks & nature centers; fees for some special programs & classes
Direct.:   (see separate listings for directions)

Strollers	*Groups*	*Food Serv.*	*Parking*	*Birthdays*
Diap. Chg.	*Picnic*	*Food Nearby*	*Pub. Trans.*	*Handicap. Access*

Cleveland Metroparks Zoo and RainForest
Area: **South**   City: **Cleveland**   Ages: **All**   Cost: **$–$$**

The RainForest, the Zoo's splashiest attraction, ranks as one of the city's most advanced interactive educational institutions. It's also a lot of fun. Upon entering, visitors are directed past a roaring waterfall and up a winding staircase to enter an Indiana Jones–style jungle laboratory, complete with microscopes and a computer. Outside the lab, the action really begins: anteaters roam behind glass fences; birds are free to fly above or walk across the floor. Good news for families with small children: there are places to climb up for good views and low-level portholes to see inside caves.

On the lower level, after meeting a colony of bats, you come upon a rain forest "island" that literally explodes into a rainstorm every few minutes. (Our then-toddler cowered. As with many children his age, thunderclaps are not his favorite noise.) The exhibits downstairs tends to be more serious. Interspersed throughout the animal habitats are displays explaining the importance of the rain forest in the ecosystem and how the forest is endangered.

Not surprisingly, the RainForest is one of the city's most popular attractions, and it is sometimes crowded, especially on school and summer holidays, despite the convoluted hourly visiting schedules. We found it best to visit either early or late. Because a limited number of visitors are allowed in at any time, advance ticket purchase is recommended—and may be necessary on busy weekends.

Despite all the attention given to the RainForest, don't overlook the zoo. Its lower level is accessible via the main gate, on the same level as the RainForest. From there you can easily get to the recently spruced-up waterfowl lake. Also accessible from the main gate are the lions, elephants, bird house, and the zoo train ride.

The Zoo Adventure Series, for children ages 3–12, introduces animals and their habitats. The most popular program of the series is Breakfast with Animals. Families get either a full breakfast or a snack, depending on the size of the featured animal. This series is a lot of fun,

NATURE & OUTDOORS

very popular, and often fills quickly, because Zoo members are offered advanced registration.

Address: 3900 Brookside Park Dr. (Wildlife Way)
Phone: (216) 661-7511; office: 661-6500
WWW: http://www.clemetzoo.com
Season: Year-round
Hours: Zoo: daily 9 a.m.–5 p.m.; RainForest: daily 10 a.m.–5 p.m., Wed 10 a.m.–9 p.m.; both closed Christmas and New Year's Day
Prices: Zoo: $5 adults, $3 ages 2–11, no charge under age 2; Free Mon 9 a.m.–noon for Cuyahoga County & Hinckley Township. residents (except holidays); RainForest (includes Zoo): $7 adults, $4 ages 2–11, Free under age 2
Direct.: I-71 to exit for Fulton Rd.; south on Fulton Rd. (becomes Fulton Pkwy.); left (east) on Brookside Park Dr. (Wildlife Way); main entrance on left.

NATURE & OUTDOORS

- Strollers
- Diap. Chg.
- Groups
- Picnic
- Food Serv.
- Food Nearby
- Parking
- Pub. Trans.
- Birthdays
- Handicap. Access

Courtesy of Cleveland Convention & Visitors Bureau

Concord Woods Nature Park (Lake Metroparks)
Area: **Far East**   City: **Concord Township**   Ages: **All**   Cost: **FREE**

The administrative offices of Lake Metroparks are located here on a 20-acre park with hiking trails, a playground, and picnic areas with grills, fireplaces, and shelters.

Address: 11211 Spear Rd.
Phone: (216†) 256-PARK; (216†) 639-PARK
WWW: http://www.harborcom.net/parks/parkinfo.html
Season: Year-round
Hours: Daily dawn–dusk; office: Mon–Fri 8 a.m.–4:30 p.m.
Prices: FREE
Direct.: I-90 to Exit 200 (SR 44); south on SR 44; left (east) on Auburn Rd., under bridge (I-90) and to the top of the hill; right (east) on Spear Rd. to end .

- Strollers
  Diap. Chg.
- Groups
- Picnic
  Food Serv.
- Food Nearby
- Parking
  Pub. Trans.
  Birthdays
- Handicap. Access

Crown Point Ecology Learning Center

Area: **Far South**   City: **Bath**   Ages: **6 & up**   Cost: **$$**

A non-profit activity of the Sisters of Saint Dominic, staffed by certified organic farmers, this 130-acre farm includes a barn (where summertime activities are held) and the Orchard House (winterized for colder months). A vast variety of children's programming is offered year-round. Past events have ranged from flower printing and art projects to canning and herb growing.

Address: 3220 Ira Rd.
Phone: (330) 666-9200
Season: Year-round
Hours: Program hours vary, office hours 9 a.m. to 5 p.m.
Prices: Vary
Direct.: I-77 to Exit 143 (Wheatley Rd.); west on Wheatley; south on Brecksville Rd. (becomes Cleveland-Massillon Rd. after Everett Rd.); left (east) on Ira Rd. for 3/4 mile; on right.

• Strollers   • Groups   Food Serv.   • Parking   Birthdays
  Diap. Chg.   • Picnic   • Food Nearby   Pub. Trans.   Handicap. Access

NATURE &
OUTDOORS

Cuyahoga Valley National Recreation Area (CVNRA)

Area: **South**   City: **Brecksville**   Ages: **All**   Cost: **FREE–$$$**

Covering 33,000 acres along 22 miles of the Cuyahoga River between Cleveland and Akron, this great nearby natural resource offers woods, prairies, freshwater ponds . . . and plenty of opportunities for outdoor recreation.

The Ohio and Erie Canal Towpath Trail, completed in 1993, is a 20-mile multi-use trail stretching from Rockside Rd. in Independence to Bath Rd. north of Akron. It runs the length of the park and follows the remnants of the old canal.

The new Environmental Education Center (3675 Oak Hill Rd., Peninsula)—open only to school groups and private parties—has introduced A River Runs Through It, a full-fledged environmental curriculum equipped with computers. For information, call 800-642-3297.

For families, the centrally located special events site is used for outdoor entertainment during the summer, most notably the annual Cuyahoga Valley Festival, which includes crafts, exhibits, games, a hands-on children's tent, and several days of music.

Visitors to the Cuyahoga Valley National Recreation Area may want to begin at either the Happy Days Visitor Center or the Canal Visitor Center (see separate listings for each).

Address: 15610 Vaughn Rd. (park headquarters)
Phone: (800) 433-1986
WWW: http://www.nps.gov/cuva
Season: Year-round

Hours: Vary; see individual listings
Prices: FREE; fee for train & special events
Direct.:   (See individual park listings for directions)

Cuyahoga Valley Scenic Railroad
Area: **South**   City: **Peninsula**   Ages: **All**   Cost: **$$$**

The Cuyahoga Valley Scenic Railroad offers scenic rides on vintage, climate-controlled railway coaches (from the 1930s and 1940s) through the Cuyahoga Valley National Recreation Area (CVNRA). Rides vary in length from 16 to 52 miles. Stops include Hale Farm and Village, the Canal Visitor Center in the CVNRA, downtown Akron, and Stan Hywet Hall and Gardens (see separate listings).

Courtesy of Cuyahoga Valley Scenic Railroad

There are several routes. The main ones are: Independence (departing from Old Rockside Rd., west of Canal Rd.) to Hale Farm and Village; and Independence (departing from the station at Ira and Riverview roads) to Akron (Howard and Ridge streets). The Scenic Ltd. travels between Independence and Peninsula.

Special rides include the Valley Explorer, a naturalist-led, 41-mile, five-hour round-trip tour departing at Independence and stopping for lunch in Akron before returning. This trip promises a close-up look at wildlife, including beaver, deer, and waterfowl, with impromptu, unscheduled stops. The most popular ride for youngsters, the Polar Express, boasts Santa Claus aboard. Running from late November through December, the trip is 24 miles and a child-friendly 90–120 minutes long. It also includes hot chocolate, Christmas carols, and stories.

Other seasonal and family-oriented train runs include special fall foliage trips, a Christmas Tree Adventure, and a warm-weather Bike and Hike.

Address: Boarding sites:
Canal Visitor Center: Hillside & Canal Rds.
Main Station, Independence: Canal & Old Rockside Rds. (near I-77)
Akron: Riverview & Ira Rds. (near Hale Farm)
Peninsula: Off SR 303 in downtown Peninsula at Historic Railroad Depot.
Phone: (216†) 657-2000; (800) 468-4070
Season: Mid-Feb–Dec
Hours: Vary
Prices: Prices vary according to destination: $11–20 adults, $10–18 seniors, $7–12 ages 3-12. Group discounts available; special prices for Nature Train & Polar Express
Direct.: Main Station: I-77 to Exit 155 (Rockside Rd.); east on Rockside Rd.; left on Canal Rd., then left on Old Rockside Rd. (Call for directions to other boarding sites.)

● Strollers	● Groups	● Food Serv.	● Parking	● Birthdays
Diap. Chg.	Picnic	Food Nearby	Pub. Trans.	● Handicap. Access

NATURE & OUTDOORS

Deep Lock Quarry Metro Park (Metro Parks Serving Summit County)
Area: **Far South**   City: **Peninsula**   Ages: **All**   Cost: **FREE**

Fishing is permitted on this reservation encircled by more than 15 miles of gentle loop trails. It is the site of the deepest lock on the Ohio & Erie Canal.

Address: Riverview Rd.
Phone: (330) 867-5511
Season: Year-round
Hours: Dawn–dusk
Prices: FREE
Direct.: I-271 to SR 303; east on SR 303 to Riverview Rd.; right (south) for 3/4 mile.

Strollers	Groups	Food Serv.	● Parking	Birthdays
Diap. Chg.	● Picnic	● Food Nearby	Pub. Trans.	Handicap. Access

East Harbor State Park
Area: **Farther West**   City: **Lakeside**   Ages: **All**   Cost: **FREE–$$**

The nearly mile-long sandy beach at East Harbor State Park offers swimming with a lifeguard on duty, boating, and fishing. For children, there is also a playground and seven miles of clearly marked hiking trails through marsh and wooded areas. Nature programs are taught by specialists, hired by the Ohio Department of Natural Resources, for families and children ages 10 and up during mornings from Memorial Day to Labor Day. Programs range from Swamp Stomps to observing birds and bugs. (Participate in three and earn a badge.) No pre-registration is necessary. An indoor recreation room with video games is open from 8 a.m. to 10 p.m.

Winter activities include three trails for a total of 3-1/2 miles of cross-country skiing with a good view of the harbor. Access to Blackberry Trail (1/2 mile) is at the campground office; Middle Harbor Trail (2 miles) starts at Exit Rd.; Red Bird Trail (1 mile) starts at the campground boat ramp. Snowmobile access to frozen Lake Erie is possible from the beach, the campground boat ramp, and the water plant.

The 1,831-acre park is set up with 570 sites for tents and recreational vehicles. Facilities include bathhouses with flush toilets and showers, laundry, telephone, a small grocery store, ice, food service, and fire rings. A "Rent-A-Camp" program is also offered.

Address: 1169 N. Buck Rd.
Phone: (419) 734-4424
Season: Year-round, fully operational Apr–Oct
Hours: Daily 6 a.m.–11 p.m.; lifeguard daily Memorial Day–Labor Day 11 a.m.–8 p.m.
Prices: Park admission FREE; fee for campsite
Direct.: SR 2 across Sandusky Bay bridge to exit for SR 53; north on SR 53; east on SR 163; north on SR 269 to marked entrance.

• Strollers	• Groups	• Food Serv.	• Parking	Birthdays
Diap. Chg.	• Picnic	• Food Nearby	Pub. Trans.	• Handicap. Access

Edgewater Park (Cleveland Lakefront State Park)
Area: **West**   City: **Cleveland**   Ages: **All**   Cost: **FREE**

This 100-acre park offers swimming at a 900-foot sandy Lake Erie beach, as well as a fishing pier, boating, a fitness trail, and plenty of space for general recreation (such as kite flying). A boat ramp is located just east of Edgewater marina. Two side-by-side pavilions are reservable for large family or group outings. Call park offices for information.

There is a playground with slides and jungle gyms. During the summer months, a naturalist program (which in the past has covered animals, geology, and plants) involves children in conservation projects and other nature activities. Edgewater is also the site for the annual July Fourth Festival of Freedom fireworks extravaganza.

Address: 6700 Memorial Shoreway
Phone: (216) 881-8141
Season: Year-round
Hours: Lifeguard noon–dusk daily Memorial Day–Labor Day
Prices: FREE
Direct.: West Memorial Shoreway (SR 2) to exit for Edgewater Park/Edgewater Marina. Or, take exit for Lake Ave./West Blvd.; right on Edgewater Dr.; right to west entrance for Edgewater Park.

Strollers	• Groups	• Food Serv.	• Parking	Birthdays
Diap. Chg.	• Picnic	• Food Nearby	• Pub. Trans.	• Handicap. Access

Eldon Russell Park (Geauga Park District)
Area: **Far East**   City: **Troy Township**   Ages: **All**   Cost: **FREE**

Bring your own canoe and paddle on the Cuyahoga River, which runs through this 132-acre park. There are hiking trails (cross-country skiing in the winter), fishing areas, and picnic facilities.

Address: 16315 Rapids Rd.
Phone: (216†) 285-2222, (216†) 564-7131, (216†) 834-1856
Season: Year-round
Hours: Daily 6 a.m.–11 p.m.
Prices: FREE
Direct.: I-90 to Exit 200 (SR 44); south on SR 44; left (east) on SR 87; right (south) on Rapids Rd. (just before town Square in Burton); entrance on left (east) side. US 422 to exit for SR 44 (Ravenna Rd.); north on SR 44; right (east) on Pond Rd.; right (south) on Rapids Rd.; entrance on left (east) side.

| • *Strollers* | • *Groups* | *Food Serv.* | • *Parking* | *Birthdays* |
| *Diap. Chg.* | • *Picnic* | *Food Nearby* | *Pub. Trans.* | *Handicap. Access* |

NATURE &
OUTDOORS

Euclid Beach (Cleveland Lakefront State Park)
Area: **East**   City: **Cleveland**   Ages: **All**   Cost: **FREE**

The 500-foot beach at Euclid Park is sandy and popular for swimming. It is mainly a day-use picnic area. Facilities include bathhouses equipped with showers, restrooms, and changing areas.

Address: 16300 Lakeshore Blvd.
Phone: (216) 881-8141
Season: Year-round
Hours: Daily 6 a.m.–11 p.m.; lifeguard noon–dusk daily Memorial Day–Labor Day
Prices: FREE
Direct.: I-90 to exit for Nottingham Rd.; north on Nottingham; left (west) on Lakeshore Blvd; right (north) on E. 169 to park area.

| *Strollers* | *Groups* | • *Food Serv.* | • *Parking* | *Birthdays* |
| *Diap. Chg.* | • *Picnic* | • *Food Nearby* | • *Pub. Trans.* | • *Handicap. Access* |

Euclid Creek Reservation (Cleveland Metroparks)
Area: **East**   City: **Euclid**   Ages: **All**   Cost: **FREE**

Euclid Creek Reservation is home to a quarry featuring the only remaining exposure of bluestone in the area. It also offers all-purpose trails (including cross-country ski trails), five picnic areas, ball fields, and designated sledding (at Kelly Picnic Area).

Address: Euclid Creek Pkwy. (south of Euclid Ave.)
Phone: (216) 351-6300
Season: Year-round
Hours: Daily 6 a.m.–11 p.m.
Prices: FREE

Direct.: I-90 to exit for Nottingham Rd.; south on Nottingham (becomes Highland Rd.); continue south on Highland to Euclid Creek Reservation entrance, on right (west) side.
I-271 to Exit 36; right (west) on Wilson Mills Rd.(becomes Monticello Blvd. past Richmond Rd.); continue west on Monticello; look for signs for entrances to Euclid Creek Reservation before Green Rd.

- *Strollers*   • *Groups*   *Food Serv.*   • *Parking*   *Birthdays*
    Diap. Chg.   • *Picnic*   • *Food Nearby*   • *Pub. Trans.*   • *Handicap. Access*

NATURE & OUTDOORS

F. A. Seiberling Naturealm (Metro Parks Serving Summit County)
Area: **Far South**   City: **Akron**   Ages: **All**   Cost: **FREE**

This nature center boasts some of the best exhibits in the area. Stuffed owls and prairie dogs stare down at toddlers, and no, the rope in front of them does not stop kids from petting these inanimate animals. Please-touch exhibits range from turtles to leaf bark. Among our favorites are an interactive computer game in which users are asked to match footprints to their owners, and leaves to their trees. The best display, however, was a bug's-eye view of a typical pond from under the water. This room boasts crayfish blown up from their regular size to the size of a 5-year-old.

Bird-watchers can sit in front of a huge picture window overlooking a series of birdfeeders, trees, and a manmade babbling brook. Like most kids, ours cared less about the birds than about the huge black binoculars on the window sill. The naturealm also has paths, including a rock-and-herb garden and a tree walk. Both are less than half a mile long and are handicap- as well as family-friendly.

Address: 1828 Smith Rd.
Phone: (330) 865-8065
Season: Year-round
Hours: Mon–Sat 10 a.m.–5 p.m., Sun noon–5 p.m.; grounds open from 8 a.m. to sunset
Prices: FREE
Direct.: I-77 southbound to Exit 138 (Ghent Rd.); Ghent Rd. south to Smith Rd.; left (east) on Smith past Sand Run Rd.; on right.
I-77 northbound to exit for Smith Rd.; east on Smith.

- • *Strollers*   • *Groups*   *Food Serv.*   • *Parking*   *Birthdays*
    • *Diap. Chg.*   • *Picnic*   • *Food Nearby*   *Pub. Trans.*   • *Handicap. Access*

Fairport Harbor Lakefront Park (Lake Metroparks)
Area: **Far East**   City: **Fairport Harbor**   Ages: **All**   Cost: **FREE–$$**

Activities at the 20-acre Fairport Harbor Lakefront Park include fishing, picnic areas with grills and shelters, a large playground, and volleyball courts.

Special for families is the Sunday in the Park summer concert series. For kids, there are organized programs for infants to high-school age, such as Beach Babies playtime, sand crafts, obstacle courses, Hobie Cat lessons, and sailing.

At the beach, rental equipment is available for volleyball, badminton, softball, Wiffle ball, soccer, horseshoes, frisbee, and bocce. Facilities also include restrooms, changing rooms, and showers.

Address: 2 High St.
Phone: (216†) 256-PARK; hotline: (216†) 639-9972
WWW: http://www.harborcom.net/parks/parkinfo.html
Season: Year-round, fully operational Memorial Day–Labor Day
Hours: Daily dawn–dusk; lifeguards 11 a.m.–7 p.m. daily (in season)
Prices: FREE admission; $2 parking; fees for some classes
Direct.: SR 2 to exit for Fairport Harbor/Richmond Rd.; north on Richmond (becomes High St. after East St.); continue north on High St. to park entrance.

- Strollers   Groups   • Food Serv.   • Parking   • Birthdays
- Diap. Chg.   • Picnic   Food Nearby   Pub. Trans.   • Handicap. Access

Findley State Park
Area: **Far West**   City: **Wellington**   Ages: **All**   Cost: **FREE–$$**

The big attraction here is Findley Lake. At 93 acres and with a relatively shallow depth (up to 25 feet) it offers a sandy beach, swimming with a lifeguard on duty, and boating—with boat rentals. Fishing, mainly for bass, bluegill, catfish, and northern pike, is also available. Bait is sold at the concession stand, but bring your own rod and reel. Because this state park was originally a state forest, the 10 miles of well-marked hiking trails are heavily wooded.

In the winter months, 6 miles of ski trails run through rolling wooded terrain suitable for both beginning and advanced cross-county skiers. Approximately half the trail is groomed. Access points are provided at the park office and the camp check-in station (no ski rental is available). There is also ice-skating on the lake.

There is a playground for children, and nature programs are offered from Memorial Day to Labor Day. There are no age restrictions for most of the programs, and older children can earn Junior Naturalist badges by attending three courses at any state park or combination of parks. There is no need to register.

The park has 272 tent and recreational vehicle sites. Park facilities include fire rings, flush and pit toilets, showers, laundry, phone, and a small grocery store. The "Rent-A-Camp" program is also offered.

Address: 25381 SR 58
Phone: (216†) 647-4490
Season: Year-round, fully operational Apr–Oct
Hours: Daily 6 a.m.–11 p.m.; 24 hrs. on request

NATURE &
OUTDOORS

Prices: FREE park admission; fee for campsites
Direct.:   I-480 to exit for SR 10/US 20; west on SR 10/US 20; south on SR 58; 2 miles
               south of Wellington.

- Strollers   • Groups   • Food Serv.   • Parking   Birthdays
  Diap. Chg.   • Picnic   Food Nearby   Pub. Trans.   • Handicap. Access

Firestone Metro Park (Metro Parks Serving Summit County)
Area: **Far South**   City: **Akron**   Ages: **All**   Cost: **FREE**

In addition to several hiking and fitness trails, this park has the Coventry Oaks Pavilion (off S. Main St.) available for rental. There's also play equipment, a sledding hill, and cross-country skiing (when conditions permit). Little Turtle Pond is reserved for fishing for ages 15 and under. The park contains a river, two ponds, and a marsh in its 255 acres.

Address: Harrington and Warner Rds.
Phone: (330) 867-5511
Season: Year-round
Hours: Dawn–dusk
Prices: FREE
Direct.:   I-77 to I-277/US 224; take Exit 3 (S. Main St.); right (south) on S. Main; follow S.
               Main, Swartz Rd., or Harrington Rd. to park entrances.

    Strollers   Groups   Food Serv.   • Parking   Birthdays
  • Diap. Chg.   • Picnic   • Food Nearby   Pub. Trans.   Handicap. Access

French Creek Nature Center (Lorain County Metroparks)
Area: **Far West**   City: **Sheffield Village**   Ages: **All**   Cost: **FREE–$**

The French Creek Nature Center has two rooms of natural history displays with several interactive exhibits (a hollowed-out tree to climb into, cards to flip, buttons to push) and a few live animals (a rather big snake, turtles, and frogs).

For ages 4–5 with parents, the Park Pals program includes a short hike, simple crafts, and a discussion with a nature focus. Other workshops are designed for school-age kids and can include tree identification, making milk carton birdfeeders, and nature art. Organized hikes are offered year-round for all age levels. Registration is required for most activities, and these programs are popular.

The Nature Center is located in the French Creek Reservation (listed separately).

Address: 4530 Colorado Ave. (SR 611)
Phone: (216†) 949-5200; (800) LCM-PARK
Season: Year-round
Hours: Daily 8 a.m.–4:30 p.m.

NATURE &
OUTDOORS

Prices: FREE; fees for some classes & special events
Direct.:   I-90 to Exit 151 to SR 611 (Lorain-Avon Rd.); west on SR 611 (Colorado Ave.) for
              2-1/2 miles (past SR 301) to nature center entrance.

● Strollers   ● Groups   Food Serv.   ● Parking   Birthdays
● Diap. Chg.   Picnic   ● Food Nearby   Pub. Trans.   ● Handicap. Access

French Creek Reservation (Lorain County Metroparks)
Area: **Far West**   City: **Sheffield Village**   Ages: **All**   Cost: **FREE**

Hiking trails, picnic areas with shelters, large playground, French Creek Nature Center (listed separately).

The trails here are ideal for younger hikers because they are well-marked and include some very short loops over the creek, through the woods, and back to the Nature Center.

Address: Between E. River & Abbe Rds. on French Creek Rd.
Phone: (800) LCM-PARK
Season: Year-round
Hours: Daily 8 a.m.–dusk
Prices: FREE
Direct.:   I-90 to Exit 151 (SR 611/Lorain-Avon Rd.); west on SR 611 (Colorado Ave.) for 2-
              1/2 miles to nature center entrance; -or-
              I-90 to Exit 151 (SR 611/Lorain-Avon Rd.); west on SR 611 to Abbe Rd.; left
              (south) on Abbe Rd. to French Creek Rd.; right (west) on French Creek; on right.

● Strollers   ● Groups   Food Serv.   ● Parking   Birthdays
  Diap. Chg.   ● Picnic   ● Food Nearby   Pub. Trans.   ● Handicap. Access

Furnace Run Metro Park (Metro Parks Serving Summit County)
Area: **South**   City: **Richfield**   Ages: **All**   Cost: **FREE**

There are 3.2 miles of trails within the 890 acres of this park. (Though two-thirds of the park is off-limits, an annual Stream Stomp allows a glimpse into the restricted area.) During winter months there is ice-skating on Brushwood Lake and cross-country skiing.

Address: 4955 Townsend Rd.
Phone: (330) 867-5511
Season: Year–round
Hours: Dawn–dusk
Prices: FREE
Direct.:   I-77 southbound to Exit 147 (Miller Rd.); left (east) on Miller; right (south) on SR
              21 past I-77 overpass; right on Townsend Rd.; on right.
              I-77/SR 21 northbound to Exit 143 (Wheatley Rd.); west on Wheatley; right
              (north) on Cleveland-Massillon/Brecksville Rd.; left on Townsend Rd.; on right.

  Strollers   Groups   Food Serv.   ● Parking   Birthdays
● Diap. Chg.   ● Picnic   ● Food Nearby   Pub. Trans.   Handicap. Access

Gardenview Horticultural Park
Area: **Southwest**   City: **Strongsville**   Ages: **All**   Cost: **$**

Gardenview, a public, not-for-profit horticultural park, is a throwback to a time before shopping malls and developments. Gardenview's member gardeners are committed to preserving and demonstrating the art of English cottage gardening and of traditional perennial borders. Ten acres of crabapple trees and six acres of gardens are ribboned with winding paths that make for a beautiful and peaceful break from the outside world.

Address: 16711 Pearl Rd. (US 42)
Phone: (216†) 238-6653
Season: Apr 1–mid-Oct
Hours: Sat–Sun noon–6 p.m. (non-members); members admitted any time 7 days a week; groups by appt.
Prices: Adults $5, children $3; $25 membership
Direct.:   I-71 to Exit 234 (US 42); south on US 42 (Pearl Rd.) for 3 miles; on left.

- Strollers   ● Groups   Food Serv.   ● Parking   Birthdays
- Diap. Chg.   Picnic   ● Food Nearby   ● Pub. Trans.   Handicap. Access

Garfield Park Nature Center (Cleveland Metroparks)
Area: **South**   City: **Garfield Hts.**   Ages: **All**   Cost: **FREE–$$**

Kids particularly enjoy the collection of live animals—turtles, fish, frogs, toads, and snakes, as well as a beehive—at this nature center. Programs designed for young children include Forest Adventures and Night Crawlers (ages 3–5); Junior Naturalists (ages 6–7); and Explorers (ages 8–10). All are led by naturalists and include stories, short hikes, and crafts. Registration is required for all programs. Check the *Emerald Necklace* monthly newsletter for details.

Address: 11350 Broadway Ave.
Phone: (216) 341-3152
Season: Year-round
Hours: Daily 9:30 a.m.–5 p.m. except Thanksgiving, Christmas, New Year's Day
Prices: FREE; fees for special programs
Direct.:   I-480 to Exit 23 (Bedford Freeway/Broadway Ave./SR 14); north on Broadway Ave.; on right (west) side.

- Strollers   ● Groups   Food Serv.   ● Parking   Birthdays
- Diap. Chg.   ● Picnic   ● Food Nearby   Pub. Trans.   ● Handicap. Access

Garfield Park Reservation (Cleveland Metroparks)
Area: **South**   City: **Garfield Hts.**   Ages: **All**   Cost: **FREE**

The nature trails here are especially good for youngsters because Garfield Park is one of the smaller reservations in the Cleveland

10 Great Things to Do...

For a Birthday Party

- ⊙ Rent a rec department pool for an hour or two.

- ⊙ Tour the farm and take a pony ride at Burnett's Pet Farm in Olmsted Township. (p. 79)

- ⊙ Bring your own cake and have your run of the Rainbow Children's Museum. (p. 59)

- ⊙ Relax while the kids take on the Cleveland Metroparks Zoo and Rainforest. (p. 85)

- ⊙ Climb the playmazes and throw the foam balls at one of the area's indoor playgrounds.

- ⊙ Meet some of the area's indigenous animals at the Lake Erie Nature and Science Center. (p. 108)

- ⊙ Tour the Olympia Gourmet Chocolate factory and make your own molded candy. (p. 204)

- ⊙ Go to a Crunch game for special treatment & party favors. (p. 192)

- ⊙ Have a beach blanket party with all the trimmings at Fairport Harbor Beach. (p. 92)

- ⊙ Take your group on a fall Hayride at the Chalet in the Cleveland Metroparks. (p. 162)

Metroparks' Emerald Necklace. The Ridgetop trail and the North Ravine trail cover only about 1/2 mile each. Also located on the park grounds are a small public garden, a loop all-purpose trail, ball fields, four picnic areas, Iron Spring Wildlife Preserve, and the Garfield Park Nature Center (see separate listing).

Address: Garfield Park Dr.
Phone: (216) 351-6300; nature center: (216) 341-3152
Season: Year-round
Hours: Daily 6 a.m.–11 p.m.
Prices: FREE
Direct.:   I-480 to Exit 23 (Bedford Freeway/Broadway Ave./SR 14); north on Broadway Ave. to reservation entrance (Garfield Park Dr.) on left (west) side.

● Strollers   ● Groups   ● Food Serv.   ● Parking   Birthdays
● Diap. Chg.   ● Picnic   ● Food Nearby   Pub. Trans.   ● Handicap. Access

Geauga Park District
Area: **Far East**   City: **Chardon**   Ages: **All**   Cost: **FREE**

More than 4,600 acres of forests, wetlands, lakes, rivers, and streams make up this excellent park system, complete with fishing, hiking, and picnic areas throughout. Expansion plans include a 926-acre Headwaters Park (opened recently) and the 792-acre West Woods track (to open in 1998). Also part of the park are Auburn's Beartown Lakes Reservation and 410 acres of the White Pine Bog Forest in the Burton Wetlands, jointly administered with the Nature Conservancy (public access to the wetlands, however, is restricted).

Maps and directions to the park area are available from the park office. For updated lists of special events, ask to be added to the mailing list for the bimonthly newsletter.

The following Geauga Park District facilities are described separately in this book:

Bessie Benner Metzenbaum Park
Big Creek Park and Donald W. Meyer Nature Center
Eldon Russell Park
Swine Creek Reservation
Walker C. Best Preserve
Whitlam Woods

Address: 9160 Robinson Rd.
Phone: (216†) 285-2222, (216†) 564-7131, (216†) 834-1856
Season: Year–round
Hours: Dawn–dusk
Prices: FREE
Direct.:   (See individual park listings)

Geneva State Park
Area: **Farther East**   City: **Geneva**   Ages: **All**   Cost: **FREE–$$$**

The beachfront at Geneva State Park is a 1,500-foot-wide mix of sand and rock. The park offers swimming with lifeguards on duty, boating and fishing; a marina with a bait shop; boat trailer parking; six launching ramps; and 91 tent and RV sites. Facilities include flush toilets, showers, laundry, telephone, and fire rings. The Ohio Department of Natural Resources also offers "Rent-A-Camp" and "Rent-A-RV" programs. Seasonal cabins are open May–Sep. Call for reservations.

There is a playground for children, and there are seven miles of hiking trails (but the trails are not well marked). Rangers also caution that the wooded trails go through areas in which hunting is permitted.

Winter recreation includes five miles of cross-country skiing trails that are mainly flat and excellent for beginners. Access to the trail is at the park office. The staging area for the 3-1/2-mile trail is located on Lake Rd. across from Deer Lake Golf Course on the north end of the park. (Park at the old park office lot.) No equipment rental is available.

NATURE & OUTDOORS

Address: Padanarum Rd.
Phone: (216†) 466-8400
Season: Year-round, fully operational Apr–Oct
Hours: Rangers: 24 hours Sat–Sun; lifeguard: Mon–Fri noon–6 p.m.; Sat–Sun 1 p.m.–7 p.m. Memorial Day–Labor Day
Prices: Free park admission; fee for campsites
Direct.: I-90 to Exit 218 for SR 534; north on SR 534; left (west) on N. Center Rd. to Padanarum Rd.; right (north) on Padanarum to park entrance.

	Strollers	● Groups	● Food Serv.	● Parking	Birthdays
	Diap. Chg.	● Picnic	● Food Nearby	Pub. Trans.	● Handicap. Access

Girdled Road Reservation, South (Lake Metroparks)
Area: **Far East**   City: **Concord**   Ages: **All**   Cost: **FREE**

This 643-acre reservation has all-purpose trails (including hiking, horseback riding, cross-country skiing), fishing, ball and game fields, picnic areas with grills and shelters, and a playground.

Address: Radcliffe Rd. at SR 608
Phone: (216†) 256-PARK
WWW: http://www.harborcom.net/parks/parkinfo.html
Season: Year-round
Hours: Daily dawn–dusk
Prices: FREE
Direct.: I-90 to exit for SR 44; south on SR 44 for 1.5 miles; left (east)on Girdled Rd. for 2.5 miles; right (south) on SR 608 for 2 miles; left (east) on Radcliffe Rd. for 1/3-mile.

● Strollers	● Groups	Food Serv.	● Parking	Birthdays
Diap. Chg.	● Picnic	● Food Nearby	Pub. Trans.	Handicap. Access

NATURE & OUTDOORS

Goodyear Heights Metro Park (Metro Parks Serving Summit County)
Area: **Far South**   City: **Akron**   Ages: **All**   Cost: **FREE**

Goodyear Heights is a 410-acre playground for children and adults. The park has a ball field, fishing, hiking and fitness trails, play equipment, open and closed shelters, sledding, ice-skating, restrooms, and cross-country skiing. Pavilion and shelter rental is also an option.

Address: 589 Frazier Ave.
Phone: (330) 867-5511
Season: Year–round
Hours: Dawn–dusk
Prices: FREE
Direct.: I-77 to I-76 (after split on Akron's east side) to Exit 26 (SR 91); north on SR 91 for 1/2 mile; left on Newton; on right.

| Strollers | Groups | Food Serv. | • Parking | Birthdays |
| • Diap. Chg. | • Picnic | • Food Nearby | • Pub. Trans. | Handicap. Access |

Gorge Metro Park (Metro Parks Serving Summit County)
Area: **Far South**   City: **Cuyahoga Falls**   Ages: **All**   Cost: **FREE**

This 205-acre park contains several gentle hiking trails, play equipment, an open shelter, and restrooms. The 3.2-mile Highbridge Trail connects with Cascade Valley Metro Park.

Address: 1160 Front St.
Phone: (330) 867-5511
Season: Year–round
Hours: Dawn–dusk
Prices: FREE
Direct.: I-271 to Exit 18 (SR 8); south on SR 8; right on Broad St. in Cuyahoga Falls for 2 blocks; left (south) on Second St. (it will merge with Front St.); watch for Gorge Metro Park sign on right (sharp right turn); entrance just before Cuyahoga River bridge.
SR 8 northbound to exit for Howe Ave.; south on Howe; right (north) on Front St. to Cuyahoga River bridge; entrance on left at traffic light.

| Strollers | Groups | Food Serv. | • Parking | Birthdays |
| Diap. Chg. | • Picnic | • Food Nearby | • Pub. Trans. | Handicap. Access |

Hach-Otis State Nature Preserve
Area: **East**   City: **Willoughby Twp.**   Ages: **School-age**   Cost: **FREE**

Open to the public since 1944, this 82.4-acre sanctuary and interpretive nature preserve is owned by the Cleveland Audubon Society and managed by the Ohio Department of Natural Resources. Two loop trails provide dramatic overlooks on the Chagrin and Grand rivers. (The 150-foot South Trail bluff rim can be unstable, so it's not good for youngsters.) Nature programs, such as the popular full-moon night hikes, are scheduled year-round by Audubon Society members.

Address: SR 174 & Skyline Dr
Phone: (216†) 563-9344; (614) 265-6453 (Ohio Dept. of Natural Resources)
Season: Year–round
Hours: Dawn–dusk
Prices: FREE
Direct.: I-90 to Exit 189 (SR 91); south on SR 91; left (east) on US 6; left (north) on SR 174 (Chagrin River Rd.); right on Skyline Dr.; follow to end.

Strollers	Groups	Food Serv.	• Parking	Birthdays
Diap. Chg.	Picnic	• Food Nearby	Pub. Trans.	Handicap. Access

NATURE & OUTDOORS

Hampton Hills Metro Park (Metro Parks Serving Summit County)
Area: **Far South**   City: **Akron**   Ages: **All**   Cost: **FREE**

Hampton Hills offers a ball field and soccer field, hiking trails (which are rather steep), and restrooms.

Address: Akron-Peninsula Rd. at Steels Corners Rd.
Phone: (330) 867-5511
Season: Year–round
Hours: Dawn–dusk
Prices: FREE
Direct.: I-77 to exit for Ghent Rd.; north on Ghent; right (east) on Yellow Creek Rd.; (becomes West Bath Rd); east on W. Bath past Akron-Peninsula Rd. to park entrance on left (north) side.

Strollers	Groups	Food Serv.	• Parking	Birthdays
Diap. Chg.	• Picnic	• Food Nearby	Pub. Trans.	Handicap. Access

Happy Days Visitor Center (CVNRA)
Area: **South**   City: **Peninsula**   Ages: **All**   Cost: **FREE–$$$**

Built in the 1930s by the Civilian Conservation Corps as a day camp, the Happy Day Visitor Center of the Cuyahoga Valley National Recreation Area now houses a few exhibits including a slide show about the park's history. Park publications are available here, and rangers are always on hand. Three other CCC structures are nearby: Ledges Shelter, with open playing fields and trails leading to rock ledges; the Octagon Shelter, with playing fields and picnic areas; and Kendall Lake Shelter, a winter sports shelter and picnic area (see separate listing). In all, there are 52 square miles of parkland to explore.

Special programs are offered year-round for children ages 3–6 and for older school-age children. They typically include short hikes, talks, and an activity. The Young Naturalist Series, for example, is a year-round program that offers both indoor instruction and field experience to children ages 9–12. There are workshops on family camping, hiking, biking, and canoeing. Special Olympics–related events are held here annually. A schedule of events is published quarterly; call for details.

Address: SR 303
Phone: (800) 257-9477; (216†) 650-4636
Season: Year-round
Hours: Daily 8 a.m.–5 p.m.; closed Mon–Tue Nov through Mar
Prices: FREE; fee for special events
Direct.: I-271 to SR 8; south on SR 8 to exit for SR 303; right (west) on SR 303; on left.

- • Strollers   • Groups   Food Serv.   • Parking   Birthdays
- • Diap. Chg.   • Picnic   Food Nearby   Pub. Trans.   • Handicap. Access

NATURE & OUTDOORS

Headlands Beach State Park (Cleveland Lakefront State Park)
Area: **Far East**   City: **Mentor**   Ages: **All**   Cost: **FREE**

If you are looking for a large expanse of soft sand and shallow water, you will find it here. Headlands, Ohio's largest natural sandy beach, stretches for a mile and is bounded by the last remaining natural sand dunes along the shores of Lake Erie.

Summer weekends are popular for swimming, fishing, windsurfing (lessons and rentals available), and sand volleyball (equipment rental available). Lawn chairs and umbrellas can also be rented. There is a first-aid station.

There are also three miles of well-marked hiking trails, including the northern terminus of the Buckeye Trail and several trails through the Mentor Marsh Nature Preserve. Naturalist programs are held here in the summer.

During winter months, there are designated areas for sledding, ice-skating, and cross-country skiing.

Address: 9601 Headlands Rd.
Phone: (216†) 352-8082
Season: Year–round
Hours: Mon–Sat sunrise–sunset; lifeguard on duty Mon–Fri 11 a.m.–7 p.m.; Sat–Sun noon–8 p.m. Memorial Day–Labor Day
Prices: FREE
Direct.: SR 2 to exit for SR 44/Headlands Beach State Park; north on SR 44 for 2 miles.

- • Strollers   • Groups   • Food Serv.   • Parking   Birthdays
-   Diap. Chg.   • Picnic   • Food Nearby   Pub. Trans.   • Handicap. Access

Helen Hazen Wyman Park (Lake Metroparks)
Area: **Far East**   City: **Painesville**   Ages: **All**   Cost: **FREE**

Fishing, ball fields, playground, picnic areas with fire pits, grills, and shelters on 60 acres.

Address: SR 86

Phone: (216†) 256-PARK
WWW: http://www.harborcom.net/parks/parkinfo.html
Season: Year–round
Hours: Daily dawn–dusk
Prices: FREE
Direct.:   I-90 to Exit 200 (SR 44); north on SR 44 to exit for SR 84; right (east) on SR 84 for
               2.5 miles; sharp right (south) on SR 86 for 1 mile; on left.

● *Strollers*   ● *Groups*   *Food Serv.*   ● *Parking*   *Birthdays*
  Diap. Chg.   ● *Picnic*   ● *Food Nearby*   *Pub. Trans.*   *Handicap. Access*

Hell Hollow Wilderness Area (Lake Metroparks)
Area: **Far East**   City: **Leroy**   Ages: **All**   Cost: **FREE**

Hiking trails, game fields, picnic areas with playgrounds, grills, shelters, and fire pits on 643 acres.

Address: Brockway Rd.
Phone: (216†) 256-PARK
WWW: http://www.harborcom.net/parks/parkinfo.html
Season: Year–round
Hours: Daily dawn–dusk
Prices: FREE
Direct.:   I-90 to Exit 205 (Vrooman Rd.); south on Vrooman for 1/2 mile; left (east) on
               Carter for 2 miles; left (north) on Paine Rd. to Blair Rd.; right (east) on Blair to
               Ford Rd.; right (east) on Ford; right (south) on Trask Rd. to Brockway Rd.; bear
               right (south) on Brockway; entrance on right before Leroy Center Rd.

● *Strollers*   ● *Groups*   *Food Serv.*   ● *Parking*   *Birthdays*
  Diap. Chg.   ● *Picnic*   ● *Food Nearby*   *Pub. Trans.*   *Handicap. Access*

Hidden Valley Park (Lake Metroparks)
Area: **Far East**   City: **Madison**   Ages: **All**   Cost: **FREE**

All-purpose trails (hiking, cross-country skiing), fishing, designated sledding area, canoe access, picnic areas with grills, shelters, fire pits, and playground on 147 acres.

Address: 4880 Klasen Rd.
Phone: (216†) 256-PARK
WWW: http://www.harborcom.net/parks/parkinfo.html
Season: Year–round
Hours: Daily 9 a.m.–dusk
Prices: FREE
Direct.:   I-90 to SR 528 (south) for 1.5 miles; right (west) on Klasen Rd.; park is near end
               of road on left.

● *Strollers*   ● *Groups*   *Food Serv.*   ● *Parking*   *Birthdays*
  Diap. Chg.   ● *Picnic*   ● *Food Nearby*   *Pub. Trans.*   ● *Handicap. Access*

NATURE & OUTDOORS

Hinckley Reservation (Cleveland Metroparks)
Area: **South**   City: **Hinckley**   Ages: **All**   Cost: **FREE–$$**

Best known as the place where the buzzards summer (there is even a mid-March celebration of their return), Hinckley Reservation offers swimming (with lifeguards on duty) at Hinckley Lake and Ledge Lake, changing rooms, restrooms, and concessions. Hinckley Lake Boathouse on West Drive has a boat launch and offers rentals (canoes, electric motorboats, kayaks, in-line skates) available April 1st to November 1st.

There are also all-purpose trails, cross-country ski trails, sledding (off State Rd.—lit at night), skating on Hinckley Lake, fishing and ice fishing on Hinckley, Judge's, and Ledge lakes, and eight picnic areas. Whipp's Ledges rock formation overlooks Hinckley Lake from a height of 350 feet.

Address: Off Bellus and State Rds.
Phone: (216) 351-6300; boathouse: (216†) 278-2122
Season: Year-round (lifeguard on duty early Jun–Labor Day)
Hours: Reservation: 6 a.m.–11 p.m. daily; lifeguard 9 a.m.–9 p.m. daily (seasonal)
Prices: FREE; some rental fees
Direct.: I-71 to exit for SR 303; east on SR 303; right (south) on SR 3; left (east) on Bellus Rd.; on right.

- *Strollers*   ● *Groups*   ● *Food Serv.*   ● *Parking*   *Birthdays*
  Diap. Chg.   ● *Picnic*   ● *Food Nearby*   ● *Pub. Trans.*   ● *Handicap. Access*

Hogback Ridge (Lake Metroparks)
Area: **Far East**   City: **Madison**   Ages: **All**   Cost: **FREE**

Hiking trails (including the All People's Trail), fishing, picnic areas with grills and shelters on 418 acres.

Address: Emerson Rd.
Phone: (216†) 256-PARK
WWW: http://www.harborcom.net/parks/parkinfo.html
Season: Year-round
Hours: Daily dawn–dusk
Prices: FREE
Direct.: I-90 to Exit 212 (SR 528); south on SR 528 (Madison Rd.); left (east) on Griswold; north on Emerson Rd.

- ● *Strollers*   ● *Groups*   *Food Serv.*   ● *Parking*   *Birthdays*
  Diap. Chg.   ● *Picnic*   ● *Food Nearby*   *Pub. Trans.*   ● *Handicap. Access*

Holden Arboretum
Area: **Far East**   City: **Kirtland**   Ages: **All**   Cost: **$**

Encompassing over 3,100 acres, Holden is the largest private arboretum in the United States. Its wide, well-marked trail system helps make it a family-friendly place. There are signs posted on each trail explaining the ecosystems, wildflowers, and birds—making it easier to answer children's questions. Even better, youngsters can receive a loaner backpack with an audio tape and an activity kit for the hike. (A parent must leave behind a driver's license as collateral.)

Holden also boasts fine parent-and-child programs. During the fall, for example, one program invites youngsters to collect leaves, berries, and bark and use them to prepare dye baths to color tee-shirts. Campfire story and song programs are a big hit with all ages. Advanced registration is required for all classes, and be forewarned that classes are popular and class sizes are limited. Most have a seasonal theme; look for bird feeding, snowshoeing, tracking, and gardening. The class schedule is available quarterly.

During weekday visits, you will likely encounter a school group. Last year, more than 9,000 children visited Holden Arboretum on field trips.

Address:	9500 Sperry Rd.
Phone:	(216†) 256-1110; (216†) 946-4400
Season:	Year-round
Hours:	Tue–Sun 10 a.m.–5 p.m.
Prices:	$4 adults, $2 ages 6–15, $3 seniors w/ Buckeye Card, FREE under age 6
Direct.:	I-90 to Exit 193 for SR 306; south on SR 306 to Kirtland-Chardon Rd. (splits off); bear left (east) on K-C Rd. (SR 615) to Sperry Rd.; left on Sperry; on left.

- Strollers
- Diap. Chg.
- Groups
- Picnic

Food Serv.
- Food Nearby

- Parking

Pub. Trans.

Birthdays
- Handicap. Access

Huntington Reservation (Cleveland Metroparks)
Area: **West**   City: **Bay Village**   Ages: **All**   Cost: **FREE**

This popular and sandy Lake Erie beach has a shallow walk-in and sandbars—helpful for new swimmers. There are picnic tables and grills, a small playground, bathhouse, and restrooms. On a clear day the downtown skyline is easily visible to the east.

Huntington Reservation also has hiking trails, ball fields, sledding (east of Porter Creek Dr.), the Lake Erie Nature and Science Center (off Porter Creek Dr.—see separate listing), and Baycrafters (see separate listing).

Address:	Porter Creek Dr.
Phone:	(216) 351-6300
Season:	Year–round (lifeguard on duty early June–Labor Day
Hours:	Daily 6 a.m.–11 p.m.; lifeguard 9 a.m.–9 p.m. daily (seasonal)
Prices:	FREE
Direct.:	I-90 to Exit 159 (Columbia Rd./SR 252); north on Columbia Rd. to dead end; left (west) on Lake Rd. approx. 2 miles.

- Strollers
  Diap. Chg.
- Groups
- Picnic
- Food Serv.
- Food Nearby
- Parking
- Pub. Trans.

Birthdays
- Handicap. Access

Indian Hollow Reservation (Lorain County Metroparks)
Area: **Far West**   City: **Grafton**   Ages: **All**   Cost: **FREE**

Hiking trails, horseshoe courts, picnic areas with shelters, play-ground.

Address: Parsons Rd.
Phone: (216†) 458-5121; (800) LCM-PARK
Season: Year-round
Hours: Daily 8 a.m.–dusk
Prices: FREE
Direct.: I-480 west to end (becomes SR 10/US 20); west on SR 10/US 20; south on SR 57; west on Parsons Rd.; on right.

- ● *Strollers*   ● *Groups*   *Food Serv.*   ● *Parking*   *Birthdays*
  Diap. Chg.   ● *Picnic*   ● *Food Nearby*   *Pub. Trans.*   *Handicap. Access*

Indian Point Park (Lake Metroparks)
Area: **Far East**   City: **Leroy**   Ages: **All**   Cost: **FREE**

Hiking trails, fishing, picnic areas with grills on 261 acres.

Address: Seeley Rd.
Phone: (216†) 256-PARK
WWW: http://www.harborcom.net/parks/parkinfo.html
Season: Year–round
Hours: Daily dawn–dusk
Prices: FREE
Direct.: I-90 to Exit 205 (Vrooman Rd.); north on Vrooman for 1 mile; right (east) on Seeley Rd. (gravel road); on left.

- ● *Strollers*   *Groups*   *Food Serv.*   ● *Parking*   *Birthdays*
  Diap. Chg.   ● *Picnic*   ● *Food Nearby*   *Pub. Trans.*   *Handicap. Access*

Kelleys Island State Park
Area: **Farther West**   City: **Kelleys Island**   Ages: **All**   Cost: **FREE–$$**

The 1-1/2 mile sandy beach at Kelleys Island State Park offers swimming (no lifeguards), boating (with boat launch), and fishing—mainly for small-mouthed bass and walleye. Amazing glacial grooves and Inspiration Rock are among the must-see sites on the island. There is also a playground for children and five or six miles of well-marked wooded hiking trails. Also of interest is an abandoned quarry that can be explored for fossils. Swimming in the quarry is prohibited, except during special group arrangements. The 4-H club, for example, learns to scuba dive here. A naturalist program includes hikes and nature talks for children. During summer months there are also Saturday night movies, geared toward the family, that focus on nature.

The park is set up for 129 tent and recreational vehicle sites. Facilities include bathhouse with flush toilets, showers and changing rooms, telephone, and fire ring. The "Rent-A-Camp" program is offered May 15 through September 15. Call ahead for availability information.

Address: North side of Kelleys Island
Phone: (419) 797-4530; Neuman Cruise & Ferry Line: (800) 876-1907; Kelleys Island
Ferry Line: (419) 798-9763
WWW: http://winslo.ohio.gov/ohswww/places/grooves.html (or "inscrock.html")
Season: Year-round; fully operational Apr–Oct
Hours: First aid & rangers: daily, 24 hrs.
Prices: FREE park admission; fee for campsites.
Direct.: SR 2 west to Sandusky Bay Bridge; north on SR 269; east on SR 163 to
Marblehead; Neuman Cruise & Ferry Line and Kelleys Island Ferry leave from
well-marked docks in Marblehead.

| • Strollers | Groups | Food Serv. | • Parking | Birthdays |
| Diap. Chg. | • Picnic | • Food Nearby | Pub. Trans. | • Handicap. Access |

NATURE & OUTDOORS

Kendall Lake Area & Winter Sports Center (CVNRA)
Area: **South**   City: **Peninsula**   Ages: **All**   Cost: **FREE**

The Kendall Area is one of the oldest parts of the Cuyahoga Valley National Recreation Area; the center was built by the Civilian Conservation Corps in the late 1930s. It's particularly popular in winter, especially around Kendall Lake, as it is a hub for sledding and tubing. Snowshoes are available for a fee. You must leave your driver's license behind for collateral. There are well-marked all-purpose trails, and snowshoeing and cross-country ski trails that go through woods, meadows, and several caves, and near sandstone rock ledges.

In the summer, there is fishing in the lake; there are also ball playing fields and picnic areas. The center is used for special workshops, such as boomerang construction and bird-watching (snowshoe instruction in winter). Nearby are open recreation areas for kite flying and frisbee throwing.

Address: Truxell Rd.
Phone: (800) 257-9477; (216†) 650-4636
Season: Winter
Hours: Shelter: Sat–Sun 10 a.m.–5:00 p.m. (some holidays) in Jan & Feb
Prices: FREE
Direct.: I-271 to Exit 8 (SR 8); south on SR 8 to exit for SR 303/Akron-Cleveland Rd.;
straight (south) on Akron-Cleveland Rd.; right (west) on Kendall Park Rd.
(becomes Truxell Rd.); on left.

| Strollers | • Groups | Food Serv. | • Parking | Birthdays |
| • Diap. Chg. | • Picnic | Food Nearby | Pub. Trans. | • Handicap. Access |

Lake Erie Nature and Science Center

Area: **West**   City: **Bay Village**   Ages: **All**   Cost: **FREE–$**

The Lake Erie Nature and Science Center is everything a nature center should be: cozy, with lots of little critters sliding, sniffing, and scurrying about. It is well stocked with deer, rabbits, ducks, and chickens outside; turtles, iguanas, snakes, and fish inside. Many animals in the center's collection have been brought in wounded or sick by area residents and nursed back to health. This is a wonderful place for smaller children. It is popular, but never really crowded.

Year-round special nature programs for children begin with ages 3–4, and typically include crafts, songs, stories, and exploring the adjacent trails.

The Schuele Planetarium offers programs geared for a family audience or smaller children. Annual family events range from seminars on wildlife to hands-on crafts and storytelling around a seasonal theme.

The Nature Center is located on the Metroparks' Huntington Reservation (see separate listing), so there are also trails here that lead through the woods and along the creek. Ask for directions if you want to make the longer hike that ends up on Lake Erie at Huntington Beach.

Address: 28728 Wolf Rd.
Phone: (216†) 871-2900
WWW: http://bbs2.rmrc.net/~lensc/
Season: Year-round
Hours: Mon–Sat 10 a.m.–5 p.m.; Sun 1–5 p.m.; planetarium: 1st & 3rd Saturdays of each month
Prices: Free admission; planetarium: $3, $1 under age 10 & seniors, free for members
Direct.: I-90 to exit for Columbia Rd. N. (SR 252); north on Columbia; right (west) on Wolf Rd. about 2.5 miles; on right.

- Strollers   ● Groups   Food Serv.   ● Parking   ● Birthdays
  Diap. Chg.   ● Picnic   Food Nearby   ● Pub. Trans.   ● Handicap. Access

Lake Farmpark (Lake Metroparks)

Area: **Far East**   City: **Kirtland**   Ages: **All**   Cost: **$–$$$**

Lake Farmpark offers the best way to see, chase, and pet farm animals short of buying your own farmstead. In addition to the main building, which features a daily milking demo (a hands-on original) and changing exhibits about life on the farm, there is a huge barn and open barnyard a short hike down the road. The easiest way to get to the barn—and an event in itself—is to ride the farm's horse-drawn covered wagon, which leaves every 15 minutes from the back of the main building.

The barn is home to baby farm animals (chickens, pigs, goats, lambs) and is where you'll spend most of your time—especially when there are newborns. The amiable staff makes a point of ensuring that each child has seen and touched enough. (Our son talked for months about the baby chick that hopped and peeped in his hands.) The barn also houses quarter horses and a large show ring that is used for special exhibits and farm machinery demonstrations.

In addition to being a wonderful place for families, this is also one of the few places that opens at 9:00 a.m. on Sundays.

Each month brings a new activity or special event, such as bluegrass concerts, tractor displays, a fall harvest festival, and country lights and decorations during the winter holidays. For younger visitors, special programs include Chores at the Crack of Dawn for ages 8–12 with an adult, a farm life series for preschoolers, and a variety of short-term summer camps.

Remember: this is a farm, so shoes will get dusty or muddy.

NATURE & OUTDOORS

Address: 8800 Chardon Rd. (US 6)
Phone: (216†) 256-2122
WWW: http://harborcom.net/parks/farmpark.html
Season: Year-round; closed Christmas & New Year's Day, Mondays in January and February.
Hours: Daily 9 a.m.–5 p.m.
Prices: $5, $4 seniors, $3.50 ages 2–11, no charge under age 2
Direct.: I-90 to exit for SR 306; south on SR 306 for 4 miles; left (east) on Chardon Rd. (US 6) for 1 mile; on south side.

● Strollers	● Groups	● Food Serv.	● Parking	● Birthdays
● Diap. Chg.	Picnic	Food Nearby	Pub. Trans.	● Handicap. Access

Lake Metroparks
Area: **Far East**   City: **Various**   Ages: **All**   Cost: **FREE–$$$**

Lake Metroparks offers a wide array of first-class recreational opportunities, nature programs, and many other family-oriented activities year-round at various scenic park facilities. The headquarters for Lake Metroparks is located adjacent to Concord Woods Nature Park in Concord Township (see separate listing). Registration for activities is held at Lake Farmpark (see separate listing).

These Lake Metroparks are featured separately in this book:

Chagrin River Park	Indian Point Park
Chapin Forest Reserv. & Pine Lodge	Lake Farmpark
Children's Schoolhouse & Nature Ctr.	Lakeshore Reservation
Concord Woods Nature Park	Mason's Landing Park
Fairport Harbor Lakefront Park	Paine Falls Park
Girdled Road Reservation, South	Painesville Township Park
Helen Hazen Wyman Park	Parson's Gardens
Hell Hollow Wilderness Area	Penitentiary Glen Reservation
Hidden Valley Park	Riverview Park
Hogback Ridge	Veterans Park

Address: Registration Offices: Lake Farmpark (see separate entry)8800 Chardon Rd.(US 6)
Phone: (216†) 256-PARK; class registration: (800) 669-9226; cross-country ski hotline: (216†) 256-2255
WWW: http://www.harborcom.net/parks/parkinfo.html
Season: Year-round
Hours: Daily 9 a.m.–dusk
Prices: Fees for classes & special events
Direct.: (See individual park listings.)

Lakeshore Reservation (Lake Metroparks)
Area: **Far East**   City: **Perry**   Ages: **All**   Cost: **FREE**

Hiking trails (including an All People's Trail), fishing, sculpture garden, picnic areas with grills on 86 acres.

Address: 4799 Lockwood Rd.
Phone: (216†) 256-PARK
WWW: http://www.harborcom.net/parks/parkinfo.html
Season: Year-round
Hours: Daily dawn–dusk
Prices: FREE
Direct.: SR 2 east to merge with US 20; east on US 20 to Perry; north on Antioch Rd. for 1.5 miles; right (east) on Lockwood Rd.; on left.

- Strollers   • Groups   Food Serv.   • Parking   Birthdays
  Diap. Chg.   • Picnic   • Food Nearby   Pub. Trans.   • Handicap. Access

Lorain County Metropolitan Park District
Area: **West**   City: **Various**   Ages: **All**   Cost: **FREE–$**

Lorain County Metroparks include eight varied facilities that offer families a glimpse of native wildlife, Ohio history and outdoor experiences. Maps of the parks and various trails are available at any of the parks. For updated lists of special events and programs, ask to be added to the mailing list of the bimonthly newsletter, "The Arrowhead."

These Lorain County Metroparks are featured in this book:

Black River Reservation   French Creek Reservation
Caley National Wildlife Woods   Indian Hollow Reservation
Carlisle Reservation and Visitors Center   Mill Hollow-Bacon Woods Memorial Park
Charlemont Reservation   Schoepfle Arboretum
French Creek Nature Center

Address: Park offices: 12882 Diagonal Rd., LaGrange, OH
Phone: (800) LCM-PARK or (216†) 458-5121
Season: Year-round
Hours: Daily dawn–dusk
Prices: Fees for classes & special events
Direct.: (See individual park listings.)

Lorain Lakeview Park
Area: **Far West**   City: **Lorain**   Ages: **All**   Cost: **FREE**

Families have enjoyed 42-acre Lorain Lakeview park since it was taken over by the city in 1916. There is an elegance to the setting: a boardwalk overlooking the lakefront stretches 1,200 feet; rose gardens, a fountain, and a latticed gazebo provide the setting for outdoor concerts on Sundays in the summer.

There is swimming in Lake Erie off a sandy beach and fishing off nearby Municipal Pier. The park is set up for lawn bowling, softball, baseball, beach volleyball, and tennis. Bring your own equipment, and call in advance to reserve a court. (The tennis courts are lit for night use.) There is a playground right on the beach. In summertime, craft programs run daily for school-age children. In winter, depending on weather conditions, ice-skating is offered on a small pond.

Address: W. Erie Ave. at Lakeview Dr. & Parkview Ave. (just east of SR 58)
Phone: (216†) 244-9000
Season: Year-long
Hours: Daily sunrise–11 p.m.; lifeguard Memorial Day–Labor Day 11 a.m.–7 p.m.
Prices: FREE
Direct.: SR 2 to exit for SR 58 (Leavitt Rd.); north on SR 58.; right (east) on W. Erie Ave.; left on Lakeview Dr.

Strollers	• Groups	• Food Serv.	Parking	Birthdays
• Diap. Chg.	• Picnic	• Food Nearby	Pub. Trans.	Handicap. Access

Mason's Landing Park (Lake Metroparks)
Area: **Far East**   City: **Perry**   Ages: **All**   Cost: **FREE**

Fishing, canoe access, picnic areas with grills on 133 acres.

Address: Vrooman Rd.
Phone: (216†) 256-PARK
WWW: http://www.harborcom.net/parks/parkinfo.html
Season: Year-round
Hours: Daily dawn–dusk
Prices: FREE
Direct.: I-90 to Exit 205 for Vrooman Rd.; north on Vrooman for 1.5 miles; on left.

• Strollers	• Groups	Food Serv.	• Parking	Birthdays
Diap. Chg.	• Picnic	• Food Nearby	Pub. Trans.	Handicap. Access

Mentor Marsh State Nature Preserve
Area: **Far East**   City: **Mentor**   Ages: **All**   Cost: **FREE**

Although it is just 30 miles due east from downtown Cleveland, Mentor Marsh is really a world away. This state nature preserve is co-owned by the Cleveland Museum of Natural History and is a national

NATURE &
OUTDOORS

natural landmark. It occupies 644 acres teeming with beaver, mink, deer, fox, and 125 species of birds. Of course, spotting them behind the eight-foot-tall reeds, hidden ponds, and feeder streams requires some patience, timing, and luck.

There are five self-guided tours ranging from the blacktopped New-house Overlook Trail—just one-tenth of a mile—to the more robust Zimmerman Trail, which crosses streams, shallow ravines, and swamp forests. At two miles in length through an especially soggy part of the preserve, the Zimmerman Trail might not be well suited to families with small children. Also, as this is a marsh, mosquitoes thrive here. (The handy "Mentor Marsh State Nature Preserve" brochure and map available at Mentor Marsh House does a good job of sizing up the trails.)

The area is rich in history as well as wildlife. The marsh began under a glacier before becoming a small lake and later evolving into a mean-dering branch of the Grand River. The area was once home to Native American tribes and also to surveyor crews occupying the area at the time Moses Cleaveland settled Cleveland.

Address:	5185 Corduroy Ave.
Phone:	(216†) 257-0777
Season:	Apr–Oct (Nature Center); trails open year-round
Hours:	Sat–Sun noon–5 p.m., trails dawn–dusk
Prices:	FREE
Direct.:	SR 2 (past split from I-90 in Lake County) to exit for SR 44; north on SR 44; follow signs.

Strollers	● Groups	Food Serv.	● Parking	Birthdays
Diap. Chg.	● Picnic	Food Nearby	Pub. Trans.	● Handicap. Access

Metro Parks Serving Summit County
Area: **Far South**   City: **Akron**   Ages: **All**   Cost: **FREE**

This 6,700-acre park system has 11 developed parks, more than 86 miles of trails (some stroller and wheelchair accessible), and nature programs for all ages. The Bike & Hike Trail, which also allows skiing, is an easy, traffic-free trail that follows old railroad right-of-ways. Partici-pants in the annual Fall Hiking Spree hike 8 of 12 designated trails to earn a walking staff or a metal shield for their staff. A seasonal informa-tion line gives details about Metroparks conditions (330-865-8060). A program information line lists upcoming programs and special events (330-865-8064).

The following park facilities are described separately in this book:

NATURE &
OUTDOORS

Cascade Valley Metro Park	Hampton Hills Metro Park
Deep Lock Metro Park	Munroe Falls Metro Park
Firestone Metro Park	F. A. Seiberling Metro Park
Furnace Run Metro Park	O'Neil Woods Metro Park
Goodyear Heights Metro Park	Sand Run Metro Park
Gorge Metro Park	Silver Creek Metro Park

Address: 975 Treaty Line Rd.
Phone: (330) 867-5511
Season: Year-round
Hours: 8 a.m.–4:30 p.m. (office); dawn–dusk (trails)
Prices: FREE
Direct.: (See individual park listings.)

NATURE &
OUTDOORS

Mill Hollow-Bacon Woods Memorial Park
(Lorain County Metroparks)
Area: **Far West**   City: **Brownhelm Township**   Ages: **All**   Cost: **FREE**

Here you will find hiking trails, picnic areas with shelters, open play-ing fields, a designated sledding hill, and duck ponds. Three well-marked trails ideal for young hikers provide views of the Vermilion River Valley, shale cliffs, and sandstone formations. Self-guided-tour maps are available with information about each trail; seasonally printed guides offer help with identification of a few common plants and ani-mals.

Also on the park grounds is the Benjamin Bacon Museum (open Memorial Day through mid-October and for holiday special events). Originally a homestead built in 1845, the museum preserves furnish-ings and artifacts of daily life from that period.

Recent additions to the park include the Carriage Barn, open year-round (staffed by a park district naturalist) and featuring educational displays and information. An amphitheater has been added for an all-ages summer concert series and educational lectures.

Address: N. Ridge & Vermilion Rds.
Phone: (216†) 458-5121; (800) LCM-PARK
Season: Year-round
Hours: Daily 8 a.m.–dusk; nature center, museum: Fri–Sun & holidays 1–5 p.m.
Prices: FREE
Direct.: SR 2 to exit for Vermilion/Sunnyside Rds.; left (south) off highway; follow signs; right (west) on Jerusalem Rd.; left (south) on Vermilion Rd.; right (west) on N. Ridge Rd.; on right.

● *Strollers*	● *Groups*	*Food Serv.*	● *Parking*		*Birthdays*
● *Diap. Chg.*	● *Picnic*	● *Food Nearby*	*Pub. Trans.*		● *Handicap. Access*

NATURE & OUTDOORS

Mill Stream Run Reservation (Cleveland Metroparks)
Area: **West**   City: **Strongsville**   Ages: **All**   Cost: **FREE–$$**

Trails in the Mill Stream Run Reservation are well marked and cover a variety of terrain to accommodate hikers and cross-country skiers. Hayrides through the reservation and square dancing are offered at the Chalet in October on Sundays 1–4 p.m. and during Haywagon Hoedown celebrations (which also include square dancing) on Saturdays 6–10 p.m. Hayrides are available year-round to groups and for parties.

From November through February (no snow necessary), a pair of 1,000-foot toboggan chutes open for a thrilling ride. This is not for the faint of heart—or for children under 42 inches tall. Inside the Chalet, two large stone fireplaces (and a large-screen TV) serve as popular winter warm-up spots. Year-round, the Chalet can be reserved for large picnics. There are grills, a playground, and a sand volleyball court.

Baldwin and Wallace Lakes, formed from former quarries, offer boating (non-motorized), fishing, and swimming. Paddleboats can be rented at Wallace Lake Concessions, off Valley Pkwy. south of Bagley Rd., (216-826-1682), from Memorial Day to Labor Day. In winter, there is skating on both lakes (Wallace Lake is lit at night).

There are also ball fields, the Strongsville Wildlife Area, nine picnic areas, and sledding at Pawpaw Picnic Area (lit at night).

Address: Valley Pkwy. (S. of Bagley Rd., N. of Drake Rd.)
Phone: (216) 351-6300; Chalet: (216†) 572-9990; Wallace Lake: (216†) 826-1682
Season: Year-round; tobogganing Nov–Feb; swimming early June–Labor Day (lifeguards on duty), 9 a.m.–9 p.m.
Hours: Reservation: daily 6 a.m.–11 p.m.; Chalet: Thu 6–10 p.m., Fri 6–10:30 p.m., Sat 10 a.m.–10:30 p.m.; Sun noon–10 p.m. (holiday hours are longer; Chalet is sometimes closed during private rental)
Prices: FREE; fee for tobogganing & hayrides
Direct.: I-71 to Exit 231 (SR 82); east on SR 82 (Royalton Rd.) for 1/2 mile; left (north) on Valley Pkwy.

● *Strollers*   ● *Groups*   ● *Food Serv.*   ● *Parking*   ● *Birthdays*
   Diap. Chg.   ● *Picnic*   *Food Nearby*   *Pub. Trans.*   ● *Handicap. Access*

Mosquito Lake State Park
Area: **Farther East**   City: **Cortland**   Ages: **All**   Cost: **FREE–$$**

Mosquito Lake, the second-largest artificial lake in Ohio (it covers 7,800 acres with an average depth of 10 feet), offers swimming with lifeguards on duty, sandy beaches, boating, fishing (14-foot aluminum fishing boats are available for rental), a playground, and hiking trails. (There are also horse trails, but no horses available to the public.)

Kids can enjoy nature classes taught by a naturalist, and there is an amphitheater where wildlife programs are held Saturday nights during the summer.

During the winter months, cross-country ski trails (3–4 miles) range from open meadow to mature woodland starting at the main park entrance and traveling through the campground area. Fourteen miles of frozen lake surface are available for snowmobiling. No rentals are available.

The park is a popular place for summer overnights and is set up with 234 tent and recreational vehicle sites. Facilities include bathhouses with flush toilets and showers, a telephone, and fire rings.

Address: 1439 SR 305
Phone: (330) 637-2856
Season: Year-round; fully operational Apr–Oct
Hours: First aid & rangers: 24 hrs.; lifeguard on duty daily 11 a.m.–7 p.m. Memorial Day–Labor Day
Prices: FREE park admission; fee for campsites
Direct.: I-271 to Exit 27 (US 422); east on US 422 to SR 305 east. 10 miles northeast of Warren.

Strollers	Groups	Food Serv.	• Parking	Birthdays
Diap. Chg.	• Picnic	Food Nearby	Pub. Trans.	• Handicap. Access

NATURE & OUTDOORS

Munroe Falls Metro Park (Metro Parks Serving Summit County)
Area: **Far South**   City: **Munroe Falls**   Ages: **All**   Cost: **$**

Munroe Falls offers a ball field, hiking trail, fishing, play equipment, three open shelters, sledding hill, soccer field, swimming lake, tennis court, volleyball court, cross-country skiing, and restrooms.

Address: 521-605 S. River Rd.
Phone: (330) 867-5511
Season: Memorial Day–Labor Day: swimming available (fee charged). Rest of park open year-round (free)
Hours: Daily 10 a.m.–9 p.m. swimming area (Aug & Sep close at 8 p.m.)
Prices: $3 adults, $2 for children 2-12, under 2 Free
Direct.: I-271 to Exit 18; south on SR 8 to exit for Graham Rd./Silver Lake/Stow; east on Graham Rd.; right (south) on SR 91 to Munroe Falls; left (east) on S. River Rd. for 1 mile; on right.

• Strollers	• Groups	• Food Serv.	• Parking	Birthdays
• Diap. Chg.	• Picnic	• Food Nearby	Pub. Trans.	• Handicap. Access

Nickel Plate Beach
Area: **Farther West**   City: **Huron**   Ages: **All**   Cost: **$**

Nickel Plate is a popular summer picnic spot because of its mile-long natural sand beach. Swimmers can enjoy the waters of Lake Erie, but there are no lifeguards, only buoys designating the swimming area. Volleyball nets are set up around the area; balls can be rented from the concession stand. There is also a small playground.

Address: Nickel Plate Dr.
Phone: (419) 433-5568
Season: Memorial Day through Labor Day
Hours: Dawn–dusk
Prices: Parking: $1 motorcycles, $2 cars, $3 campers, $10 season pass
Direct.: SR 2 to exit for Berlin Rd.; north on Berlin; right on Tiffin Rd. to dead-end with Nickel Plate Dr.

Strollers	• Groups	• Food Serv.	• Parking	Birthdays
Diap. Chg.	• Picnic	• Food Nearby	Pub. Trans.	Handicap. Access

NATURE & OUTDOORS

North Chagrin Nature Center (Cleveland Metroparks)
Area: **East**   City: **Mayfield Village**   Ages: **All**   Cost: **FREE–$**

North Chagrin Nature Center, located in the North Chagrin Reservation (see separate listing), houses an indoor play area that offers environment-oriented games and puzzles. The live snake and turtle exhibits are a child-pleaser. Adults as well as children are likely to learn something from the displays of bird photographs, antlers, and wetlands wildlife; they are targeted to all ages and teach about the ecosystem of the surrounding area.

We visited on a wintry day and so spent most of our time playing indoors with the big wooden Concentration game. Its removable wooden blocks cover pairs of outdoor scenes that children have to remember and match.

EarthWords (216-449-0511), the nature center's bookstore, is well stocked with nature picture books and stories about the environment and animals. A storytime is offered twice a month featuring environmental themes.

Outside the nature center, friendly ducks waddle nearby. Accustomed to curious children, they are not shy about asking for handouts. However, no feeding allowed!

For older children (and parents), in-line skates are available here for rental in the summer. Smooth trails offer an easy hike, too.

Address: 3037 SOM Center Rd. (North Chagrin Reservation)
Phone: (216†) 473-3370
Season: Year-round
Hours: 9:30 a.m.–5 p.m. daily except Thanksgiving, Christmas, New Year's Day
Prices: FREE; fees for some special programs
Direct.: I-271 to Exit 34 (Mayfield Rd.); east on Mayfield; north on SR 91 (SOM Ctr. Rd.); Sunset Lane entrance off SR 91 in Mayfield Village.

• Strollers	• Groups	Food Serv.	• Parking	Birthdays
• Diap. Chg.	• Picnic	• Food Nearby	Pub. Trans.	• Handicap. Access

10 Great Things to Do...

With Older Kids:

- ◉ Attend rehearsal at the Cleveland Orchestra. (p. 143)

- ◉ Climb the walls at the Cleveland Rock Gym. (p. 164)

- ◉ Bundle up and take on the toboggan run at Mill Stream Run Reservation. (p. 114)

- ◉ Stargaze at the Cleveland Museum of Natural History's Planetarium. (p. 37)

- ◉ Climb ladders and squeeze through hatches on the USS COD. (p. 69)

- ◉ Sign up for a class at the Cleveland Center for Contemporary Art and make a sculpture together. (p. 35)

- ◉ Root for the home team at an Indians, Cavaliers, Crunch, or Lumberjacks game. (p. 191–193)

- ◉ Explore the Lake Metroparks on a guided hike.

- ◉ Get dressed up and attend one of the plays offered in the young people's series at Playhouse Square. (p. 153)

- ◉ Pack up your sleeping bags and head to Kelleys Island State Park for an overnight camping trip. (p. 106)

North Chagrin Reservation (Cleveland Metroparks)

Area: **East**   City: **Mayfield Village, Willoughby Hills, Gates Mills**
Ages: **All**   Cost: **FREE–$$**

All-purpose trails (including Buttermilk Falls), fishing and ice fishing (Oxbow Lagoon), ball fields, basketball court, ice-skating (at Strawberry Pond and Oxbow Lagoon—both lit at night), sledding hills (at the River Grove Winter Recreation Area and Old River Farm Picnic Area—both lit at night), five picnic areas, and Manakiki Public Golf Course. A Junior Naturalist program includes a hike and instruction around a theme for grade-schoolers. Check the *Emerald Necklace* newsletter for registration information.

Squire's Castle is fun to investigate before or after a picnic. It is also the site of an annual Halloween celebration with songs and stories.

The North Chagrin Nature Center is located here (separate listing).

Address: Buttermilk Falls Pkwy.
Phone: (216) 351-6300; nature center: (216†) 473-3370
Season: Year-round
Hours: Daily 6 a.m.–11 p.m.
Prices: FREE
Direct.: I-271 to Exit 34 (Mayfield Rd.); east on Mayfield; north on SR 91 (SOM Center Rd.); Sunset Lane entrance off SR 91 in Mayfield Village.

- Strollers   • Groups   • Food Serv.   • Parking   Birthdays
- Diap. Chg.   • Picnic   • Food Nearby   Pub. Trans.   • Handicap. Access

O'Neil Woods Metro Park (Metro Parks Serving Summit County)

Area: **Far South**   City: **Bath Twp.**   Ages: **All**   Cost: **FREE**

O'Neil Woods is a hilly 274 acres, known for deer and birds.

Address: Martin Rd.
Phone: (330) 867-5511
Season: Year-round
Hours: Dawn–dusk
Prices: FREE
Direct.: I-271 to Exit 12; east on SR 303 to Peninsula; right (south) on Riverview Rd. (at light just before bridge over the Cuyahoga River) past Everett Rd. and Indigo Lake; right on Ira Rd.; left (southwest) on Martin Rd.; on left.

  Strollers   Groups   Food Serv.   • Parking   Birthdays
  Diap. Chg.   • Picnic   • Food Nearby   Pub. Trans.   Handicap. Access

Paine Falls Park (Lake Metroparks)

Area: **Far East**   City: **Leroy**   Ages: **All**   Cost: **FREE**

Hiking trails and picnic areas with grills on 56 acres near a scenic waterfall.

Address: Paine Rd.

Phone: (216†) 256-PARK
WWW: http://www.harborcom.net/parks/parkinfo.html
Season: Year-round
Hours: Daily dawn–dusk
Prices: FREE
Direct.: I-90 to exit for Vrooman Rd.; south on Vrooman for 1/2 mile; left (east) on Carter road for 2 miles; left (north) on Paine Rd. for 1/2 mile.

| • Strollers | • Groups | Food Serv. | • Parking | Birthdays |
| Diap. Chg. | • Picnic | • Food Nearby | Pub. Trans. | Handicap. Access |

Painesville Township Park (Lake Metroparks)
Area: Far East   **City: Painesville Township**   **Ages: All**   **Cost: FREE–$$**

Family events at the 37-acre Painesville Township Park include ballroom and country dances and picnics held in the community center. Programs for kids include a Jazzer Kamp for ages 4–11 and sessions in arts and crafts, fitness, and food preparation centered around holidays. Nearby are softball fields, playgrounds, and picnic areas.

Address: 1025 Hardy Rd.
Phone: (216†) 256-PARK; community center info: (216†) 354-3885; softball info: (216†) 639-9951
WWW: http://www.harborcom.net/parks/parkinfo.html
Season: Year-round
Hours: Daily dawn–dusk
Prices: Vary
Direct.: SR 2 to exit for SR 535/Fairport-Nursery Rd./Bacon Rd.; west on Fairport-Nursery Rd. for 1 mile; right (north) on Hardy Rd. for 1 mile.

| • Strollers | • Groups | • Food Serv. | • Parking | Birthdays |
| Diap. Chg. | • Picnic | • Food Nearby | • Pub. Trans. | • Handicap. Access |

Parsons Gardens (Lake Metroparks)
Area: East   **City: Willoughby**   **Ages: All**   **Cost: FREE**

Picnic areas, rental garden plots on seven acres.

Address: Erie Rd.
Phone: (216†) 256-PARK
WWW: http://www.harborcom.net/parks/parkinfo.html
Season: Year-round
Hours: Daily dawn–dusk
Prices: FREE
Direct.: SR 2 to exit for Lost Nation Rd.; west on St. Clair St. for 1/2 mile; left (south) on Erie Rd.

| • Strollers | • Groups | Food Serv. | • Parking | Birthdays |
| Diap. Chg. | • Picnic | • Food Nearby | Pub. Trans. | Handicap. Access |

NATURE & OUTDOORS

Penitentiary Glen Reserv. & Nature Ctr. (Lake Metroparks)
Area: **Far East**   City: **Kirtland**   Ages: **All**   Cost: **FREE–$$**

The 385-acre Penitentiary Glen has all-purpose trails (including hiking, horse, and cross-country ski trails, and an All People's Trail), and picnic areas with grills. Its wildlife center and amphitheater make it an especially popular family park.

Family programs such as star searches (the astronomical kind), family hikes, slide shows, and lectures in the auditorium are scheduled throughout the year. Programs for children include orienteering for school-age children, fishing workshops for ages 10 and up, and hikes for preschoolers and up.

The annual Bug Day is a popular all-ages family event with a bug show, exhibits, bug bingo, and other buggy games.

Lake Shore Live Steamers offers free 10-minute, volunteer-operated public train rides on miniature-scale trains that run on a 1/2-mile track through a wooded section of the glen on selected weekends throughout the summer.

Inside a separate wildlife center is a quiet area off limits to the public, where injured animals can recover. Outside, when weather permits, a red-tailed hawk, other birds, and squirrels can be observed in the animal yard.

Address: 8668 Kirtland-Chardon Rd.
Phone: Nature center: (216†) 256-1404; wildlife helpline: (216†) 256-2131
WWW: http://www.harborcom.net/parks/parkinfo.html
Season: Year-round
Hours: Nature center: daily 9 a.m.–5 p.m.; wildlife center: daily 9 a.m.–5 p.m.; gift shop: Tue–Sun noon–5 p.m.; closed Mon
Prices: Free; fees for some classes & special programs
Direct.: I-90 to exit for SR 306; south on SR 306 for 1 mile; left (east) on Kirtland-Chardon Rd. for 2 miles; on left.

- Strollers   Groups   Food Serv.   • Parking   Birthdays
- Diap. Chg.   • Picnic   Food Nearby   Pub. Trans.   • Handicap. Access

Portage Lakes State Park
Area: **Far South**   City: **Akron**   Ages: **All**   Cost: **FREE–$$**

A string of 13 lakes—all slightly different but averaging about 20 feet in depth—offers swimming with a lifeguard on duty, boating, and fishing. There is an area designated for boat launching on each lake. Turkey Foot Lake has a sandy beach ideal for swimmers and sun-worshippers. There are five miles of marked hiking trails that pass mainly through wooded areas, and 104 tent and trailer sites. Facilities include pit toilets, telephone, and fire rings.

A variety of classes are taught in the offices, on the beach, or at the campgrounds by a naturalist during the summer. Programming and schedules change, so call ahead. Also, the Astronomy Club of Akron offers monthly evening programs at the observatory.

In winter, cross-country skiing is available if you bring your own equipment. Snowmobiles can use lake surfaces throughout the lake chain. Access is from designated boat launch areas, but exercise caution and consult with a park employee about ice thickness.

Address: 5031 Manchester Rd.
Phone: (330) 644-2220
Season: Year-round
Hours: First aid: 24 hrs.; office: Mon–Fri 8 a.m.–noon, 1–5 p.m.
Prices: FREE park admission; fee for campsites
Direct.:   Located off SR 93.

- Strollers   • Groups   Food Serv.   • Parking   Birthdays
- Diap. Chg.   • Picnic   • Food Nearby Pub. Trans.   • Handicap. Access

Punderson State Park
Area: **Far East**   City: **Newbury**   Ages: **All**   Cost: **FREE–$$$**

Punderson is truly a park for all seasons. In summer, it is set up for 201 tent and recreational vehicle sites (all with electrical hookups). Twenty-six cabins are also available for rental, usually by the week in the summer. The 90-acre lake is the largest natural lake in the area; it has a sandy-bottomed swimming beach with lifeguards on duty. Rowboats, paddleboats, canoes, and electric motors can be rented. (Bring your own equipment and license if you want to fish.) There are also several playgrounds, tennis courts, an 18-hole golf course, a shuffleboard area, and 14 miles of well-marked hiking trails. The "Rent-A-Camp" and "Rent-A-RV" programs are also available.

In the winter months, there is cross-country skiing (rentals available) on two designated trails stretching eight kilometers through thick woods and around the perimeter of the golf course. Equipment can be rented at the chalet; call ahead for details. Winter sports also include ice-skating on the lake and tobogganing on a sledding hill (bring your own equipment). Several roads and trails are open to snowmobilers.

The naturalist program here is the same as at other state parks, including Saturday movies and campfires, with a naturalist on site various days from Memorial Day through Labor Day.

Park facilities include flush toilets, showers, laundry, telephone, and fire rings. The Manor House, once a private residence, is a resort lodge with 31 rooms, an outdoor pool, and a restaurant and lounge that are open to the public.

Address: 11755 Kinsman Rd. (SR 87)
Phone: (216†) 564-2279; chalet: (216†) 564-5246; lodge front desk: (216†) 564-9144; lodge & cabin rental: (800) 282-7275
Season: Year-round

Hours: First aid & rangers: 24 hrs.
Prices: FREE park admission; fee for campsites, cabins, and lodge accommodations
Direct.:   I-271 to Exit 29 (Chagrin Blvd./SR 87); east on SR 87 (Kinsman Rd.); 2 miles past SR 44.

| ● Strollers | ● Groups | ● Food Serv. | ● Parking | Birthdays |
| ● Diap. Chg. | ● Picnic | ● Food Nearby | Pub. Trans. | ● Handicap. Access |

Pymatuning State Park
Area: **Farther East**   City: **Andover Township**   Ages: **All**   Cost: **FREE–$$$**

In summer, the big attraction at Pymatuning is the 14,650-acre reservoir lake with three swimming beaches (Main Beach, near the offices; Cabin Beach, near the cabins, and Campground Beach, reserved for campers). Kids will especially like the fish hatchery tour, with its spillway and "duck walk"—so named because the ducks walk the spillway in search of fish. There is also a small waterfowl museum and a nature program that includes hikes, workshops, wildlife clinics, and fishing derbies. An amphitheater features movies and slide shows for overnighters.

Three miles of hiking trails are well marked, but be sure to pick up an interpretive brochure at the main office before you set out. The Beaver Dam trail loops for just under a mile and leads past a stream where, appropriately enough, beavers are busy building dams.

In winter months, there are cross-country ski trails and snowmobiling; bring your own equipment.

The park is set up with 373 campsites, most with electrical hookups, and 60 cabins. There is some playground equipment near the campgrounds. Pontoons and motorized boats can be rented.

Address: Pymatuning Lake Rd.
Phone: Office: (216†) 293-6030; cabin rental: (800) 282-7275
Season: Year-round
Hours: Daily 8 a.m.–11 p.m.; lifeguard on duty Sat–Sun 11 a.m.–7 p.m. Memorial Day–Labor Day
Prices: FREE; fees for campsite & cabin rental
Direct.:   I-271 to Exit 34 (US 322/Mayfield Rd.); east on US 322 to Simons, OH; left (north) on Pymatuning Lake Rd. into park.

| Strollers | ● Groups | ● Food Serv. | ● Parking | Birthdays |
| Diap. Chg. | ● Picnic | Food Nearby | Pub. Trans. | ● Handicap. Access |

Quail Hollow State Park
Area: **Farther South**   City: **Hartville**   Ages: **All**   Cost: **FREE**

The main attraction at Quail Hollow is the 12-mile system of hiking trails. The trails are well marked and travel through forest and field, meadow and swamp. There is a small wildlife pond here, but no swimming is allowed. A naturalist is on duty year-round, but programs for kids (ages 9–14) are offered only during summer. Although four miles of bridle trails are available, horses are not. Bring your own mount.

During winter months, you can cross-country ski on several miles of interpretive, hiking, and bridle trails with gently rolling terrain. Ski rental is available through the park office, and there is a winter warm-up center at the manor house.

Campsites are available for organized groups only.

Address:	13340 Congress Lake Ave.
Phone:	(330) 877-6652
Season:	Year-round
Hours:	Daily 6 a.m.–11 p.m.
Prices:	FREE
Direct.:	I-77 to Exit 118 (SR 241) in Green; left (north) on SR 241; right (east) on SR 619 to Hartville; left (north) on Prospect (becomes Congress Lake Rd.); on right.

● Strollers   ● Groups   ● Food Serv.   ● Parking   Birthdays
  Diap. Chg.   ● Picnic   ● Food Nearby   Pub. Trans.   ● Handicap. Access

NATURE & OUTDOORS

Riverview Park (Lake Metroparks)
Area: **Far East**   City: **Madison**   Ages: **All**   Cost: **FREE**

This 45-acre park includes hiking trails, fishing, sledding areas, picnic areas with fire pits and grills, and overnight camping.

Address:	Bailey Rd.
Phone:	(216†) 256-PARK
WWW:	http://www.harborcom.net/parks/parkinfo.html
Season:	Year-round
Hours:	Daily dawn–dusk
Prices:	FREE
Direct.:	I-90 to exit for SR 528; south on SR 528 for 1 mile; left (east) on River Rd.; right on Bailey Rd.

● Strollers   ● Groups   Food Serv.   ● Parking   Birthdays
  Diap. Chg.   ● Picnic   ● Food Nearby   Pub. Trans.   Handicap. Access

Rocky River Nature Center (Cleveland Metroparks)
Area: **Southwest**   City: **North Olmsted**   Ages: **All**   Cost: **FREE–$**

Inside the nature center are a few small animal displays (turtles, frogs, and fish) and a topographical map of the area. A huge stone fireplace is the site for special storytimes. Each month there are programs for children. The Fun to Be Three program and Fundays (for 4–5-year-olds) are great ways to introduce younger kids to nature. They typically include a short hike, a nature talk, and a make-and-take craft, all centered around a specific topic. Junior and Senior Leafkickers (ages 6–8 and 9–12 respectively) are programs of topic-related hikes guided by naturalists. All of these programs are very popular and reservations are required. Check the *Emerald Necklace* newsletter for details.

The Rocky River Nature Center is located in the Cleveland Metroparks Rocky River Reservation (listed separately).

Address: 24000 Valley Pkwy.
Phone: (216†) 734-6660
Season: Year-round
Hours: Daily 9:30 a.m.–5 p.m. except Thanksgiving, Christmas, New Year's Day
Prices: FREE; fees for some special programs
Direct.: I-480 to exit for Clague Rd.; south on Clague; right on Mastick Rd.; left on Shephard Ln.; right (south) on Valley Pkwy. for 1/2 mile; on right.

- Strollers   • Groups   Food Serv.   • Parking   Birthdays
  Diap. Chg.   • Picnic   • Food Nearby   Pub. Trans.   • Handicap. Access

Rocky River Reservation (Cleveland Metroparks)
Area: **West**   City: **N. Olmsted, Rocky River, Berea, Strongsville, Fairview Park, Cleveland**
Ages: **All**   Cost: **FREE**

Rocky River Reservation has an all-purpose trail, ball fields, fishing (several locations), ice fishing and ice-skating (Rocky River Lagoon), sledding hills, Little Met, Big Met, and Mastick Woods golf courses, Rocky River Stables (listed separately), nine picnic areas, Rocky River Nature Center (listed separately), and the Frostville Museum (listed separately) within its 2,540 acres.

The Emerald Necklace Marina at the northern end of the reservation near Detroit Rd. (1500 Scenic Park Dr., 216-226-3030) supplies a boat launch and trailer parking, and sells bait, tackle, and supplies. Recently rebuilt, the marina store also includes a snack bar/restaurant with a very pleasant outdoor patio. It is a great place to aim for after a family hike or bike ride.

The well-marked trails of the Rocky River Reservation are perfect for younger hikers. One short (but strenuous) walk leads up a grand staircase for a great view of the Rocky River; another winds alongside the river—a good place for waterfowl sightings. The Solar System Walk combines the natural surroundings of Cleveland Metroparks with the scientific knowledge of NASA Lewis Research Center. This 3/4-mile walk (with informational signs that describe the planets) traverses a scaled-down model of the universe. (One foot is equal to one million miles, so you can really do a lot of walking!)

▲

Address: 24000 Valley Pkwy.
Phone: (216) 351-6300; nature center: (216†) 734-6660
Season: Year-round

Hours: Daily 6 a.m.–11 p.m.
Prices: FREE
Direct.: I-480 to exit for Clague Rd.; south on Clague; right on Mastick Rd.; left on Shephard Lane; right (south) on Valley Pkwy. for 1/2 mile; on right.
Alternate entrances via SR 237 (Rocky River/Riverside Dr.) and Wooster Rd.

● Strollers	● Groups	Food Serv.	● Parking	Birthdays
Diap. Chg.	● Picnic	● Food Nearby	Pub. Trans.	● Handicap. Access

Sand Run Metro Park (Metro Parks Serving Summit County)
Area: **Far South**   City: **Akron**   Ages: **All**   Cost: **FREE**

Sand Run offers a fitness and hiking trail, ice-skating, play equipment, open shelters and closed pavilions, a sledding hill, a soccer field, and restrooms for guests. Pavilion rental is available.

Address: 1475 Sand Run Pkwy.
Phone: (330) 867-5511
Season: Year-round
Hours: Dawn–dusk
Prices: FREE
Direct.: I-77 to Exit 138 (Ghent Rd./SR 175); south on Ghent; left (east) on Sand Run Pkwy. (opposite Summit Mall).

● Strollers	● Groups	Food Serv.	● Parking	Birthdays
● Diap. Chg.	● Picnic	● Food Nearby	● Pub. Trans.	Handicap. Access

Schoepfle Arboretum (Lorain County Metroparks)
Area: **Far West**   City: **Birmingham**   Ages: **All**   Cost: **FREE**

The garden, created by Otto B. Schoepfle, contains more than 70 acres of shrubs and trees, rhododendrons, roses, hostas, and topiaries and fronts three-quarters of a mile on the Vermilion River. A winding river walk is a nice one for families—it is easy on smaller hikers.

Address: 1106 Market St.
Phone: (216†) 965-7237
Season: Year-round
Hours: Daily 8 a.m.–dusk
Prices: FREE
Direct.: SR 2 to exit for Baumhart Rd.; south on Baumhart (past Ohio Turnpike); right (west) on SR 113 for 4 miles to Birmingham; left (south) on Market St. (first road after the Vermilion River); left on Mills St. to parking area.

Strollers	Groups	Food Serv.	● Parking	Birthdays
Diap. Chg.	Picnic	● Food Nearby	Pub. Trans.	● Handicap. Access

NATURE & OUTDOORS

Seneca Caverns
Area: **Farther West**   City: **Bellevue**   Ages: **School age**   Cost: **$-$$**

Like Ohio Caverns near West Liberty, Olentangy Indian Caverns near Delaware, and Zane Caverns near Bellefontaine, Seneca Caverns is an easy way to visit the world below without becoming a mole.

The tour of Seneca Caverns, which lasts about one hour, covers about a half mile, consisting of seven rooms, or levels, the biggest being about 250 feet in length, the deepest about 110 feet under the ground.

While Seneca Caverns does not boast colorful formations, it does have a crystal-clear underground river. The configuration is unusual in that it was created when the limestone bedrock below it collapsed, resulting in its formation along a fracture plane—otherwise known as a crack in the earth. In case you're curious, the separated limestone is expected to come together again, but don't worry about it for the next million years or so. In October 1996, Seneca Caverns was declared a registered State of Ohio Natural Landmark.

The average temperature inside the cave is 54 degrees Fahrenheit. Wear a light jacket and decent walking shoes.

Address: SR 269
Phone: (419) 483-6711
Season: May–Labor Day (weekends only in May before Memorial Day, Sep–mid-Oct)
Hours: Summer hours 9 a.m.–7 p.m.; May, Sep–mid-Oct 10 a.m.–5 p.m.
Prices: Adults $7.75, children $3.50
Direct.: Ohio Turnpike (I-80/I-90) to Exit 6A (SR 4); south on SR 4; west on Seel Rd. to SR 269; cross SR 269; follow Twp. Rd. 178 west to Seneca Caverns (follow signs).

	Strollers	Groups	Food Serv.	Parking	Birthdays
	Diap. Chg.	● Picnic	Food Nearby	Pub. Trans.	Handicap. Access

(Groups ● ; Food Serv. ● ; Parking ●)

Silver Creek Metro Park (Metro Parks Serving Summit County)
Area: **Far South**   City: **Norton**   Ages: **All**   Cost: **$**

This park has a bridle trail, fishing, two hiking trails, play equipment, swimming lake, cross-country skiing, restrooms, and an open shelter.

Address: Medina Line Rd.
Phone: (330) 867-5511
Season: Open year-round; swimming Memorial Day to Labor Day
Hours: 10 a.m.-9 p.m. (in season)
Prices: $3 adults, $2 children 2-12, under 2 FREE (for swimming); other areas of the park are free
Direct.: I-77 to exit for SR 21; south on SR 21; west on SR 585 to exit for Hametown Rd.; west on Hametown; right (north) on Medina Line Rd.; on right.

● Strollers	Groups	● Food Serv.	● Parking	Birthdays
● Diap. Chg.	● Picnic	● Food Nearby	Pub. Trans.	● Handicap. Access

Sippo Lake Park (Sanders Center of Outdoor Education)
Area: **Farther South**   City: **Massillon**   Ages: **All**   Cost: **FREE**

Officially known as the Sanders Center of Outdoor Education, Sippo Lake Park is a 278-acre park with four hiking trails. The center, like other nature centers in the area, is designed to better inform visitors about endangered species, the food chain, animal classification, ecosystems, environmental pollution, and other aspects of nature study.

The center also provides medical attention to injured animals and supplies live traps for nuisance animals. The staff suggests calling ahead before bringing in animals or borrowing its traps. During spring and summer, the center opens an outdoor area for reptiles known as the reptarium.

Outside are a wide variety of activities: a marina with boat rental and a tackle and bait shop; stocked lakes; a playground; perception park designed for handicapped access; hiking trails; volleyball courts; and an observation tower. Future plans call for the extension of the Towpath Trail through all of Stark County.

Address: 800 Genoa Rd. North (Sanders Center)
Phone: (330) 477-3552 (park); (330) 477-0448 (center)
Season: Apr–Oct
Hours: May–Sep: daily 10 a.m.–5 p.m.; Apr & Oct: Tue–Thu 10 a.m.–7 p.m., Sat–Sun noon-5 p.m.
Prices: FREE
Direct.: I-77 to exit for Tuscarawas St.; west on Tuscarawas to Genoa Rd.; right on Genoa; Sanders Center is 1/2 mile on right.
Sippo Lake Park Marina: Tuscarawas St. west to Perry Dr.; right on Perry, then left at Tyner Ave. (5300 Tyner Ave. NW).

● Strollers   ● Groups   ● Food Serv.   ● Parking   Birthdays
  Diap. Chg.   ● Picnic   ● Food Nearby   Pub. Trans.   ● Handicap. Access

South Bass Island State Park
Area: **Farther West**   City: **Put-in-Bay**   Ages: **All**   Cost: **FREE–$$**

Located on the largest of the Lake Erie islands, this small park includes a half-mile-long stone beach with public swimming (no lifeguard on duty). The campground is popular because it is just west of the village of Put-in-Bay, which has many playgrounds, restaurants, and shops.

Of the 135 campsites located on a bluff overlooking Lake Erie, 32 are considered cliffside sites and are limited to tent campers (with no more than one vehicle per site). There are also four small efficiency cabins. Cabin rental is very popular and is available only by the week from Memorial Day to the last weekend in September. Cabins are rented on a lottery basis; contact the Catawba Island State Park. Facilities include showers and toilets.

NATURE & OUTDOORS

There is fishing for perch, crappies, walleye, and small-mouthed bass at various times from April to June in the shallow waters surrounding the park. Ice-fishing guides are available in winter.

If you decided to leave your car on the mainland, bikes and golf carts are available for rental, allowing you to cruise the 17 miles of road on the island.

Address: Catawba Ave.
Phone: (419) 285-2112, (419) 797-4530; Miller Boat Line: (419) 285-2421; Put-in-Bay Jet Express Boat Line: (800) 245-1538
Season: Year-round
Hours: Park: daily, sunrise–sunset; office: 8 a.m.–5 p.m.
Prices: FREE; fee for campsites
Direct.: SR 2 west to Sandusky Bay Bridge; north on SR 53 to Catawba Point; Put-in-Bay is located 3 miles from the Ohio mainland, north of Catawba Island Peninsula (see ferry info above—call for rate and schedule information).

	Strollers	*Groups*	*Food Serv.*	● *Parking*	● *Birthdays*
	Diap. Chg.	● *Picnic*	● *Food Nearby*	*Pub. Trans.*	● *Handicap. Access*

South Chagrin Reservation (Cleveland Metroparks)
Area: **Far East**   City: **Solon**   Ages: **All**   Cost: **FREE–$$**

This reservation consists of all-purpose trails (including cross-country ski trails), ball fields, and fishing and ice skating at Shadow Lake. Designated sledding hills are located off Hawthorn Pkwy., south of Solon Rd., and at the corner of Sulphur Springs Dr. and Chagrin River Rd. There are also six picnic areas.

One of the trails here leads along the Chagrin River to Squaw Rock, a large stone outcrop that bears the remains of a 19th-century carving by Henry Church. Family programs are scheduled at the WPA-era Look About Lodge (216-247-7075), a former private club that is now reopened to the public.

▲

Address: Sulphur Springs Dr. & Hawthorn Pkwy.
Phone: (216) 351-6300
Season: Year-round
Hours: Daily 6 a.m.–11 p.m.
Prices: FREE; fee for special programs
Direct.: I-271 to Exit 27 (US 422); east on 422 to exit for SR 91 (SOM Ctr. Rd.); north on SR 91; east on Sulpher Springs Dr.

● *Strollers*	● *Groups*	*Food Serv.*	● *Parking*	*Birthdays*
Diap. Chg.	● *Picnic*	*Food Nearby*	*Pub. Trans.*	● *Handicap. Access*

Swine Creek Reservation (Geauga Park District)
Area: **Far East**   City: **Middlefield Twp.**   Ages: **All**   Cost: **FREE**

Named for the hogs that once searched its bank for hickory nuts, Swine Creek passes through this 331-acre reservation, which includes a picnic area and a catch-and-release fishing pond. The lodge, with its fireplace, videos, and warm beverages, is used as a warm-up center in the winter months after skating on the pond or enjoying a sleigh ride. During March there are maple sugaring demonstrations.

Address: 16004 Hayes Rd.
Phone: (216†) 285-2222, (216†) 564-7131, (216†) 834-1856
Season: Year-round
Hours: Daily, 6 a.m.–11 p.m.
Prices: FREE
Direct.: I-90 to Exit 200 (SR 44); south on SR 44; left (east) on SR 87 past SR 528; right (south) on Hayes Rd.; on right (west) side.
422 to exit for SR 528; north on SR 528; right (east) on Bridge Rd.; right (south) on Hayes; on right (west) side.

● Strollers   ● Groups   Food Serv.   ● Parking   Birthdays
● Diap. Chg.   ● Picnic   ● Food Nearby   Pub. Trans.   ● Handicap. Access

NATURE & OUTDOORS

The Nature Center at Shaker Lakes
Area: **East**   City: **Shaker Hts.**   Ages: **All**   Cost: **FREE–$**

The Shaker Lakes Nature Center is surrounded by eight miles of well-marked trails through wooded hillside, marshland, and gardens along the Doan Brook and Shaker Lakes. It is an ideal place for young hikers. (The 1/3-mile-long All People's Trail is also wheelchair- and stroller-accessible.)

Programs for children ages 2–11 specialize in early childhood education and explore the natural world through hikes, talks, and projects. Saturday parent-and-child classes are particularly popular, as are the summer programs. Watch for special annual events, including family holiday celebrations and a birdseed sale.

Be sure to pick up a trail map before you set out.

Address: 2600 S. Park Blvd.
Phone: (216) 321-5935
Season: Year-round
Hours: Nature center: Mon–Fri 9 a.m.–5 p.m., Sat 10 a.m.–5 p.m., Sun 1–5 p.m.; Trails: daily 6 a.m.–9 p.m
Prices: FREE; fee for special programs
Direct.: I-271 to Exit 29 (Chagrin Blvd./US 422); west on Chagrin; north on Warrensville Ctr. Rd.; left (west) on South Park Blvd. (immediately past Shaker Blvd.).

● Strollers   ● Groups   ● Food Serv.   ● Parking   ● Birthdays
  Diap. Chg.   ● Picnic   ● Food Nearby   ● Pub. Trans.   ● Handicap. Access

The Rookery (Geauga Park District)
Area: **Far East**   City: **Munson Twp.**   Ages: **All**   Cost: **FREE**

The Rookery, a 446-acre nature preserve that includes a 200-acre wetlands habitat, was purchased by Geauga Park District in 1991 and is the site of one of the largest great blue heron nesting colonies in Northeast Ohio. The Chagrin River runs through The Rookery, and there are beaver ponds, fields, forests, and an abundance of wildlife including deer, waterfowl, mink, and turtles.

Although access is currently limited to park-sponsored group programs, The Rookery is scheduled to open to the general public in fall 1997. Call ahead for information.

Address: 10110 Cedar Rd.
Phone: (216†) 285-2222, (216†) 564-7131, (216†) 834-1856
Season: Year-round
Hours: 6 a.m.–11 p.m.
Prices: FREE
Direct.: I-90 to Exit 193 (SR 306); south on SR 306 to Chesterland; east on US 322 (Mayfield Rd.); right (south) on Rockhaven.; right (west) on Cedar Rd.

Strollers	● *Groups*	*Food Serv.*	● *Parking*	*Birthdays*
Diap. Chg.	*Picnic*	*Food Nearby*	*Pub. Trans.*	*Handicap. Access*

Tinker's Creek State Park
Area: **Southeast**   City: **Aurora, Streetsboro**   Ages: **All**   Cost: **FREE**

Almost three miles of hiking trails traverse Tinker's Creek State Park, a small satellite of the West Branch State Park that includes a nature preserve. The trails are well marked, wooded, and pass by active beaver ponds. There is also a small lake for swimming. (A lifeguard is only on duty weekends.)

During winter months, a 1.5-mile cross-country ski trail combines woods and a field for a good beginner outing. No equipment rental is available.

Address: Aurora-Hudson Rd.
Phone: (216†) 562-5515
Season: Year-round
Hours: Daily dawn–dusk; lifeguard on duty weekends only
Prices: FREE
Direct.: I-480 to exit for Aurora-HudsonRd./Frost Rd. (last exit before Turnpike); left (east) on Aurora-Hudson; on left.

Strollers	*Groups*	*Food Serv.*	● *Parking*	*Birthdays*
Diap. Chg.	● *Picnic*	● *Food Nearby*	*Pub. Trans.*	*Handicap. Access*

NATURE &
OUTDOORS

Veterans Park (Lake Metroparks)
Area: **Far East**   City: **Mentor**   Ages: **All**   Cost: **FREE**

The facilities at this 93-acre park include hiking trails, fishing pier, ball fields, picnic areas, and a playground.

Address: 5740 Hopkins Rd.
Phone: (216†) 256-PARK
WWW: http://www.harborcom.net/parks/parkinfo.html
Season: Year-round
Hours: Daily dawn–dusk
Prices: FREE
Direct.: SR 2 to exit for SR 615; north on SR 615 for 1 mile; north on Center St. for 1/2 mile to light; right (east) on Hendricks Rd.; left (north) on Hopkins Rd. for 1 mile; on left.

● Strollers   ● Groups   Food Serv.   ● Parking   Birthdays
  Diap. Chg.   ● Picnic   ● Food Nearby   Pub. Trans.   ● Handicap. Access

Villa Angela (Cleveland Lakefront State Park)
Area: **East**   City: **Cleveland**   Ages: **All**   Cost: **FREE**

Villa Angela is an extension of Euclid Beach State Park. It is a 900-foot-long sand beach with a picnic area. Lifeguards are on duty Memorial Day–Labor Day. A park naturalist schedules programming for children and families in the summer.

Address: Lakeshore at E. 162 St.
Phone: (216) 881-8141
Season: Year-round
Hours: Dawn–11 p.m.
Prices: FREE
Direct.: I-90 to exit for E. 185 St./Nottingham Rd; north on E. 185; left (west) on Lakeshore Blvd.; on right. Or, I-90 to exit for Lakeshore Blvd.; east on Lakeshore; on left.

● Strollers   ● Groups   ● Food Serv.   ● Parking   Birthdays
● Diap. Chg.   ● Picnic   ● Food Nearby   ● Pub. Trans.   ● Handicap. Access

Walter C. Best Wildlife Preserve (Geauga Park District)
Area: **Southeast**   City: **Munson Twp.**   Ages: **All**   Cost: **FREE**

This 101-acre wildlife preserve has hiking trails and a 30-acre lake that's great for fishing and bird-watching.

Address: 11620 Ravenna Rd. (SR 44)
Phone: (216†) 285-2222, (216†) 564-7131, (216†) 834-1856
Season: Year-round
Hours: Daily 6 a.m.–11 p.m.
Prices: FREE

Direct.: I-90 to Exit 200 (SR 44); south on SR 44 (Ravenna Rd.) through Chardon Square; approx. 2 miles past square on right.
US 422 to SR 44 (Ravenna Rd.) north.

| • *Strollers* | • *Groups* | *Food Serv.* | • *Parking* | *Birthdays* |
| *Diap. Chg.* | *Picnic* | • *Food Nearby* | *Pub. Trans.* | • *Handicap. Access* |

West Branch State Park
Area: **Far South**   City: **Ravenna**   Ages: **All**   Cost: **FREE–$$**

NATURE & OUTDOORS

The central attraction at West Branch State Park is the 2,650-acre Kirwan Lake maintained by the Army Corps of Engineers. Speedboaters and water-skiers often frequent the murky waters because there are no restrictions on engine horsepower. There is also a small sandy swimming beach with a lifeguard on duty. Fishing is allowed.

Kids will enjoy the playground and four short one-mile hiking trails. In summer, a naturalist offers various programs for children, and there are Friday-night family movies. There is no need to register.

For more hiking, there is an 8.5-mile stretch of the Buckeye Trail. Even though this trail is well marked, the park manager suggests picking up a trail guide at the office.

In winter, West Branch offers 20 miles of cross-country ski trails that are generally hilly and wooded, as well as 25 miles of snowmobiling trails, which are straight and fairly level. (No rental equipment is available.)

The park is set up with 103 tent and recreational vehicle sites. Park facilities include pit toilets, telephone, and fire rings.

Address: Rock Spring Rd.
Phone: (330) 296-3239
Season: Year-round; fully operational Apr–Oct
Hours: Rangers: 24 hrs.
Prices: FREE park admission; fee for campsites
Direct.: I-271 to exit for I-480/SR 14; east on SR 14; east on SR 5.; right (south) on Rock Spring Rd. for 1 mile; on right.

| *Strollers* | *Groups* | • *Food Serv.* | • *Parking* | *Birthdays* |
| *Diap. Chg.* | • *Picnic* | • *Food Nearby* | *Pub. Trans.* | • *Handicap. Access* |

Whitlam Woods (Geauga Park District)
Area: **Far East**   City: **Hambden Twp.**   Ages: **All**   Cost: **FREE**

This 110-acre park includes 1-1/2 miles of hiking trails through scenic forests and ravines.

Address: 12500 Pearl Rd.
Phone: (216†) 285-2222, (216†) 564-7131, (216†) 834-1856
Season: Year-round

Hours: Daily 6 a.m.–11 p.m.
Prices: FREE
Direct.: I-90 to Exit 200 (SR 44); south on SR 44 for 3 miles; left (east) on Clark Rd.; right (south) on Robinson Rd.; left (east) on Pearl Rd.; on left.
US 422 to SR 44 north through Chardon; take North St./Ravenna Rd. out of the square for 1-1/4 miles; right (east) on Woodin Rd. for 1 mile; left (north) on Robinson Rd.; right (east) on Pearl Rd; on left.

Strollers	● Groups	Food Serv.	● Parking	Birthdays
Diap. Chg.	Picnic	Food Nearby	Pub. Trans.	Handicap. Access

NATURE & OUTDOORS

Courtesy of Lake County Metroparks

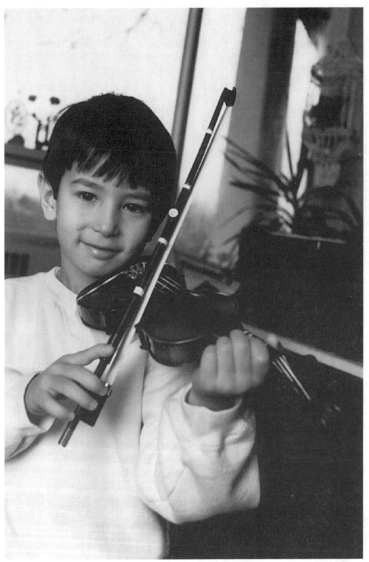

Performing Arts

Apart from their value in teaching us about ourselves and the world, the arts are simply a lot of fun. The benefits of exposing children to the arts, both as audience members and as participants, are sure to last them a lifetime. Taking part does not have to be expensive. There are free concerts, special performances for younger audiences, and a wide variety of classes. And, no matter what your preference may be—sculpture, puppets, the ballet—you'll find it in Greater Cleveland.

Unsure of where to get started? What follows is a comprehensive list of arts organizations with specific programming for children. As always, it's important to pick activities that are appropriate for your family. Performances intended for adults are not the best way to interest and involve children; look instead for performances aimed specifically at your children's age group. It also helps if youngsters are prepared a bit. Try talking about the program first—what is the story-line, what to expect from the experience. Many area institutions also offer programs that include both parent and child and provide a first-class way of sharing a first-time arts experience. These are especially worthwhile.

Ashtabula Arts Center
Area: **Farther East**   City: **Ashtabula**   Ages: **3 & up**   Cost: **FREE–$$$**

This well-established community arts center offers a variety of programs in theater, dance, art, and music. In addition to the school-year programs, there is a summer arts camp as well as the Grand Valley Theatre Company for school-age kids. Annual special events include the Free Kids Fest in summer, family matinee performances in the spring and fall, and the traveling Ashtabula Arts Center on Tour.

Address: 2928 W. 13 St.
Phone: (216†) 964-3396
Season: Year-round
Hours: Mon–Thu 9 a.m.–9 p.m., Fri 9 a.m.–7 p.m., Sat 9 a.m.–5 p.m.
Prices: Vary
Direct.: I-90 to Exit 223 (SR 45); north on SR 45 into Ashtabula; right (east) on Lake Rd./SR 531 past the Kent State University-Ashtabula campus; right on Norwood Rd. at flashing light; right on W. 13 St.

● *Strollers*   ● *Groups*   *Food Serv.*   ● *Parking*   *Birthdays*
  Diap. Chg.   ● *Picnic*   ● *Food Nearby*   *Pub. Trans.*   ● *Handicap. Access*

Baldwin-Wallace College Conservatory of Music
Area: **Southwest**   City: **Berea**   Ages: **3 & up**   Cost: **$$–$$$**

Well-known for its music program, the preparatory department of the Conservatory of Music at Baldwin-Wallace offers a varied program of music lessons for children starting at age 3.

Address: 96 Front St.
Phone: (216†) 826-2365 or (216†) 826-2330
Season: Year-round
Hours: Vary
Prices: Vary
Direct.: I-71 to Exit 235 (Bagley Rd.); west on Bagley; left (south) on Front St. for 2 blocks to Center St.; on corner of Front and Center.
Center.

Strollers	Groups	● Food Serv.	● Parking	Birthdays
Diap. Chg.	Picnic	● Food Nearby	● Pub. Trans.	● Handicap. Access

PERFORMING ARTS

Baycrafters
Area: **West**   City: **Bay Village**   Ages: **3 & up**   Cost: **FREE–$$$**

Devoted to the visual arts and tucked away among a collection of turn-of-the-century frame buildings on the grounds of Cleveland Metroparks Huntington Reservation, Baycrafters is a gem that nearby residents know well. Among the year-long classes offered for school-age children are painting, cartooning, clay sculpture, drama, and puppetry. A summer program includes preschoolers. Classes are kept small and are popular—so register early. Many special arts and crafts events are held throughout the year, including the Renaissance Fayre (Labor Day weekend), a true family festival. With three days of entertainment—jousting, theater, puppetry, music—in a lush meadow just a short hike from the lakefront, there is enough activity to please an all-ages group. There are also plenty of hands-on opportunities: on one visit we tried juggling, and our 3-year-old became part of a puppet show. Because this is a very popular event, be prepared for traffic congestion, especially later in the day. Call for a schedule beforehand so that you can be sure to catch the performances that look like the most fun.

Address: 28795 Lake Rd. (Cleveland Metroparks Huntington Reservation)
Phone: (216†) 871-6543
Season: Year-round
Hours: Gallery and station shop daily 1–5 p.m.; class times vary
Prices: Gallery FREE; fee for classes
Direct.: I-90 to Exit 159 (Columbia Rd./SR 252); north on Columbia; right (west) on Lake Rd.; left on Porter Creek Rd.; right into paved lot.; on left, next to Huntington Playhouse.

● Strollers	● Groups	Food Serv.	● Parking	Birthdays
Diap. Chg.	● Picnic	● Food Nearby	● Pub. Trans.	Handicap. Access

Beachwood Community Youth Theatre
Area: **East**   City: **Beachwood**   Ages: **School age & up**   Cost: **$**

For more than 15 years this community theater has offered classes, productions, and also a summer camp, primarily through the city's schools. The seasonal schedules culminate in performances four times a year. This is an inter-generational theater group for youth, teens, and adults of all ages.

Address: 2700 Richmond Rd. (Beachwood High School)
Phone: (216) 464-1070
Season: Sep–Jun
Hours: Vary for performances
Prices: $3.50 students, $4.50 adult
Direct.:   I-271 to Exit 29 (Chagrin Blvd.); west on Chagrin; right (north) on Richmond Rd.

Strollers	● Groups	Food Serv.	● Parking	● Birthdays
Diap. Chg.	Picnic	● Food Nearby	● Pub. Trans.	● Handicap. Access

PERFORMING ARTS

Beck Center for the Cultural Arts
Area: **West**   City: **Lakewood**   Ages: **3 & up**   Cost: **FREE–$$$**

Beck is a well-established arts center with an active community theater and changing exhibits throughout the year. West-side families know the place well for the variety and quality of classes offered year-round for preschoolers and up, including dance, dramatics, and a variety of fine arts. Sessions run fall, winter, spring, and summer.

Particularly popular with younger children is the Little Folks Theatre (LFT) program. LFT introduces 4- and 5-year-olds to creative dramatics and S.M.I.L.E. (Sensory Motor Integrated Learning Experience), which combines movement with positive self-image for preschoolers. As for the regular theater season, most productions would be enjoyable for older school-age children; families with younger children should look for performances by the Beck Center Theater School for Children and Teens. The school typically presents two major stage productions a year—winter and spring—performed for children and by children.

Address: 17801 Detroit Rd.
Phone: (216) 521-2540
WWW: http://www.lkwdpl.org/beck
Season: Year-round
Hours: Center: Mon–Fri 9 a.m.–5 p.m.; weekends vary; Performances: Thu–Sat 8 p.m., Sun 2 p.m.
Prices: Gallery FREE; fees for classes & performances
Direct.:   I-90 to Exit 164 (McKinley); north on McKinley (becomes Larchmont Ave. after Madison Ave.); right (west) on Detroit for 2 blocks; on left, parking in rear.

● Strollers	● Groups	Food Serv.	● Parking	● Birthdays
● Diap. Chg.	● Picnic	● Food Nearby	● Pub. Trans.	● Handicap. Access

Brecksville Center for the Arts
Area: **South**   City: **Brecksville**   Ages: **Preschool & up**   Cost: **FREE–$$$**

This growing community center offers a wide variety of arts instruction for adults and kids. While specific schedules change, classes have included ceramics, dance, painting, photography, basket weaving, paper making, quilting, calligraphy, music, kids' crafts, drawing, Ukrainian egg decorating, origami, ballroom dancing, floral design, glass bead making, seminars and workshops, and more.

Address: 8997 Highland Dr. (Old Library Building)
Phone: (216†) 526-6232
Season: Year-round
Hours: 9:30 a.m.–12:30 p.m. Mon–Fri (office hours); class schedule varies
Prices: Vary
Direct.:   I-77 to Exit 149 (SR 82); east on SR 82 (Royalton Rd.); right on Highland Dr.; on left, across from cemetery.

- • Strollers   • Groups   Food Serv.   • Parking   Birthdays
    Diap. Chg.   Picnic   • Food Nearby   • Pub. Trans.   • Handicap. Access

PERFORMING ARTS

Cain Park
Area: **East**   City: **Cleveland Hts.**   Ages: **All**   Cost: **FREE–$$$**

An extensive summer calendar of activities has made this arts park a Heights-area favorite. Exhibits, theater, concerts, and dance activities—many designed for family audiences, and some free—are scheduled, using the park's outdoor amphitheater and other facilities. A series of summer classes offered through the City of Cleveland Heights (which operates the park) for school-age children includes full- and half-day classes in theater, visual arts, music, writing, and movement. The annual Cain Park Arts Festival offers a wide variety of free entertainment, typically including one matinee children's concert and a kids' area with arts and crafts activities. Of note for older school-age children and teens, the Alma Forum series, also free, highlights different alternative art forms with a combination of lectures and performances. In winter, the hill at Cain Park is a popular site for sledding.

Be forewarned that there is no on-site parking facility, so come early for nearby street parking or take advantage of one of the city's lots and use the park's shuttle service.

Address: Superior Rd. between Lee & S. Taylor Rds.
Phone: (216) 291-5796; summer: (216) 371-3000; winter: (216) 291-2828
Season: Jun–Aug
Hours: Event times vary
Prices: Fees vary for concerts, theater, classes; some events Free
Direct.:   Superior Rd. between Lee and S. Taylor Rds.

- • Strollers   • Groups   • Food Serv.   Parking   Birthdays
    Diap. Chg.   • Picnic   • Food Nearby   • Pub. Trans.   • Handicap. Access

10 Great Things to Do...

That the Whole Family Will Enjoy

- Get stuck in a "rainstorm" at the Cleveland Metroparks Zoo RainForest. (p. 85)

- Take a canal boat ride at Roscoe Village. (p. 63)

- Tour the fish hatchery at Pymatuning State Park. (p. 122)

- Sample fresh, hot apple butter at Century Village. (p. 33)

- Romp in the sand and surf at Headlands Beach or Huntington Beach. (p. 102, 105)

- Tour the stables of the Cleveland Mounted Police. (p. 198)

- Try juggling or jousting at the Baycrafters' annual Renaissance Fayre. (p. 136)

- Build a family float with the help from the staff of the Cleveland Museum of Art for the Parade the Circle celebration. (p. 36)

- Climb mazes and play pirates at Sea World's Happy Harbor. (p. 26)

- Ride the Nature Train on the Cuyahoga Valley Scenic Railroad. (p. 88)

Chagrin Valley Youth Theatre

Area: **Southeast**   City: **Chagrin Falls**   Ages: **5 & up**   Cost: **$$–$$$**

This youth theater program is designed to introduce children ages 10–18 to music, drama, and performance in live theater productions. Each year's series of workshops—typically two eight-week sessions—culminates in a student performance.

Address: 40 River St.
Phone: (216†) 247-8955
Season: Year-round
Hours: Shows: Fri–Sat 8 p.m.; box office: Tue–Sat 1–6 p.m.
Prices: Vary
Direct.: I-271 to Exit 29 (Chagrin Blvd.); east on Chagrin (stay on Chagrin after Lander Rd.); Chagrin becomes W. Orange in Chagrin Falls; right on Division to River St.; left on River.

- Strollers   • Groups   Food Serv.   • Parking   • Birthdays
  Diap. Chg.   Picnic   • Food Nearby   • Pub. Trans.   • Handicap. Access

Clague Playhouse

Area: **West**   City: **Westlake**   Ages: **School-age**   Cost: **$$-$$$**

Clague Playhouse offers performances and theater classes for children and teens in basic theatrical techniques, including lighting, makeup, costuming, props, set work, acting, music, and stage direction. The auditorium seats 93.

Address: 1371 Clague Rd.
Phone: (216†) 331-0403
Season: Year-round
Hours: Wed–Sat 1 p.m.–6 p.m.
Prices: $10 adults, $9 seniors & students, $7 group discount
Direct.: I-90 to exit for Clague Rd.; south on Clague 1 mile.
I-480 to exit for Clague Rd.; north on Clague 3 miles; behind Clague Museum.

- Strollers   • Groups   Food Serv.   • Parking   Birthdays
  Diap. Chg.   Picnic   • Food Nearby   • Pub. Trans.   • Handicap. Access

Cleveland Ballet

Area: **Downtown**   City: **Cleveland**   Ages: **3 & up**   Cost: **$–$$$**

Taking a youngster to the ballet may seem daunting, but the Cleveland Ballet has paved the way for a more child-friendly experience over the past few years. Special prices, special school matinees, a Kids Club, children's parties, and family days have been offered. Each December, many Cleveland families include in their holiday tradition the annual performance of *The Nutcracker*, a wonderful introduction to dance for school-age children.

Classes offered through the School of Cleveland Ballet begin with ages 4–10 and are held once or twice a week as part of the Community Program. Classes become more serious and advanced, with instruction in technique and pointe, for ages 10–18, with sessions held two to six times per week in the Preprofessional Training Program. Recently the school added ballet for figure skaters and gymnasts, with a focus on balance and poise. A special summer session offers a variety of dance experiences for ages 4–18.

To everyone's delight, students get an opportunity to perform small roles (the mice, no less) in *The Nutcracker*.

Address: 1375 Euclid Ave., Suite 330 (offices); State Theatre: 1519 Euclid Ave.
Phone: (216) 621-2260; school: (216) 621-3633
Season: Year-round
Hours: Box office: Mon–Fri 10 a.m.–4:30 p.m.
Prices: Vary
Direct.: I-90 to Exit 173B (Chester Ave./US 322); west on Chester to E. 17; left (south) on E. 17 to Euclid Ave. (US 20); right on Euclid; on right.

● Strollers   ● Groups   ● Food Serv.   ● Parking   Birthdays
   Diap. Chg.   Picnic   ● Food Nearby   ● Pub. Trans.   ● Handicap. Access

PERFORMING ARTS

Courtesy of the Cleveland Ballet

Cleveland Institute of Music
Area: **Near East**   City: **Cleveland**   Ages: **3 & up**   Cost: **FREE–$$$**

Founded in 1920 to provide world-class education in music, the Cleveland Institute of Music delivers just that. For children ages 3–18, the Preparatory and Community Education divisions offer classes in instruments, voice, theory, and movement (Dalcroze Eurythmics). For school-age students, performance experience includes two Suzuki

Studies string orchestras, a percussion ensemble, and the Cleveland Youth Wind Symphony.

Many of the Institute's regular free concerts are matinees and would be interesting to older children. They are very popular, and seating is on a first-come, first-served basis. Be prompt. Recently, the Institute introduced a special series of family concerts to expose younger children to the performing arts. More children's events are promised for the future.

Branches:

22441 Lorain Rd., Fairview Park, (216†) 734-3120

32000 Chagrin Blvd., Pepper Pike, (216) 831-0697

21600 Shaker Blvd., Shaker Heights, (216) 283-2699

Address: 11021 East Blvd.
Phone: (216) 791-5000
WWW: http://www.cwru.edu/CIM
Season: Year-round
Hours: Vary
Prices: Vary
Direct.: I-90 to Exit 177; south on Martin Luther King, Jr. Blvd.; cross E. 105 St. and stay left around traffic circle; right on East Blvd.

- Strollers   ● Groups   ● Food Serv.   ● Parking   Birthdays
  Diap. Chg.   ● Picnic   ● Food Nearby   ● Pub. Trans.   ● Handicap. Access

PERFORMING ARTS

Cleveland Music School Settlement
Area: **Near East**   City: **Cleveland**   Ages: **3 & up**   Cost: **FREE–$$$**

The Cleveland Music School Settlement is one of the largest community music schools in the country. It is committed to providing music education to everyone—regardless of age, skill, background, or means. The performing arts department offers private lessons as well as classes in a variety of musical styles. The Early Childhood Department includes a preschool day school.

Classes in music and dance for preschoolers include Suzuki-method violin and piano for ages 3–8, Music Explorers (Orff-Schulwerk) for ages 3–6, and movement (Dalcroze Eurythmics) for ages 3–6. There is also ballet, drama, kinderdance, tap, and more. A Music Builders summer camp is especially popular.

Young musicians should look into the youth orchestra, which has two groups: one for ages 7–11, one for ages 12–18. Rehearsals are on Saturday mornings, and performances are scheduled three times a year. For families interested in attending performances, the school regularly offers free concerts that feature faculty, students, and guest artists.

Branch: 19000 Libby Rd., Maple Heights, (216) 662-6227

Address: 11125 Magnolia Dr.
Phone: (216) 421-5806
Season: Year-round

Hours: Office: 9 a.m.–7:30 p.m.
Prices: Vary
Direct.: I-90 to Exit 177; south on Martin Luther King, Jr. Blvd.; cross E. 105 St., stay left
around traffic circle; right on East Blvd.; left on E. 108 St.; right on Magnolia Dr.

| • Strollers | • Groups | Food Serv. | • Parking | Birthdays |
| • Diap. Chg. | Picnic | • Food Nearby | • Pub. Trans. | • Handicap. Access |

Cleveland Orchestra
Area: **Near East**   City: **Cleveland**   Ages: **3 & up**   Cost: **$–$$$**

The Cleveland Orchestra, established in 1918, is a venerable institution and a world-class musical experience. Its offerings for children are extensive and popular; families with any interest at all in music should check them out.

For school-age children or teenagers, performances by the Cleveland Youth Orchestra are especially suitable. They offer a traditional concert experience, but at more affordable prices than those of the regular orchestra.

Families with preschoolers flock to the Musical Rainbows series. Designed specifically for ages 3–6, each program lasts 30 minutes and focuses on individual instruments as demonstrated by orchestra members. In addition to demonstration, explanation, and audience participation, there are also stories using the instruments.

Key Concerts, for ages 5–9, last an hour and feature the entire orchestra playing shorter pieces; preconcert activities include hands-on projects and entertainment—sometimes even a few surprise visitors.

Another good way to introduce your children to the orchestra is to attend one of the free public concerts scheduled throughout the year. These are very popular but are not recommended for young children because crowds are often very large. The orchestra performs outdoors during the summer months at Blossom Music Center adjacent to the Cuyahoga Valley National Recreation Area. Picnics are allowed—even encouraged—for the summertime performances under the stars.

Address: Severance Hall, 11001 Euclid Ave.
Blossom Music Center: 1145 W. Steels Corners Rd. (Cuyahoga Falls).
Phone: (216) 231-1111, (800) 686-1141
WWW: http://www.clevedorch.com; http://www.cris.com/~jadato/orch.htm
Season: Mid-Sep–late May (Severance); Jul–Aug (Blossom)
Hours: Vary
Prices: Vary
Direct.:   Severance: I-90 to Exit 177; south on Martin Luther King, Jr. Blvd.; left (east) on
Euclid Ave.
Blossom: I-271 to Exit 18 (SR 8); south on SR 8; west on Steel Corners Rd.

| Strollers | • Groups | • Food Serv. | • Parking | Birthdays |
| Diap. Chg. | • Picnic | • Food Nearby | • Pub. Trans. | • Handicap. Access |

PERFORMING ARTS

PERFORMING ARTS

Cleveland Play House
Area: **Near East**   City: **Cleveland**   Ages: **5 & up**   Cost: **$$$**

Founded in 1915, the Play House is as the oldest not-for-profit professional theater in the country and now includes four separate theaters. Its regular performance series may not be suitable for younger audiences, but a separate schedule of plays has been developed for school-age children. It offers lower-priced tickets and matinees in the smaller 120-seat Studio One Theatre.

For children interested in learning more about the theater, classes in the fall, winter, and spring cover improvisation, writing, dance, and drama. Curtain Pullers offers acting and technical theater classes for children ages 5 and up on Saturdays during the school year, with sessions running 10 weeks. Camp Cleveland Play House, a popular summer program, is organized by age: Creative Drama for ages 5–7; Creative Workshops or Performance Workshops for ages 8–12; and Performance Workshops and Writing for ages 13–17.

Address: 8500 Euclid Ave.
Phone: Box office: (216) 795-7000; Education Dept.: (216) 795-7010
Season: Year-round
Hours: Vary
Prices: Vary
Direct.:   I-90 eastbound to exit for Carnegie Ave.; right (east) on Carnegie; on left.
                    I-90 westbound to exit for E. 55; south on E. 55; left (east) on Carnegie Ave.; on left.

● Strollers   ● Groups   ● Food Serv.   ● Parking   Birthdays
   Diap. Chg.   ● Picnic   ● Food Nearby   ● Pub. Trans.   ● Handicap. Access

Cleveland Public Theatre
Area: **Near West**   City: **Cleveland**   Ages: **5 & up**   Cost: **$–$$**

The Cleveland Public Theatre, a showcase for alternative and experimental theater, often presents works specifically designed for a family audience. Neighborhood residents know it for children's classes in theater arts and alternative workshops in scriptwriting, costume design, mime, movement, and yoga.

Address: 6415 Detroit Ave.
Phone: (216) 631-2727
WWW: http://www.en.com/cpt
Season: Year-round
Hours: Vary
Prices: Vary
Direct.:   I-90 to Exit 167 for West Blvd.; north on West Blvd.; right (east) on Detroit Ave.; on right.

● Strollers   ● Groups   ● Food Serv.   ● Parking   Birthdays
● Diap. Chg.   Picnic   ● Food Nearby   ● Pub. Trans.   ● Handicap. Access

Cleveland Signstage Theatre
Area: **Near East**   City: **Cleveland**   Ages: **5 & up**   Cost: **$–$$**

Formerly the Fairmount Theatre of the Deaf, this troupe mounts three main shows a year, at least one of which is geared toward the entire family. The traveling Deaf Awareness Show is available for school presentations including a question-and-answer session with the actors after the performance.

Address: 8500 Euclid Ave.
Phone: (216) 229-2838 (voice), (216) 229-0341 (tty)
Season: Year-round
Hours: Vary
Prices: Vary
Direct.: I-90 eastbound to exit for Carnegie Ave.; right (east) on Carnegie; on left.
I-90 westbound to exit for E. 55; south on E. 55; left (east) on Carnegie Ave.; on left.

● *Strollers*   ● *Groups*   *Food Serv.*   ● *Parking*   *Birthdays*
   Diap. Chg.   *Picnic*   ● *Food Nearby*   ● *Pub. Trans.*   ● *Handicap. Access*

PERFORMING ARTS

Cudell Fine Arts Center
Area: **Near West**   City: **Cleveland**   Ages: **All**   Cost: **FREE–$$**

Part of the City of Cleveland's Department of Recreation, this community arts group offers after-school classes for ages 7–17 in drawing, painting, ceramics, and sewing. There are also special series for parent and child, family workshops designed for younger children, and even an introductory arts program aimed at home-schooled children.

The best part is that all classes are free, with materials provided by the City of Cleveland and Cudell.

Address: 10013 Detroit Ave.
Phone: (216) 664-4183; Studio: 664-4103
Season: Year-round
Hours: Mon–Fri 12:30 p.m.–9 p.m., Sat 9:30 a.m.–6 p.m.
Prices: FREE
Direct.: I-90 to Exit 167 (West Blvd.); north on West Blvd. to Detroit Ave.; at intersection of West and Detroit.

● *Strollers*   ● *Groups*   *Food Serv.*   ● *Parking*   *Birthdays*
   Diap. Chg.   ● *Picnic*   *Food Nearby*   ● *Pub. Trans.*   ● *Handicap. Access*

Cuyahoga Valley Youth Ballet
Area: **Far South**   City: **Cuyahoga Falls**   Ages: **All**   Cost: **$$$**

For two decades, the Cuyahoga Valley Youth Ballet has been auditioning and training young dancers for performances. Each season it also commissions a new ballet, combining young talent with new dance interpretations. Dancers rehearse every weekend and enroll in a rigorous schedule of classes; it is no wonder alumni go on to dance professionally.

Address: 2315 State Rd. (studio—performance locations vary)
Phone: (330) 928-6479 (studio)
Season: Oct–May
Hours: Vary
Prices: Vary
Direct.: I-271 to Exit 18 (SR 8); south on SR 8; take exit for Hudson/SR 303, but go straight on Akron-Cleveland Rd. (becomes State Rd.); studio on State Rd.

- Strollers   • Groups   • Food Serv.   • Parking   Birthdays
  Diap. Chg.   Picnic   • Food Nearby   • Pub. Trans.   • Handicap. Access

PERFORMING ARTS

DANCECleveland
Area: **Downtown**   City: **Cleveland**   Ages: **5 & up**   Cost: **$$–$$$**

DANCECleveland brings in different modern dance productions from across the country throughout the year. Performances are staged at the Ohio Theater and Palace Theater in Playhouse Square. Families should be on the lookout for Young People's Concerts—a matinee series for school-age children offered irregularly. DANCECleveland also performs at Cain Park (see separate listing) in the summer, providing a more relaxed opportunity to see modern dance with your children.

Address: 1148 Euclid Ave., Suite 311 (Playhouse Square)
Phone: (216) 861-2213; Box office: (216) 771-4444
Season: Year-round
Hours: Vary
Prices: Vary
Direct.: I-90 to Exit 173B (Chester Ave./US 322); west on Chester to E. 17; left (south) on E. 17 to Euclid Ave. (US 20); right on Euclid; on right.

  Strollers   • Groups   • Food Serv.   • Parking   Birthdays
  Diap. Chg.   Picnic   • Food Nearby   • Pub. Trans.   • Handicap. Access

Dobama Theatre
Area: **East**   City: **Cleveland Hts.**   Ages: **5 & up**   Cost: **FREE–$$$**

Participation is the focus at Dobama, from the acting classes for older kids (ages 7–15) to the Marilyn Bianchi Kids' Playwriting Festival (ages 7–17). Entries in this annual playwriting festival are judged on the basis of imagination and human values as much as on playwriting skill. All festival entrants are invited to a special preview performance of the winning contestant's play.

Address: 1846 Coventry Rd.
Phone: (216) 932-6838

Season: Year-round
Hours: Vary
Prices: Vary
Direct.: I-90 to Exit 173B (Chester Ave/US 322); east on Chester; left (east) on Euclid Ave.
(US 20); right on Mayfield Rd. (US 322); right (south) on Coventry Rd.; on right.

- Strollers   • Groups   Food Serv.   • Parking   Birthdays
  Diap. Chg.   Picnic   • Food Nearby   • Pub. Trans.   Handicap. Access

Fairmount Fine Arts Center
Area: **Far East**   City: **Russell Township**   Ages: **2-1/2 & up**   Cost: **FREE–$$$**

Concert series, youth theater, and young people's music recitals are just some of the special events scheduled here year-round. But even more popular with families are the class offerings for kids, from preschool age up. The choices are terrific: dance, music, art, and theater as well as gymnastics and karate. The Summer Arts Camp is a good way to sample them all.

Address: 8400 Fairmount Rd.
Phone: (216†) 338-3171
Season: Year-round
Hours: Mon–Thu 9 a.m.–8 p.m.; Fri 9 a.m.–4:30 p.m.; Sat 9 a.m.–1 p.m.
Prices: Vary
Direct.: I-271 to Exit 29 (Chagrin Blvd./SR 87); east on SR 87 (becomes Pinetree Rd.,
then S. Woodland Rd); left (north) on SR 306; left (west) on Fairmount Blvd.

  Strollers   • Groups   Food Serv.   • Parking   • Birthdays
• Diap. Chg.   • Picnic   • Food Nearby   Pub. Trans.   Handicap. Access

Fine Arts Association
Area: **East**   City: **Willoughby**   Ages: **1-1/2 & up**   Cost: **$–$$$**

This local institution is a gem for families. Special performances for children, by children, are included in each theater season—with moderate prices and matinees scheduled.

Classes for preschoolers and up, both during the school year and in the summer, include painting, drawing, and pottery. (This is one of few such places where children as young as age 2 are welcome.) For older ones, there is instruction in cartooning, calligraphy, and portrait painting.

There's more: As part of a comprehensive program of private music lessons, children as young as age 4 are started in Suzuki-method violin and piano instruction. (Ages 2–3 can join Happy Fingers class with a parent.) Dance lessons are offered for the very young to adult, along with drama. A special summer drama camp is particularly popular.

Other annual special events include Discovery Day in July, an art,

PERFORMING ARTS

dance, drama, and music open house. Santa's Workshop in December features hands-on art projects, storytelling, live musical entertainment, and a visit from you-know-who. Both are open and free to the public.

Address: 38660 Mentor Ave.
Phone: (216†) 951-7500
Season: Year-round
Hours: Vary
Prices: Vary
Direct.: SR 2 to exit for Willoughby/Vine St.; east on Vine (becomes Mentor Ave./US 20 past Erie St.) across Chagrin River; about 1/4 mile after bridge, look for the entrance of Andrews School on right (south) side of Mentor Ave.; enter Andrews School campus; FAA building is at the far driveway on left.

● Strollers   Groups   Food Serv.   ● Parking   Birthdays
   Diap. Chg.   Picnic   ● Food Nearby   Pub. Trans.   ● Handicap. Access

Courtesy of Fine Arts Association

Firelands Association for the Visual Arts
Area: **Far West**   City: **Oberlin**   Ages: **3-adult**   Cost: **FREE–$$$**

Founded in 1979 to provide exhibitions and art classes for kids and adults, FAVA offers photography, clay sculpting, painting, drawing, theater, and music. A regular art appreciation program for preschoolers includes a free guided look at the Allen Memorial Art Museum. It is available for preschool groups as well. Call for current schedule of classes and exhibitions. FAVA's home, the recently restored New Union Center for the Arts, was built in 1874 and is listed on the National Register of Historic Places.

Address: 39 S. Main St.
Phone: (216†) 774-7158
Season: Year-round

PERFORMING ARTS

Hours: Office: Tue–Sat noon–5 p.m., Sun 2–4 p.m.; gallery shop: Tue–Sat 10 a.m.–5 p.m., Sun 1–5 p.m.
Prices: Admission FREE for exhibitions; class fees vary
Direct.: I-480 to exit for SR 511; west on SR 511; south on SR 58 (S. Main St.) into Oberlin; in the New Union Center for the Arts in downtown Oberlin.

- Strollers   • Groups   Food Serv.   • Parking   Birthdays
  Diap. Chg.   • Picnic   • Food Nearby   Pub. Trans.   • Handicap. Access

Great Lakes Theater Festival
Area: **Downtown**   City: **Cleveland**   Ages: **2 & up**   Cost: **$$$**

The Great Lakes Theater Festival is one of the few American theater companies dedicated to classic drama. Its annual family favorite is *A Christmas Carol*, based on the Charles Dickens novel. Of special note to teachers: productions for schoolchildren are previewed in detailed teachers' guides.

Address: 1501 Euclid Ave. (Performances at the Ohio Theatre, 1519 Euclid, Playhouse Square)
Phone: (216) 241-5490
Season: Oct–May
Hours: Vary
Prices: Vary
Direct.: I-90 to Exit 173B (Chester Ave./US 322); west on Chester to E. 17 St.; left (south) on E. 17; right on Euclid Ave. (US 20).

  Strollers   • Groups   • Food Serv.   • Parking   Birthdays
  Diap. Chg.   Picnic   • Food Nearby   • Pub. Trans.   • Handicap. Access

PERFORMING ARTS

Heights Youth Theatre
Area: **East**   City: **University Hts.**   Ages: **All**   Cost: **$$–$$$**

Heights Youth Theatre, the oldest children's theater in this area, offers classes for children ages 4–18 in improvisation, dance, and stage production. For preschoolers there are dance and drama classes. A summer camp program culminates in an on-stage performance.

Productions for kids by kids are performed in the Wiley Middle School auditorium. For birthday parties, rooms can be reserved prior to shows (bring your own cake, decorations, and party favors).

Audition schedules are often hard to find, especially for those not living in the neighborhood, so if you're interested, call the office.

Address: 2155 Miramar Blvd. (Office at Bd. of Education)
         2181 Miramar Blvd. (performance site)
Phone: (216) 371-7406; (216) 591-0128 (performance information)
Season: Oct–May; winter holidays
Hours: Sat–Sun 2 p.m.
Prices: Vary; group rates available

Direct.: Performances at Wiley Middle School Auditorium, 2181 Miramar Blvd., 1 block east of Cedar and Warrensville Center Rds.

● Strollers	● Groups	Food Serv.	● Parking	Birthdays
Diap. Chg.	Picnic	● Food Nearby	● Pub. Trans.	● Handicap. Access

Irish Music Academy of Cleveland
Area: **Near West**   City: **Lakewood**   Ages: **School-age**   Cost: **$-$$$**

The Irish Music Academy was founded in 1993 to preserve and develop Irish traditional music in Greater Cleveland. Classes include voice, bodhran, button accordion, concertina, fiddle, flute, guitar, hammered dulcimer, harp, mandolin, piano accompaniment, piano accordion, tenor banjo, tin whistle, and uilleann pipes.

Address: 16920 Detroit Ave.
Phone: (216) 529-1996
Season: Year-round
Hours: Lessons: Mon & Wed 5 p.m.-9 p.m., Sat 10 a.m.-1 p.m.; office hours Mon, Wed, Fri 1-5 p.m.
Prices: Vary
Direct.: I-90 to Exit 164 (McKinley Ave.); north on McKinley (becomes Larchmont Ave. after Madison Ave.); east on Detroit Ave. for 2 blocks; on left.

Strollers	Groups	Food Serv.	● Parking	Birthdays
Diap. Chg.	Picnic	● Food Nearby	● Pub. Trans.	Handicap. Access

Karamu Performing Arts Theater
Area: **Near East**   City: **Cleveland**   Ages: **3 & up**   Cost: **$$–$$$**

Founded in 1915 by graduates of Oberlin College as the Playhouse Settlement, this theater has become known nationwide for its focus on interracial theater and arts. It was renamed Karamu House in 1941 after the Swahili word for the center of the community and place of enjoyment. Karamu is especially active in the schools, and for its work the group received an award from the American Alliance of Theater in Education in 1993.

There are actually two theaters here, as well as a small cabaret, exhibit galleries, and classrooms. The annual program includes theater for young audiences and classes for preschoolers and up in drama, theater, dance, and music. A popular summer day camp offers a broad program in arts and culture for kids ages 6–12.

Address: 2355 E. 89 St.
Phone: (216) 795-7077
Season: Year-round
Hours: Vary
Prices: Vary

Direct.:   I-90 to Exit 173B (Chester Ave./US 322); east on Cheste; right (south) on E. 89 St. for four blocks; on left.

• Strollers	• Groups	Food Serv.	• Parking	Birthdays
Diap. Chg.	Picnic	• Food Nearby	• Pub. Trans.	Handicap. Access

Lorain County Community College
Area: **Far West**   City: **Elyria**   Ages: **5 & up**   Cost: **$$–$$$**

Lorain County Community College's College for Kids is a growing resource for area families. For school-age children, year-round Saturday classes are offered in music, dance, karate, language, computers, visual arts, outer space, and dinosaurs. The school year is divided into three eight-week sessions; a special session during the summer allows students to mix and match coursework. Summer programs are one week long, usually in the morning. Looking for performances? Try the student matinee series, offerings of professional performing arts (improvisation, opera, and music) especially designed for young people.

Address: 1005 Abbe Rd.
Phone: (800) 995-5222; College for Kids: ext. 4093; Stocher Center Box Office: ext. 4040
WWW: http://www.lorainccc.edu
Season: Year-round
Hours: Vary
Prices: Vary
Direct.:   I-90/SR 2 to Exit 148 (SR 254); east on SR 254; right (south) on SR 301; on left.

• Strollers	• Groups	• Food Serv.	• Parking	Birthdays
Diap. Chg.	• Picnic	• Food Nearby	Pub. Trans.	• Handicap. Access

Lyric Opera Cleveland
Area: **Near East**   City: **Cleveland**   Ages: **5 & up**   Cost: **$$–$$$**

Performances by Lyric Opera are sung in English. Though probably too serious for younger school-age children, performances may appeal to older kids interested in music and theater. Two special programs tour schools each year and perform for grades K–12. Lyric Opera Cleveland regularly performs in Kulas Hall at the Cleveland Institute of Music.

Address: 11300 Juniper Ave.
Phone: Box office: (216) 231-2910; office: (216) 231-2484
Season: Summer festival season with year-round educational and community performances
Hours: Evening and matinee performances
Prices: Vary; discounts for students, seniors, and groups
Direct.:   I-90 to Exit 177; south on Martin Luther King, Jr. Blvd.; cross E. 105 St. and stay left around traffic circle; right on East Blvd.; left on Juniper.

• Strollers	• Groups	• Food Serv.	• Parking	Birthdays
Diap. Chg.	• Picnic	• Food Nearby	• Pub. Trans.	• Handicap. Access

PERFORMING ARTS

Magical Theater
Area: **Farther South**   City: **Barberton**   Ages: **5 & up**   Cost: **$$–$$$**

Founded in 1972, the Magical Theater company is specifically dedicated to introducing young people and families to theater. It offers professional performances, both in its resident theater and during a year-round travel schedule. Classes for ages 6–18 include basic acting, mime, creative dramatics, and makeup.

Address: 565 W. Tuscarawas Ave.
Phone: (330) 848-3708
Season: Oct–Jun
Hours: Office: 9 a.m.–6 p.m.; performances: times vary
Prices: $12 adults, students over 12; $6 children under 12
Direct.:   I-77 to I-76 east to Exit 16; right (south) on Barber Rd. (becomes Fourth St.) to dead end; left on Lake Ave.; right (south) on Third St.; right (west) on W. Tuscarawas for 1 block.

● Strollers   ● Groups   Food Serv.   ● Parking   ● Birthdays
  Diap. Chg.   Picnic   ● Food Nearby   ● Pub. Trans.   ● Handicap. Access

Near West Theater
Area: **Near West**   City: **Cleveland**   Ages: **5 & up**   Cost: **$–$$**

The neighborhood-based Near West Theater is committed to diversity and to involving people of all ages in its three annual productions. A professionally directed full-scale musical is usually staged by the youth group (ages 13–19) in the summer. Fridays before shows are often designated Teen Nights to allow teens to help professionals in set design, construction, and the consumption of pizza. Classes in acting and general theater skills are offered for ages 8–12.

Address: Performances: St. Patrick's Club Bldg., 3606 Bridge Ave.; offices: 4315 Bridge Ave.
Phone: (216) 651-2037 (office); (216) 732-8324
Season: Year-round
Hours: Performances: Thu–Sat 8:00 p.m., Sun 3:00 p.m.
Prices: Vary
Direct.:   I-90 to Exit 169 (W. 41 St.); north on W. 41.; right (east) on Bridge Ave.; on left.

  Strollers   ● Groups   ● Food Serv.   ● Parking   Birthdays
  Diap. Chg.   Picnic   ● Food Nearby   ● Pub. Trans.   Handicap. Access

Oberlin College
Area: **Far West**   City: **Oberlin**   Ages: **All**   Cost: **$-$$$**

Oberlin College's community arts offerings include the Little Theater, Oberlin Opera, Oberlin Dance Company, Oberlin Choristers Chamber Choir, and the Artist Recital Series. The Little Theater's season runs through the school year; past performances have included

PERFORMING ARTS

Gospel at Colonus and *Women of Troy*. School-year performances of Oberlin Opera have included *The Marriage of Figaro* and *A Midsummer Night's Dream*. The Oberlin Dance Company season culminates in a spring performance. The Oberlin Choristers Chamber Choir includes a children's choir, which performs with the Oberlin Dance Company in their annual spring performance. The Artist Recital Series held in Finney Chapel brings such programming as the Cleveland Orchestra, the London Brass, and the Emerson String Quartet.

Address:	Oberlin College, 173 W. Lorain
Phone:	(216†) 775-8169 (central ticket service)
WWW:	http://www.oberlin.edu
Season:	Year-round
Hours:	Vary
Prices:	Vary
Direct.:	I-480 west to SR 10/US 20 to SR 511 (west) into Oberlin.
	I-90 to SR 2 split; west on SR 2 to SR 58; left (south) on SR 58 into Oberlin.

● Strollers	● Groups	● Food Serv.	● Parking	Birthdays
Diap. Chg.	● Picnic	● Food Nearby	● Pub. Trans.	● Handicap. Access

Ohio Chamber Orchestra
Area: **Downtown & citywide**   City: **Cleveland**   Ages: **5 & up**   Cost: **FREE–$$$**

The Ohio Chamber Orchestra performs mainly at Cleveland State University's Waetgen Auditorium. A summer series brings the Orchestra to Cain Park in Cleveland Heights (see separate listing), where it offers free concerts geared toward the entire family.

Address:	3659 S. Green Rd. (Performances at Waetgen Auditorium, Cleveland State University, Euclid Ave. & E. 21 St.)
Phone:	(216) 464-1755
Season:	Year-round
Hours:	Vary
Prices:	Vary
Direct.:	To Waetgen Auditorium: I-90 to Exit 173B (Chester Ave./US 322); west on Chester; left (south) on E. 21; parking on right.

● Strollers	● Groups	Food Serv.	● Parking	Birthdays
Diap. Chg.	Picnic	● Food Nearby	● Pub. Trans.	● Handicap. Access

Playhouse Square Center
Area: **Downtown**   City: **Cleveland**   Ages: **3 & up**   Cost: **$–$$$**

The Palace, Ohio, and State theaters, which together make up Playhouse Square Center, were originally built in the 1920s as ornate and glamorous movie houses. Closed down and boarded up by the late 1960s, they have been brought back to their original splendor thanks to an ambitious renovation project. Every Clevelander should visit here at

least once. The regular season brings a diverse schedule of touring theater, dance, and musical performances to Playhouse Square. Many are
perfect for a special family outing (albeit an expensive one).

Younger, squirmier children will do better to attend one of the special performances offered through the Children's Theater Series. This
series is created especially for children ages 3 and up and typically
includes classic fairy tales, music, and mime, with matinee performances and lower prices (not to mention an audience of peers with the
same fidgety habits).

The Playhouse Square theaters are also home to regularly scheduled
performances of the Great Lakes Theater Festival, DANCECleveland,
the Cleveland Opera, and the Cleveland Ballet (see separate listings).

For a great lesson in both Cleveland history and the arts, check out
the free guided tours of the theater complex.

PERFORMING ARTS

Address:	1519 Euclid Ave. (Playhouse Square)
Phone:	(216) 771-4444; Advantix: (216) 241-6000
Season:	Year-round
Hours:	Vary
Prices:	Vary
Direct.:	I-90 to Exit 173B (Chester Ave./US 322); west on Chester; left (south) on E. 17 St.; right on Euclid Ave. (US 20); on right.

Strollers	• Groups	• Food Serv.	• Parking	Birthdays
Diap. Chg.	Picnic	• Food Nearby	• Pub. Trans.	• Handicap. Access

Shore Cultural Centre

Area: **East**	City: **Euclid**	Ages: **3 & up**	Cost: **FREE–$$$**

The Shore Cultural Centre, housed in a school built in 1913, offers a
full and varied schedule of classes in the arts for all ages, from toddlers
to seniors. For school-age children these include theater, art, pottery,
and calligraphy. Special holiday workshops and hands-on classes are
geared for preschoolers and their parents. Classes are offered year-
round; the summer program is particularly popular. The old school's
two gymnasiums are used for a variety of events (including community
theater), many of them suitable for older children; instrumental and
voice lessons for children are available. The building is also home to the
national Cleveland-Style Polka Hall of Fame.

Address:	291 E. 222 St.
Phone:	(216) 289-8578
Season:	Year-round
Hours:	Mon–Fri 8:00 a.m.–11 p.m.; Sat 8 a.m.–3 p.m.
Prices:	Vary
Direct.:	I-90 to exit for Babbitt Rd.; north on Babbitt; right on Shore Centre Dr.

• Strollers	• Groups	Food Serv.	• Parking	Birthdays
Diap. Chg.	Picnic	• Food Nearby	• Pub. Trans.	• Handicap. Access

Weathervane Community Playhouse
Area: **Far South**   City: **Akron**   Ages: **3 & up**   Cost: **$$–$$$**

Weathervane's mainstage productions may not always be suitable for young audiences, but there is usually something going on here for children. Classroom instruction culminates in performances, including three shows a year by youths, for youths. Separately, ProjectSTAGE brings performances to area high schools with question-and-answer sessions with performers.

Popular class offerings for ages 3–18 cover such areas as creative movement, improvisation, theater games, and advanced acting. Fall-winter sessions last for 16 weeks; spring sessions last 8 weeks. A special 2-week summer workshop includes all-around classes and a culminating performance.

Assisted Listening Devices are available for the hearing impaired at performances.

Address: 1301 Weathervane Ln.
Phone: (330) 836-2626
Season: Year-round
Hours: Curtain times: Thu–Sat 8 p.m., Sun 2:30 or 7:30 p.m.; class times vary
Prices: Vary
Direct.: I-77 to Exit 138 (Ghent Rd.); right (south) on Ghent off highway; left (east) on Smith Rd.; right (south) on Merriman Rd.; left on Weathervane Ln.

Strollers	• Groups	Food Serv.	• Parking	Birthdays
• Diap. Chg.	Picnic	• Food Nearby	• Pub. Trans.	• Handicap. Access

PERFORMING ARTS

Wildwood Cultural Center
Area: **Far East**   City: **Mentor**   Ages: **Pre-K–Adult**   Cost: **FREE–$**

Wildwood is located in a turn-of-the-century English Tudor mansion on 34 acres. Opened in 1980, the center has established itself in the community with a varied schedule of classes in arts, cooking, and music for youth and adults; changing exhibits; wellness programs; and special events, such as an annual Christmas concert and a summer arts festival. Sessions run fall, winter, spring, and summer. (The mansion is also available for private rental for events such as conferences or reunions.)

Address: 7645 Little Mountain Rd.
Phone: (216†) 974-5735
Season: Year-round
Hours: Vary
Prices: Vary
Direct.: I-90 to Exit 193 (SR 306); left (north) on SR 306; right (east) on SR 84 (Johnny Cake Ridge Rd.); left (north) on Little Mountain Rd. for 1 mile; on right.

Strollers	• Groups	Food Serv.	• Parking	Birthdays
Diap. Chg.	• Picnic	• Food Nearby	Pub. Trans.	• Handicap. Access

Sports & General Recreation

How can parents pick the best sports activities for their children? Maturity levels, development, and age all contribute to readiness for a specific sport. Generally, T-ball, soccer, gymnastics, swimming, cycling, and skating are great for younger children. They all emphasize the development of hand-eye coordination, agility, and strength. Besides, for fun and exercise, what's better than sports?

When it comes down to signing your children up for activities, begin by taking their interests to heart. Ask them: Why do you want to play? And a reminder: don't forget to check the weekly practice and game schedule—those 5 a.m. ice-hockey practices can be hard to manage.

The following list should help narrow your search for sporting activities.

Alpine Valley

Area: **Far East**　　City: **Chesterland**　　Ages: **3 & up**　　Cost: **$$$**

The seven slopes at Alpine Valley are reached by chair lift, J-bar, and rope tow. For beginning skiers, there are group lessons in the early morning and evening; each class is open to ages 4 and up. There are two "Bunny" classes on Saturday and Sunday (9 a.m.–1 p.m. and 1–5 p.m., respectively) for ages 7–12. Cost includes lift tickets, equipment rental, one-hour group lesson, and three hours of ski time. For even younger skiers, Uncle Bob's Preschool Ski School for ages 4–6 involves four weeks of lessons intended to help children learn the basics and to give their parents instructional tips on how to teach their kids. (An adult on skis must attend.) Private lessons are also available. Equipment rental prices are reduced for ages 6 and under. The annual WinterFest includes snow volleyball and an obstacle course.

Address:　10620 Mayfield Rd.
Phone:　(216†) 285-2211; ski line recording: (216†) 729-9775 (during season)
Season:　Winter (natural & artificial snow)
Hours:　Mon–Fri 1–10:30 p.m.; Sat–Sun & holidays 9 a.m.–11 p.m.
Prices:　Vary; $16–27, $14–23 ages 12 & under
Direct.:　I-271 to Exit 36 (Mayfield Rd.); east on Mayfield for 10 miles .

Strollers	● Groups	● Food Serv.	● Parking	Birthdays
Diap. Chg.	Picnic	● Food Nearby	Pub. Trans.	Handicap. Access

Beachwood Municipal Pool
Area: **East**   City: **Beachwood**   Ages: **All**   Cost: **$–$$**

Kiddie pool, lessons, playground.

Address: 25125 Fairmount Blvd.
Phone: (216) 292-1974
Season: Jun–Sep
Hours: Vary
Prices: $4 per visit, $6 non-resident guests under 18, $7 adult non-resident (must be accompanied by a resident); individual family membership $15 per person, not to exceed $75; non-resident fees vary; season guest pass $60
Direct.:   Adjacent to Beachwood City Hall at intersection of Fairmount Blvd. and Richmond Rd.

- Strollers   - Groups   - Food Serv.   - Parking   - Birthdays
- Diap. Chg.   - Picnic   Food Nearby   - Pub. Trans.   - Handicap. Access

Bexley Pool (South Euclid/Lyndhurst Recreation Dept.)
Area: **East**   City: **South Euclid**   Ages: **All**   Cost: **$–$$**

Kiddie pool, slides, lessons, playground.

Address: 4194 Temple Rd.
Phone: (216) 381-0446; (216) 691-2246
Season: Jun–Sep
Hours: Vary
Prices: $4 residents, $5 non-resident guests; individual family pass $29 each, maximum $87 per family
Direct.:   From Mayfield Rd. go south on S. Belvoir Rd.; right (west) on Wrenford Rd. to Temple Rd. to entrance for Bexley Pool (in Bexley Park).

- Strollers   - Groups   - Food Serv.   - Parking   - Birthdays
  Diap. Chg.   - Picnic   Food Nearby   - Pub. Trans.   - Handicap. Access

Boston Mills and Brandywine Ski Areas
Area: **South**   City: **Peninsula**   Ages: **3 & up**   Cost: **$$$**

These two downhill ski areas are located 3 miles apart in the Cuyahoga Valley National Recreation Area. Lift tickets are good at each area, and a shuttle bus operates between them, so you can ski both on the same visit.

Half the 18 slopes are for beginners. A beginner package offered for ages 8 and up includes a lift ticket, equipment rental, and a group lesson. For skiers age 3–6 there is the Tiny Tot program, and for ages 7-12, Mogul Mites. Classes for the younger children focus on getting kids used to the equipment and the snow, and on teaching them how to stop and turn control. (Parents without skis are asked to assist the tots.) These classes are offered every weekend morning (call for times); the price includes equipment rental, lifts, and a one-hour group lesson. Private lessons are also available. For older kids, there is ski and snow-boarding instruction (the Jr. program, for ages 8–16), and rentals are available.

Address: Boston Mills: 7100 Riverview Rd.; Brandywine: 1146 Highland Rd.
Phone: Cleve: (216†) 467-2242; Akron: (330) 657-2334; Kent/Aurora: (216†) 650-9219; (800) 875-4241
WWW: http://www.bmbw.com
Season: Winter (natural & artificial snow)
Hours: Boston Mills: Mon–Thu 9:30 a.m.–11 p.m.; Fri–Sun 9:30 a.m.–1 a.m. Brandy-wine: Mon–Thu 3 p.m.–11 p.m.; Fri–Sun 8:30 a.m.–2 a.m.
Prices: Mon–Thu $28; Fri–Sun $30; $4 off for ages 12 & under w/ adult
Direct.: I-77 southbound to exit for Miller Rd.; left on Miller for 1/4 mile; right on SR 21 for 1/2 mile; left on Snowville Rd.; right, on Riverview Rd. toward Boston Mills—or left, on Riverview toward Brandywine; follow signs.
I-271 to exit for SR 8; south on SR 8; right at Highland Rd.; follow signs. Shuttle bus available from Boston Mills to Brandywine and back.

- Strollers
  Diap. Chg.
- Groups
  Picnic
- Food Serv.
- Food Nearby
- Parking
- Pub. Trans.
- Birthdays
- Handicap. Access

Courtesy of Boston Mills/Brandywine

Brainard Pool (South Euclid/Lyndhurst Recreation Dept.)
Area: **East**   City: **Lyndhurst**   Ages: **All**   Cost: **$–$$**

Kiddie pool, slides, lessons, playground.

Address: 1840 Brainard Rd.
Phone: (216†) 442-5844
Season: Jun–Sep
Hours: Vary

Prices: $4 residents, $5 non-resident guests; individual family pass $29 each, maximum $87 per family

Direct.:   Located in Brainard Park, on Brainard Rd. between Mayfield and Cedar Rds.

- **Strollers**
- *Groups*
- *Food Serv.*
- **Parking**
- **Birthdays**
  Diap. Chg.   • *Picnic*   *Food Nearby*   • *Pub. Trans.*   • *Handicap. Access*

Brecksville Stables (Cleveland Metroparks)

Area: **South**   City: **Brecksville**   Ages: **3 & up**   Cost: **$$**

The Cleveland Metroparks stables offer year-round pony rides. English saddle horseback-riding instruction includes indoor group lessons (five to a group) for ages 8 and up, and private lessons for 6- and 7-year-olds. Indoor and outdoor lessons (weather depending) are offered on weekends for all ages. A therapeutic riding program is offered on Wednesdays for the physically or mentally challenged.

A summer mini-camp is offered in one-week sessions that run every day for two hours; for younger riders (ages 4–7) there is a pony camp.

Address: 11921 Parkview Dr.
Phone: (216†) 526-6767
Season: Year-round
Hours: Vary
Prices: Vary
Direct.:   I-77 to Exit 149 (SR 82/Chippewa Rd.); east on SR 82; right (south) on Brecksville Rd. (SR 21); left (east) on Parkview Rd.; on left (north) side. Stables are near Parkview entrance.

- **Strollers**
- *Groups*
- *Food Serv.*
- **Parking**
- **Birthdays**
  Diap. Chg.   • *Picnic*   • *Food Nearby*   *Pub. Trans.*   • *Handicap. Access*

Brooklyn Recreation Center

Area: **Near West**   City: **Cleveland**   Ages: **3 & up**   Cost: **$**

Open skate times are scheduled in the morning, at lunchtime, in the afternoon, and in the evening. (Slight variations do occur to accommodate hockey games.) For preschoolers, a Tot and Parent skate is offered Wednesday mornings and Thursday afternoons. Special events include an annual Skate with Santa and an ice show.

Lessons are offered for ages 3 and up in three eight-week sessions during the season. Each lesson lasts 30 minutes and includes a special one-hour practice session. Lessons are also offered through the Brooklyn Hockey Association.

Skate rental and sharpening are offered. The rink is available for rental, and birthday parties can be arranged.

The Natatorium Swim Complex offers indoor and outdoor pools, a kiddie pool, and swim lessons. The Recreation Center also offers rac-

SPORTS & RECREATION

10 Great Things to Do...

During the Summer:

- ◉ Pilot a ship's wheel and play sea captain at the Fairport Marine Museum. (p. 43)

- ◉ Go on an "early bird" hike at the Holden Arboretum. (p. 104)

- ◉ Explore the Whipp's Ledges rock formations and take a swim at Hinckley Reservation. (p. 105)

- ◉ Stay over on a Saturday night for a movie and a campfire at Punderson State Park. (p. 121)

- ◉ Have breakfast with the animals at the Cleveland Metroparks Zoo. (p. 85)

- ◉ Hop on board one of the area's scenic railroads for a slow ride through the woods.

- ◉ Take a canal boat ride aboard the *St. Helena III* at Canal Fulton. (p. 64)

- ◉ Try juggling or jousting at Baycrafters' annual Renaissance Fayre. (p. 136)

- ◉ Enroll in a class at the Beck Center or other area arts centers. (p. 137)

- ◉ Escape the heat at Winterhurst Ice Rink. (p. 180)

quetball, roller-skating, an ice-skating gymnasium, and exercise equipment.

Address:　7600 Memphis Ave.
Phone:　(216) 351-5334 (Rec. Center); (216) 351-6781 (Natatorium)
Season:　Skating: Sep–mid-May; Natatorium: year-round (outdoor pool Memorial Day–Labor Day)
Hours:　Vary
Prices:　Skating: $1 resident w/ ID, $2 non-resident, $.50 students; swimming: $1 resident w/ ID, $3 non-resident, $2 seniors & students
Direct.:　Located west of the intersection of Ridge Rd. and Memphis Ave., across from Brooklyn City Hall and courthouse.

● Strollers　● Groups　● Food Serv.　● Parking　● Birthdays
● Diap. Chg.　Picnic　● Food Nearby　● Pub. Trans.　● Handicap. Access

Camp Hi Canoe Livery
Area: **Far East**　　City: **Hiram**　　　Ages: **4 & up**　　Cost: **$$-$$$**

　　Camp Hi offers two canoe trips: a three-hour, 7-mile excursion ($22 for two people); and a four-hour, 10-mile trip ($28 for two) on 25 miles of the upper Cuyahoga River. Primarily slow and flat, they are ideal for novices.

　　Excursions are unguided and time slots need to be reserved between 9 a.m. and 3 p.m. Limit 10 people per group.

Address:　12274 Abbott Rd.
Phone:　(330) 569-7621
Season:　Spring–fall
Hours:　Daily 9 a.m.–6 p.m.
Prices:　$11–14 per person; children as passengers in center of canoe ride free
Direct.:　I-271 to Exit 27 (US 422); east on US 422; right (south) on SR 44 (Painesville-Ravenna Rd.); left (east) on SR 82 (Twinsburg-Warren Rd.); left (north) on Abbott Rd.

Strollers　● Groups　Food Serv.　● Parking　Birthdays
Diap. Chg.　● Picnic　● Food Nearby　Pub. Trans.　Handicap. Access

Chalet Recreation Area (Cleveland Metroparks)
Area: **Southwest**　　City: **Strongsville**　　Ages: **42 inches & up**　　Cost: **$-$$**

　　A year-round recreation spot with hayrides, square dancing, ball fields and a playground, the chalet comes alive in the winter months for tobogganing. The 1,000-foot, refrigerated ice chutes offer a thrilling ride. The hike up the stairs can be chilling (mittens are required). Inside, the fireplaces are very popular indeed.

Address:　Valley Pkwy. in Mill Stream Reservation
Phone:　(216†) 572-9990
Season:　Nov–Feb

SPORTS & RECREATION

Hours: Vary
Prices: Vary
Direct.: I-71 to Exit 231 (SR 82); east on SR 82 (Royalton Rd.) for 1/2 mile to entrance for
              Mill Stream Run Reservation; left (north) on Valley Pkwy. for 1-1/4 miles to
              chalet.

- Strollers   • Groups   • Food Serv.   • Parking   • Birthdays
  Diap. Chg.   • Picnic   • Food Nearby   Pub. Trans.   • Handicap. Access

Chardon Memorial Pool
Area: **Far East**   City: **Chardon**   Ages: **All**   Cost: **$**

Kiddie pool, lessons, playground.

Address: 316 Maple Ave.
Phone: (216†) 285-2413
Season: Jun–Sep
Hours: Vary
Prices: $3, $2 under 18, no charge under age 3
Direct.: Maple Ave. at Memorial Dr. in Chardon.

- Strollers   • Groups   Food Serv.   • Parking   Birthdays
  Diap. Chg.   • Picnic   • Food Nearby   Pub. Trans.   Handicap. Access

Clague Park Pool
Area: **West**   City: **Westlake**   Ages: **All**   Cost: **$**

Kiddie pool, slides, fountain, lessons, playground.

Address: 1500 Clague Rd.
Phone: (216†) 835-6436
Season: Jun–Sep
Hours: Vary
Prices: Residents w/passes: $3.50 adults, $3 children (12 & under), Free under age 5
              with paying adult. Non-residents: $5 adults, $4.50 children (12 & under)
Direct.: On Clague Rd. between Detroit Rd. and Center Ridge Rd.

- Strollers   • Groups   • Food Serv.   • Parking   Birthdays
  Diap. Chg.   • Picnic   • Food Nearby   • Pub. Trans.   • Handicap. Access

Cleveland Heights Pavilion
Area: **East**   City: **Cleveland Hts.**   Ages: **3 & up**   Cost: **$**

The schedule of skating times changes throughout the season to accommodate lessons, hockey, and special events, such as the annual Skate with Frosty and the Halloween dress-up skate.

For preschoolers, a parent and tot session is held weekly. There are also Learn-to-Skate sessions for all ages.

SPORTS &
RECREATION

Lessons for ages 3–adult are offered throughout the season in sessions lasting six or seven weeks.

The youth hockey league for ages 4–17 is open to residents of University Heights, Cleveland Heights, and communities that do not have ice-hockey programs. Children are placed in divisions based on their birth dates.

Skate rental, sharpening, and lockers are offered. The rink is available for rental. An annual used equipment and skate sale in the summer is a hockey league fundraiser and a great way for parents to save on gear.

Address: 1 Monticello Blvd.
Phone: (216) 691-7373
Season: Sep–Apr
Hours: Vary
Prices: $2.25 adult residents w/ ID, $1.50 residents grades K–12, $3.25 non-residents
Direct.: Located at the corner of Mayfield and Superior.

- Strollers   • Groups   • Food Serv.   • Parking   • Birthdays
- Diap. Chg.   • Picnic   • Food Nearby   • Pub. Trans.   • Handicap. Access

Cleveland Rock Gym
Area: **East**   City: **Euclid**   Ages: **9 & up**   Cost: **$$$**

This unusual gym attracts both first-timers and aficionados starved for rock-climbing experiences. The two-hour introductory class covers safety and technique and includes time on the 30-foot wall with an instructor. The wood and fake stone face covering most of the side of a former warehouse can be daunting for the novice or the faint of heart.

Address: 21200 St. Clair Ave. Bldg. B-3
Phone: (216) 692-3300
Season: Year-round
Hours: Mon–Fri 4 p.m.–10 p.m., Sat–Sun noon–6 p.m.
Prices: $15 per person for introduction to climbing sessions Tue–Thu; $50 Sat morning belay class
Direct.: I-90 to exit for Nottingham Rd./E. 185; south on Nottingham; east on St. Clair Ave.; on right, Bldg. B-3 in rear.

   Strollers   • Groups   • Food Serv.   • Parking   • Birthdays
   Diap. Chg.   Picnic   • Food Nearby   • Pub. Trans.   Handicap. Access

Cumberland Pool (Cleveland Hts. Recreation Dept.)
Area: **East**   City: **Cleveland Hts.**   Ages: **All**   Cost: **$**

Kiddie pool, lessons.

Address: Cumberland Dr.
Phone: (216) 691-7390
Season: Jun–Sep

Hours: Mon–Fri 1–5 p.m., Sat–Sun 1–6 p.m.; family swim Mon–Fri 5–8 p.m.
Prices: $2 adult residents w/ ID, $1.50 student resident w/ ID, $3 non-resident guests
Direct.: From Mayfield Rd. turn south on Cumberland Dr.; pool is on right at Cumberland Park recreation building.

● Strollers   ● Groups   ● Food Serv.   ● Parking   ● Birthdays
● Diap. Chg.   ● Picnic   ● Food Nearby   ● Pub. Trans.   ● Handicap. Access

Dan Kostel Recreation Center (Garfield Hts. Recreation Dept.)
Area: **South**   City: **Garfield Hts.**   Ages: **3 & up**   Cost: **$–$$**

The daily ice schedule changes to accommodate lessons, hockey, and special events, including a Halloween skate and a skate with Santa. Skating lessons for ages 3 and up, including a preschooler-with-parent lesson, are held throughout the season in three sessions. Hockey also starts at preschool age, with season-long play. Skate rentals and skate sharpening are available. Private parties can be arranged.

Kiddie pool and lessons are also available.

Address: 5411 Turney Rd.
Phone: (216) 475-7272
Season: Pool: mid-Jun–Labor Day; skating: mid-Sep–mid-Mar
Hours: Vary
Prices: Resident ID card $4; admission with ID—$2 adult, $1.50 students/children, ages 4 and under Free with paying adult. Non-resident ID card can be purchased if enrolling in skating or swimming class
Direct.: I-480 to Exit 21 (E. 98 St.); take E. 98 south from I-480 westbound to Antenucci Dr. (or go straight—over E. 98—from I-480 eastbound); left (east) on Antenucci; left (north) on Turney Rd. over I-480; right at first light into Garfield Heights Recreation complex; follow drive to last building in complex.

Strollers   ● Groups   ● Food Serv.   ● Parking   Birthdays
Diap. Chg.   ● Picnic   ● Food Nearby   ● Pub. Trans.   ● Handicap. Access

SPORTS & RECREATION

Denison Pool (Cleveland Hts. Recreation Board)
Area: **East**   City: **Cleveland Hts.**   Ages: **All**   Cost: **$**

Kiddie pool, slides, lessons.

Address: Belvoir & Monticello Blvds.
Phone: (216) 691-7393
Season: Jun–Sep
Hours: Mon–Fri 1–5 p.m., Sat–Sun 1–6 p.m.; family swim Mon–Fri 5–8 p.m.
Prices: $2 adult residents w/ ID, $1.50 student resident w/ ID, $3 non-resident guests
Direct.: Located in Denison Park on Monticello Blvd. (at Belvoir), between Noble and Green Rds.

● Strollers   ● Groups   ● Food Serv.   ● Parking   ● Birthdays
● Diap. Chg.   ● Picnic   ● Food Nearby   ● Pub. Trans.   ● Handicap. Access

Dudley Pool (Willowick Recreation Dept.)
Area: **East**   City: **Willowick**   Ages: **All**   Cost: **$**

Water slides and playground equipment.

Address: 315 Willowick Dr.
Phone: (216†) 943-3970
Season: Jun–Sep
Hours: Mon–Fri 11 a.m.–8 p.m., Sat–Sun 11 a.m.–5 p.m.
Prices: $2 residents, $2.50 non-residents
Direct.: SR 2 to exit for E. 305; north on E. 305; right (east) on W. Willowick Dr. for 1 mile.

- ● Strollers   ● Groups   ● Food Serv.   ● Parking   ● Birthdays
- ● Diap. Chg.   ● Picnic   ● Food Nearby   Pub. Trans. ● Handicap. Access

Dunham Recreation Center (Maple Hts. Recreation Dept.)
Area: **Southeast**   City: **Maple Hts.**   Ages: **All**   Cost: **$**

Olympic-size pool, kiddie pool, slides, fountains, lessons. Pool rental available only during off-hours.

Address: 15005 Schreiber Rd.
Phone: (216) 475-1811
Season: Mid-Jun–Aug 31st
Hours: Vary
Prices: Residents: $.50, $.25 under age 18; non-residents: $4, $3 under age 18
Direct.: I-77 to exit for Rockside Rd.; east on Rockside; right (south) on Dunham Rd. to Schreiber Rd.; right (west) on Schreiber; entrance on right.

- Strollers   Groups   ● Food Serv.   ● Parking   ● Birthdays
- ● Diap. Chg.   ● Picnic   ● Food Nearby   ● Pub. Trans. ● Handicap. Access

Euclid Orr Ice Rink
Area: **East**   City: **Euclid**   Ages: **3 & up**   Cost: **$**

Open skating sessions vary to accommodate lessons and hockey games. Annual events include a Halloween Costume Skate, a Skate with Santa, and hockey tournaments. Lessons are offered for ages 3 and up in four six-week sessions; they are also available through the youth hockey program. Skate rental, skate sharpening, and lockers are available.

Address: 22550 Milton Dr.
Phone: (216) 289-8649; 289-8630
Season: Sep–early May
Hours: Vary
Prices: $3 adult residents w/ ID, $2 under 18 w/ ID, $3.50 non-residents, $2 seniors
Direct.: I-90 to exit for Babbitt Rd.; north on Babbitt; left (west) on Milton Dr.; across from Euclid YMCA.

- ● Strollers   ● Groups   ● Food Serv.   ● Parking   ● Birthdays
- Diap. Chg.   ● Picnic   ● Food Nearby   ● Pub. Trans. ● Handicap. Access

SPORTS & RECREATION

CLEVELAND DISCOVERY GUIDE

Fit by Five Preschool

Area: **West**   City: **North Olmsted**   Ages: **2-5**   Cost: **$$$**

In this large, open classroom/gym for preschoolers only, academics as well as social skills are taught in an environment featuring sports skills and exercise. Flexible program scheduling allows for families to participate one, two, or three times a week; goals are school readiness and mastery of preschool academic skills. A popular summer camp program is designed around weekly themes.

Address: 28641 Lorain Rd.
Phone: (216†) 777-8555
Season: Year-round
Hours: Mornings or afternoons
Prices: Classes start at $20 per month
Direct.: I-480 to Exit 3 (Stearns Rd.); north on Stearns; right (east) on Lorain Rd. (SR 10) for about 2 blocks; on right (south) side.

● Strollers   Groups   Food Serv.   ● Parking   ● Birthdays
● Diap. Chg.   Picnic   ● Food Nearby   ● Pub. Trans.   Handicap. Access

Foster Pool (Lakewood Recreation Dept.)

Area: **West**   City: **Lakewood**   Ages: **All**   Cost: **$**

Kiddie pool, lessons, playground. Located adjacent to the lakefront in Lakewood Park.

Address: 14532 Lake Ave.
Phone: (216) 529-4121
Season: Jun–Sep
Hours: Vary
Prices: Residents: $2.50 adult , $2 students, children 6 and under, seniors Free; non-residents: $3.50 adults, $3 students, $2 seniors and children 6 and under. Season passes: $25 resident adult ($50 non-resident), $20 students ($40 non-resident), $40 senior non-resident
Direct.: I-90 to exit for Warren Rd.; north on Warren to dead end; right (east) on Clifton Rd. for 2 blocks; left (north) on Belle Ave. across Lake Ave. and into Lakewood Park.

● Strollers   ● Groups   ● Food Serv.   ● Parking   Birthdays
● Diap. Chg.   ● Picnic   ● Food Nearby   ● Pub. Trans.   ● Handicap. Access

Grand River Canoe Livery

Area: **Far East**   City: **Rock Creek**   Ages: **Preschool & up**   Cost: **$$$**

This small livery runs trips from two to five hours in length (with the longest ones in the fall) on the Grand River, a state-designated scenic waterway that runs through Ashtabula and Lake counties. Tours are not guided. Four to seven canoes are available for large groups.

SPORTS &
RECREATION

Address: 3825 Fobes Rd.
Phone: (800) ME-CANOE, (216†) 632-2663
Season: Daily in summer; weekends spring & fall
Hours: Vary
Prices: $23 per canoe
Direct.: I-90 to exit for SR 45; south on SR 45 for 6 miles; right (west) on Fobes Rd. to end.

Strollers	● Groups	Food Serv.	● Parking	● Birthdays
Diap. Chg.	● Picnic	● Food Nearby	Pub. Trans.	Handicap. Access

Great Lakes Gymnastics
Area: **Far West**   City: **Avon Lake**   Ages: **Pre-K–adult**   Cost: **$$$**

Gymnastics classes for boys and girls in this 15,000-square-foot gymnasium feature an exercise or warm-up period to develop strength and flexibility. Classes are subdivided so that students are working on skills appropriate for their abilities. Preschoolers as young as 2 work with their parents to acquire basic gymnastic and movement-coordination skills. Kindergarten classes are divided into boys and girls, and equipment is adapted to the interests and capabilities of the age group.

Address: 33600 Pin Oak Pkwy.
Phone: (216†) 871-6239/(216†) 933-2674
Season: Year-round
Hours: Office hours 9 a.m.–1 p.m.
Prices: Vary
Direct.: I-90/SR 2 to exit for Avon Lake/SR 611; north on SR 611; right (east) on Chester Rd.; left (north) on Moore Rd.; right (east) on Pin Oak Pkwy.

Strollers	● Groups	Food Serv.	● Parking	Birthdays
Diap. Chg.	Picnic	● Food Nearby	Pub. Trans.	● Handicap. Access

Greenbrier Ice Rink (Parma Hts. Recreation Center)
Area: **South**   City: **Parma Hts.**   Ages: **3 & up**   Cost: **$**

Open skating sessions include an after-school session for families. Lessons are offered for ages 3 and up, primarily on weekends, and also through the youth hockey program. Skate rentals and lockers available.

Address: 6200 Pearl Rd.
Phone: (216†) 842-5005
Season: Sep–May, special programs during the summer
Hours: Vary
Prices: Residents: $4 adult, $2.50 student; non-residents: $5 adult, $3.50 student
Direct.: Between York & Snow Rds. in Greenbrier Commons, near police station.

● Strollers	● Groups	● Food Serv.	● Parking	● Birthdays
Diap. Chg.	● Picnic	● Food Nearby	● Pub. Trans.	● Handicap. Access

SPORTS & RECREATION

Gymboree Play Programs
Area: **East**   City: **Beachwood**   Ages: **Infant–5**   Cost: **$$–$$$**

Music, movement, fun, and games are offered here in a colorful room created for playful interaction by parents and their 3-month- to 5-year-old children. Kindermusik creative music classes for children 18 months to 5 years are also offered.

Address: 1980 S. Green Rd.
Phone: (216) 291-9969
Season: Year-round
Hours: Vary
Prices: Vary
Direct.: I-271 to Exit 32 (Brainard/Cedar Rd.); west on Cedar; right (north) on S. Green Rd.; in the Workman's Circle building, across from Notre Dame College.

- Strollers   Groups   Food Serv.   ● Parking   ● Birthdays
- Diap. Chg.   Picnic   ● Food Nearby   ● Pub. Trans.   Handicap. Access

Gymnastics Training Center
Area: **East**   City: **Warrensville Hts.**   Ages: **1 & up**   Cost: **$$–$$$**

Olympic-style instruction for boys and girls starts from age 10 months. Classes for 7–9 and 10–teen include power tumbling and competitive teams.

Address: 4505 Northfield Rd.
Phone: (216) 663-6993
Season: Year-round
Hours: Vary
Prices: Vary
Direct.: I-480 to Exit 26 (Northfield Rd./Miles Rd.); left (west) on Miles; right (north) on Northfield; on right, across from Thistledown Racetrack.

-   Strollers   Groups   Food Serv.   ● Parking   ● Birthdays
   Diap. Chg.   Picnic   ● Food Nearby   ● Pub. Trans.   ● Handicap. Access

SPORTS & RECREATION

Houston-Fisher Pool
Area: **East**   City: **Eastlake**   Ages: **All**   Cost: **$**

Kiddie pool, lessons, playground.

Address: Jakse Dr.
Phone: (216†) 951-1416;(216†) 975-4269
Season: Jun–Sep
Hours: Vary
Prices: $2 per person, $55 season pass
Direct.: SOM Ctr. Rd. to Stevens Blvd.; west on Stevens to Jakse Dr.; left (south) on Jakse.

-   Strollers   ● Groups   ● Food Serv.   ● Parking   ● Birthdays
- Diap. Chg.   ● Picnic   ● Food Nearby   Pub. Trans.   ● Handicap. Access

J. A. Hruby Natatorium
Area: **South**   City: **Brecksville**   Ages: **All**   Cost: **$$**

Olympic-size pool, kiddie pool, slides, fountains, lessons. Programs open to public (residents and non-residents).

Address: One Community Center Dr.
Phone: (216†) 546-2300
Season: Year-round
Hours: Vary
Prices: $5 (residents only); annual memberships available for residents only
Direct.: I-77 to Exit 149 (SR 82); east on SR 82; right (south) on SR 21 (Brecksville Rd.); for about 1500 feet; on left (east) side, past police station.

- Strollers
- Diap. Chg.
- Groups
- Picnic
- Food Serv.
- Food Nearby
- Parking
- Pub. Trans.
- Birthdays
- Handicap. Access

Jewish Community Center (Beachwood)
Area: **East**   City: **Beachwood**   Ages: **All**   Cost: **FREE–$$**

This neighborhood institution offers a flurry of activities for younger children and their parents. Classes are extensive. For children 4 months and up there is infant massage, music therapy, tumbling, arts and crafts, and storytelling. The preschool department (ages 2-1/2–5) offers dance, cooking, swimming, drama, and pottery. For adults, parenting classes cover nutrition, separation anxiety, and infant care. Each year there are special workshops and discussions.

In summer, there are a number of camps designed around age groups and special activities. Of special interest to parents is Family Place. Specifically designed for parents with children up to age 3-1/2, it provides a drop-in center with parent-child activities and support from other parents and staff.

Special events here are also popular, with a concentration on traditional Jewish holidays. Chanukah is celebrated with a program including music, arts, crafts, and food for the entire family. A new meeting and catering facility holds up to 500 people for large gatherings.

Address: 26001 S. Woodland Rd.
Phone: (216) 831-0700
Season: Year-round
Hours: Vary
Prices: Vary
Direct.: Located between Richmond & Brainard on S. Woodland.

- Strollers
- Diap. Chg.
- Groups
- Picnic
- Food Serv.
- Food Nearby
- Parking
- Pub. Trans.
- Birthdays
- Handicap. Access

SPORTS & RECREATION

Jewish Community Center (Cleveland Hts.)

Area: **East**   City: **Cleveland Hts.**   Ages: **All**   Cost: **FREE–$$**

See previous listing for Jewish Community Center, Beachwood for details. Extended day care (all-day preschool program) and After-school Kid Center classes available.

Address: 3505 Mayfield Rd.
Phone: (216) 382-4000
Season: Year-round
Hours: Vary
Prices: Vary
Direct.: Located between Warrensville & Taylor, across from Severance Center.

- Strollers   • Groups   • Food Serv.   • Parking   • Birthdays
- Diap. Chg.   • Picnic   • Food Nearby   • Pub. Trans.   • Handicap. Access

KIDSPORTS

Area: **Southeast**   City: **Bainbridge**   Ages: **6 mos.–adult**   Cost: **$$$**

A Wee Sports Gym is stocked with soft equipment for children ages 6 months to 5 years. Certified instructors teach a variety of children's classes, including Baby Club (ages 6–12 months), Tot Club (12–24 months), Mini Club (2–3 years), Romp and Roll (preschoolers), Tumble and Fun (4–6 years), Introduction to Games (6–8 years), Fun to Be Fit (8–12), Soccer, Gymnastics, Karate, Basketball, Aerobics, and Pre-conditioning. A separate Wee Sports Village allows children to experience creative play in four different rooms: grocery store/bank, gas station/hardware store, restaurant/kitchen, and clothing store/puppet theater. While your kids are getting in shape, you can too. The fitness center is stocked with Trotter equipment, virtual reality machines, and PACE hydraulic equipment. A full range of classes is offered.

Address: 8185 E. Washington St.
Phone: (216†) 543-1111
Season: Year-round
Hours: Mon–Sat 8 a.m.–8 p.m., Sun 1 p.m.–6 p.m.
Prices: Vary, by membership (starting at $35)
Direct.: I-480 and/or I-271 to Exit 27 (US 422); east on US 422; left (north) for 3 miles on SR 306 in Bainbridge; left (west) for 1 mile on Washington St.; on left.

- Strollers   • Groups   • Food Serv.   • Parking   • Birthdays
- Diap. Chg.   Picnic   • Food Nearby   • Pub. Trans.   • Handicap. Access

SPORTS & RECREATION

Lake Erie Gymnastics School

Area: **Far East**   City: **Mentor**   Ages: **2 yrs–school age**   Cost: **$$–$$$**

This gymnastics school includes team-level instruction for boys and girls through their high-school years. Special classes are designed for preschoolers ages 2–5. Also available: recreational gymnastics instruction for 1st grade through high school; evening classes in high-school cheerleading and tumbling (combined).

Address: 8785 East Ave.
Phone: (216†) 255-0228
Season: Year-round
Hours: Vary
Prices: Vary
Direct.:   SR 2 to exit for Center St. (SR 615); south on Center to Station St.; left (east) on Station to East Ave.; bear to left onto East Ave.; on left.

- ● *Strollers*
  Diap. Chg.
- ● *Groups*
  Picnic
- *Food Serv.*
- ● *Food Nearby*
- ● *Parking*
  Pub. Trans.
- ● *Birthdays*
- ● *Handicap. Access*

Lakeland Community College
Area: **Far East**   City: **Kirtland**   Ages: **3 & up**   Cost: **$$$**

Lakeland's College for Kids has courses in creative arts, ballet, aikido, and computers. Quarterly sessions run for 8 to 12 weeks, depending on the type of class. Also offered are 8 weeks of summer camps and a week-long mini-camp offered in early spring, designed around recreational and educational activities, arts, and crafts. College for Teens programs offer a variety of educational and leisure activities for junior and senior high school students, including Computer-Aided Design, Criminalistics, Theater, Video Production, Hands-On Science, and more. All classes are offered quarterly; there are also spring and summer camps. An annual two-day jazz festival showcases area high school bands.

Address: 7700 Clocktower Dr.
Phone: (216†) 953-7116
Season: Year-round
Hours: Vary
Prices: Vary
Direct.:   I-90 to Exit 193 (SR 306); south on SR 306; left (east) on Clocktower Dr.

- *Strollers*
  Diap. Chg.
- *Groups*
  ● *Picnic*
- ● *Food Serv.*
  ● *Food Nearby*
- ● *Parking*
  ● *Pub. Trans.*
- *Birthdays*
  ● *Handicap. Access*

Little Gym
Area: **West**   City: **North Olmsted**   Ages: **4 mos.–12 years**   Cost: **$$$**

This child-friendly fitness and development center offers age-appropriate instruction in gymnastics, sports skills, karate, and fitness. Programs are designed to build self-confidence and self-esteem. Weekend birthday parties are available.

Address: 24140 Lorain Rd.
Phone: (216†) 734-4900

SPORTS & RECREATION

Season: Year-round
Hours: Mon–Fri 9 a.m.–7:30 p.m.; Sat 9:00 a.m.–1 p.m.; class times vary
Prices: Vary
Direct.: I-90 to Exit 159 (SR 252/Columbia Rd); south on SR 252; left (east) on Lorain Rd./SR 10
I-480 to Exit 6 (Great Northern Blvd.); north on Great Northern; right (east) on Lorain Rd.

Strollers	● *Groups*	*Food Serv.*	● *Parking*	● *Birthdays*
Diap. Chg.	*Picnic*	● *Food Nearby*	● *Pub. Trans.*	*Handicap. Access*

Lyndhurst Pool (South Euclid/Lyndhurst Recreation Dept.)
Area: **East**   City: **Lyndhurst**   Ages: **All**   Cost: **$–$$**

Kiddie pool, lessons, playground.

Address: 1331 Parkview Dr.
Phone: (216) 691-2246
Season: Jun–Sep
Hours: Vary
Prices: $4 residents, $5 non-resident guests; individual family pass $29 each, maximum $87.00 per family
Direct.: From Mayfield Rd. in Lyndhurst turn north onto Parkview Dr. (east of Richmond Rd.); near Lyndhurst City Hall.

Strollers	● *Groups*	*Food Serv.*	● *Parking*	● *Birthdays*
Diap. Chg.	● *Picnic*	*Food Nearby*	● *Pub. Trans.*	*Handicap. Access*

SPORTS & RECREATION

Madison Pool
Area: **West**   City: **Lakewood**   Ages: **All**   Cost: **$**

Kiddie pool, fountain, slide, lessons, playground.

Address: Madison Ave.
Phone: (216) 221-0627
Season: Jun–Sep
Hours: Vary
Prices: Residents: $2.50 adult , $2 students, children 6 and under, seniors FREE; non-residents: $3.50 adults, $3 students, $2 seniors and children 6 and under. Season passes: $25 resident adult ($50 non-resident), $20 students ($40 non-resident), $40 senior non-resident
Direct.: I-90 to exit for Bunts Rd.; north on Bunts; right (east) on Madison Ave.

● *Strollers*	● *Groups*	● *Food Serv.*	● *Parking*	● *Birthdays*
● *Diap. Chg.*	● *Picnic*	● *Food Nearby*	● *Pub. Trans.*	● *Handicap. Access*

Manry Pool (Willowick Recreation Dept.)
Area: **East**   City: **Willowick**   Ages: **All**   Cost: **$**

Kiddie pool (free to the public), swim lessons, playground.

Address: 30100 Arnold Dr.
Phone: (216†) 944-1575
Season: Jun–Sep
Hours: Mon–Fri 1 p.m.–5 p.m., 6 p.m.–8 p.m.; Sat–Sun 11 a.m.–5 p.m.
Prices: $2 residents, $2.50 non-residents
Direct.: SR 2 to exit for E. 305; north on E. 305; left on Arnold Dr.

• Strollers   • Groups   • Food Serv.   • Parking   Birthdays
• Diap. Chg.   • Picnic   • Food Nearby   Pub. Trans.   Handicap. Access

Mentor Civic Arena and Waterpark
Area: **Far East**   City: **Mentor**   Ages: **All**   Cost: **$**

Open skating sessions include after-school skates Monday through Thursday, luncheon skates, and evening skates on weekends, with special hours during the winter holidays. Skating lessons for ages 3 and up are offered in several sessions through the season, including a mini-session during the winter holidays. Skate rentals, sharpening, and lockers are available; the rink can be rented for private parties.

The facility also has a kiddie pool, slides, and lessons.

Address: 8600 Munson Rd.
Phone: (216†) 974-5730; (216†) 255-1777;(216†) 255-1100 (City Hall)
Season: Pool: Memorial Day–Labor Day; skating: year-round
Hours: Vary
Prices: Pool: $3.50, $3 ages 4–17, no charge under age 3; skating: $3.50, $3 ages 17 & under
Direct.: SR 2 to exit for SR 615; north on SR 615 past Mentor High School; right (east) on Civic Center Blvd. at first light after high school; right on Munson Rd.

• Strollers   • Groups   • Food Serv.   • Parking   • Birthdays
• Diap. Chg.   • Picnic   • Food Nearby   • Pub. Trans. • Handicap. Access

Courtesy of Mentor Recreation Dept.

North Olmsted Recreation Center
Area: **West**   City: **North Olmsted**   Ages: **3 & up**   Cost: **$**

The ice-skating schedule here varies; open sessions are held most afternoons and weekend evenings (October to mid-April). Special events include a Halloween skate and a Skate with Frosty and Santa. A hockey mini-camp is also offered in late December. Skating lessons for ages 3 and up are offered in five sessions during the season. Hockey lessons for ages 4–8 are also offered through the Hockey Club's Mighty Mite program. Skate rentals, skate sharpening, and lockers are available. Birthday parties can be arranged.

Other activities here include swimming and a playground.

Address: 26000 Lorain Rd.
Phone: (216†) 734-8200
Season: Year-round
Hours: Vary
Prices: $3–$5
Direct.: Located on Lorain Rd. between Columbia and Dover Center Rds.

| • Strollers | • Groups | • Food Serv. | • Parking | • Birthdays |
| • Diap. Chg. | Picnic | • Food Nearby | • Pub. Trans. | • Handicap. Access |

Public Square Ice-Skating Rink
Area: **Downtown**   City: **Cleveland**   Ages: **3 & up**   Cost: **$**

Aside from open skating, this small rink hosts a variety of special events, such as figure-skating exhibitions and ice-carving competitions, all arranged by the Greater Cleveland Growth Association. Skate rentals are offered; the rink is available for private parties. For a complete schedule (which varies from year to year) send a self-addressed, stamped envelope to Holiday Activity Schedule, Greater Cleveland Growth Association, 50 Public Square, Cleveland, OH 44113.

Address: 200 Tower City Center, 50 Public Square (adjacent to Terminal Tower)
Phone: (216) 621-3300
Season: Fri after Thanksgiving–mid-Jan
Hours: Mon–Thu 11 a.m.–10 p.m.; Fri–Sat 11 a.m.–11 p.m.; Sun 1 p.m.–10 p.m.
Prices: $3 admission; $1 skate rental
Direct.: I-90 eastbound to Exit 171B (Ontario Ave.); north on Ontario to Public Square
I-90 westbound to Exit 173C (Superior Ave.); west on Superior to Public Square.

| Strollers | Groups | Food Serv. | Parking | • Birthdays |
| Diap. Chg. | Picnic | • Food Nearby | • Pub. Trans. | • Handicap. Access |

SPORTS & RECREATION

Courtesy of Greater Cleveland Growth Assoc.

Quail Hollow Resort and Country Club
Area: **Far East**   City: **Painesville**   Ages: **Preschool & up**   Cost: **$$**

This club offers cross-country skiing (with rentals and lessons) on eight miles of double-tracked trail through rolling hills. There are also two golf courses, an indoor/outdoor pool, and a fitness area.

Address: 11080 Concord-Hambden Rd.
Phone: (800) 792-0258, (216†) 352-6201
Season: Year-round
Hours: Resort open 24 hours/day; activity hours vary by season
Prices: Vary; special packages available
Direct.:   I-90 to Exit 200 (SR 44); south on SR 44 to first light; left on Auburn Rd. to Concord-Hambden Rd.

Strollers	● Groups	● Food Serv.	● Parking	Birthdays
Diap. Chg.	● Picnic	● Food Nearby	Pub. Trans.	Handicap. Access

Quarry Pool (South Euclid/Lyndhurst Recreation Dept.)
Area: **East**   City: **South Euclid**   Ages: **All**   Cost: **$–$$**

Water slide, baby wading pool, "mushroom" sprinklers; no diving.

Address: 711 S. Belvoir Blvd.
Phone: (216) 381-7674
Season: Jun–Sep
Hours: Mon–Fri 1:30 p.m.–8 p.m.; weekend hours vary
Prices: $4 residents, $5 non-resident guests; individual family pass $29 each, maximum $87 per family
Direct.:   Located north of the intersection of S. Belvoir and Monticello Blvds.

● Strollers	● Groups	Food Serv.	● Parking	Birthdays
Diap. Chg.	● Picnic	Food Nearby	● Pub. Trans.	Handicap. Access

Rocky River Recreation Center
Area: **West** City: **Rocky River** Ages: **All** Cost: **$–$$**

Open skating is scheduled for afternoons and evenings; hours vary to accommodate special events such as the annual Skate with Santa. For preschoolers, there is a Parent and Tot session scheduled for Wednesday afternoons. Skating lessons are offered for ages 3 and up with several six-week sessions through the season; classes last 30–45 minutes. Smaller group instruction is offered for tots; there is a special Parent and Tot Learn to Skate which includes lessons for both parent and child along with time to skate together. Youth hockey is also offered through the local league. Indoor soccer is offered during non-skating season. Skate rental, skate sharpening, and lockers are available. Birthday parties can be arranged.

The municipal pool also has a kiddie pool, slides, fountain, and lessons.

Address: 21018 Hilliard Blvd.
Phone: (216†) 356-5657; (216†) 356-5666 (evenings & weekends); (216†) 356-5660 (pool)
Season: Pool: June–Labor Day; skating: Sep–Mar; indoor soccer, Apr–Aug
Hours: Vary
Prices: Vary (call for programs & prices)
Direct.: At corner of Hilliard Blvd. & Wagar Rd. (W. 210), 1 block north of Westgate Mall.

- Strollers • Groups • Food Serv. • Parking • Birthdays
  Diap. Chg. • Picnic • Food Nearby • Pub. Trans. • Handicap. Access

Rocky River Stables (Cleveland Metroparks)
Area: **West** City: **Fairview Park** Ages: **4 & up** Cost: **$$**

Cleveland Metroparks stables offer year-round pony rides and English saddle riding lessons. There is an indoor arena and two outdoor rings for individual lessons and mini-camps for small groups. Ages 8 to 12 can attend a week-long horse camp; pony camp is available for ages 4 to 7. All lessons stress riding safety and grooming.

Address: 19901 Puritas Ave.
Phone: (216) 267-2525
Season: Year-round
Hours: Vary
Prices: Vary
Direct.: I-480 to Exit 9 (Grayton Rd.); north on Grayton to Puritas Rd.; left (west) on Puritas into Rocky River Reservation; on left before Valley Pkwy.

- Strollers • Groups Food Serv. • Parking • Birthdays
  Diap. Chg. • Picnic • Food Nearby • Pub. Trans. • Handicap. Access

SPORTS & RECREATION

Rollerworld
Area: **South**   City: **Parma**   Ages: **4 & up**   Cost: **$-$$**

This two-year-old in-line skating arena boasts youth and adult roller hockey leagues, open skate nights every Friday and Saturday, a video arcade, and skate rental.

Address: 5310 Hauserman Rd.
Phone: (216†) 843-7490
Season: Year-round
Hours: Vary
Prices: $4–$5
Direct.:   I-480 to Exit 13 (Tiedeman Rd.); south on Tiedeman for 3/4 mile (becomes Hauserman south of Brookpark Rd.); on right.

| Strollers | ● Groups | ● Food Serv. | ● Parking | ● Birthdays |
| Diap. Chg. | Picnic | ● Food Nearby | ● Pub. Trans. | Handicap. Access |

Solon Municipal Pool
Area: **Southeast**   City: **Solon**   Ages: **All**   Cost: **$**

Kiddie pool, lessons (outdoors only during summer months). Also in the summertime, a 50-meter outdoor pool and 1- and 3-meter diving boards are available. During the school year, an indoor 25-yard high school pool and 1-meter diving board are available. Open swim Saturdays 2–5 p.m., Sundays 1–4 p.m. All swim lessons and recreational swim teams for Solon residents only.

Address: 33355 Arthur Rd.
Phone: (216†) 248-0650
Season: Memorial Day–Labor Day
Hours: Mon–Fri 1 p.m.–8:45 p.m., Sat–Sun 11 a.m.–8:45 p.m.
Prices: $3 without pass; season passes: $30 individual, $70 family (Solon residents only unless accompanied by a Solon resident)
Direct.:   Corner of SOM Ctr. (SR 91) and Arthur Rds., adjacent to Board of Education Bldg.

| ● Strollers | Groups | ● Food Serv. | ● Parking | ● Birthdays |
| ● Diap. Chg. | Picnic | ● Food Nearby | Pub. Trans. | ● Handicap. Access |

Stafford Recreation Center (Maple Hts. Recreation Dept.)
Area: **East**   City: **Maple Hts.**   Ages: **All**   Cost: **$**

Kiddie pool, slides, lessons. Pool rental available only during off-hours.

Address: 5400 Mayville Rd.
Phone: (216) 663-8738
Season: Memorial Day–Labor Day
Hours: Vary
Prices: Residents: $.50, $.25 under age 18; non-residents: $4; $3 under age 18

SPORTS & RECREATION

Direct.: I-480 to exit for Warrensville Ctr. Rd.; south on Warrensville; right (west) on Libby Rd. for one block; left (south) on Mayville to end.

Strollers	● Groups	● Food Serv.	● Parking	● Birthdays
● Diap. Chg.	● Picnic	● Food Nearby	● Pub. Trans.	● Handicap. Access

Thornton Park (Shaker Hts. Recreation Dept.)
Area: **East**   City: **Shaker Hts.**   Ages: **All**   Cost: **$–$$**

Open skating is typically scheduled for weekdays, with morning, afternoon, and evening sessions; weekend afternoons; and a Sunday evening family skate. Hours vary for special events, such as the annual hockey tournament and ice show. Skating classes are offered for ages 3 and up with several sessions through the year. Youth Hockey is also offered through the Shaker Youth Hockey Association. Skate rental, skate sharpening, and lockers are offered. The rink is available for private rental, and birthday parties can be arranged.

The swimming pool also has a kiddie pool, slides, fountain, and lessons.

Address: 20701 Farnsleigh Rd.
Phone: (216) 491-1290
Season: Year-round; pool Memorial Day–Labor Day
Hours: Vary
Prices: Vary
Direct.: Farnsleigh Rd. east of Warrensville Ctr. Rd., near Van Aken Shopping Center.

● Strollers	● Groups	● Food Serv.	● Parking	● Birthdays
● Diap. Chg.	● Picnic	● Food Nearby	● Pub. Trans.	● Handicap. Access

Victory Pool (South Euclid/Lyndhurst Recreation Dept.)
Area: **East**   City: **South Euclid**   Ages: **All**   Cost: **$–$$**

Kiddie pool, slides, lessons.

Address: 1352 Victory Dr.
Phone: (216) 381-0435
Season: Jun–Sep
Hours: Vary
Prices: $4 residents, $5 non-resident guests; individual family pass $29 each, maximum $87 per family
Direct.: From Mayfield Rd. turn north on Victory Dr. 1 block west of Green Rd.

● Strollers	Groups	Food Serv.	● Parking	● Birthdays
Diap. Chg.	● Picnic	● Food Nearby	● Pub. Trans.	Handicap. Access

SPORTS & RECREATION

Winterhurst Municipal Ice Rink
Area: **West**   City: **Lakewood**   Ages: **3 & up**   Cost: **$**

This indoor rink is among the largest in the country. Open skating sessions vary widely to accommodate special events, which include hockey tournaments, figure-skating competitions, speed skating, and skating derbies. For families, each year there is a Halloween Costume Skate, Pizza skates, Skate with Santa, and a Skate with the Easter Bunny. For preschoolers, a parent and tot session is offered Tuesday mornings.

Skating lessons are offered for ages 3 and up in seven-week sessions four times a year. Lessons are also available through the Winterhurst Ice Hockey Association. Skate rentals, skate sharpening, and lockers are available. The rink is available for private rental. Birthday parties can be arranged.

Address: 14740 Lakewood Heights Blvd.
Phone: (216) 529-4236
Season: Year-round
Hours: Vary
Prices: Vary—call or pick up brochure for more details
Direct.:   I-90 to Exit 165(Warren Rd.); at intersection of Lakewood Heights Blvd. and Warren Rd. north of I-90.

- Strollers
  Diap. Chg.
- Groups
  Picnic
- Food Serv.
  Food Nearby
- Parking
  Pub. Trans.
- Birthdays
  Handicap. Access

YMCAs of Greater Cleveland
(See individual listings for location information.)

For swimming lessons, a summer day camp, a T-ball league, or karate classes for your kids, check out the neighborhood YMCA. While the facilities vary, general offerings are similar (most have indoor pools, large gyms, and fitness centers). YMCA members and non-members alike can sign up for classes that are offered year-round.

The parent-child Indian Guides program forms new tribes each September with groups of five or more from ages 5–15. Holidays generally bring special events and family parties.

YMCA, Broadway Branch
Area: **Near East**   City: **Cleveland**   Ages: **All**   Cost: **$$–$$$**

Swimming pool, gym, fitness room, summer day camp.

Address: 11300 Miles Ave.
Phone: (216) 341-1860
Season: Year-round
Hours: Mon–Fri 8:00 a.m.–9:00 p.m.
Prices: Vary

10 Great Things to Do...

Early in the Morning:

- ◉ Take a sunrise swim at Headlands Beach or Huntington Beach. (p. 102, 105)

- ◉ Watch for early birds at Holden Arboretum. (p. 104)

- ◉ Shop for groceries and goodies at the West Side Market. (p. 207)

- ◉ Have an outdoor breakfast at a Metroparks picnic pavilion. (p. 84)

- ◉ Grab a donut and attend rehearsals at the Cleveland Institute of Music. (p. 141)

- ◉ Have breakfast with the animals at the Cleveland Metroparks Zoo. (p. 85)

- ◉ Help with the chores at Lake Farmpark. (p. 108)

- ◉ Take an early hike through any of the Metroparks.

- ◉ Sign up for a family swim at one of the area YMCAs. (p. 180)

- ◉ Visit your neighborhood library. (p. 209)

Direct.:   I-480 to Exit 26 for Miles Ave.; west on Miles.

● *Strollers*   ● *Groups*   *Food Serv.*   ● *Parking*   ● *Birthdays*
  Diap. Chg.   *Picnic*   ● *Food Nearby*   ● *Pub. Trans.*   ● *Handicap. Access*

YMCA, Brooklyn Branch
Area: **Near West**   City: **Cleveland**   Ages: **All**   Cost: **$$–$$$**

Swimming (including youth swim), gym, fitness room, handball and racquetball courts, day camp, game rooms. Also available: all-day preschool care and other preschool programs.

Address: 3881 Pearl Rd.
Phone: (216) 749-2355
Season: Year-round
Hours: Mon–Fri 6 a.m.–10 p.m.; Sat 8 a.m.–5 p.m.; Sun noon-5 p.m.
Prices: Vary
Direct.:   One block south of the intersection of Denison Ave. & Pearl Rd.

● *Strollers*   ● *Groups*   ● *Food Serv.*   ● *Parking*   ● *Birthdays*
  Diap. Chg.   *Picnic*   ● *Food Nearby*   ● *Pub. Trans.*   *Handicap. Access*

YMCA, Central Branch (Painesville)
Area: **Far East**   City: **Painesville**   Ages: **All**   Cost: **$$–$$$**

Swimming pool, gym, fitness room, track, racquetball and handball courts, day camp. Other special facilities include the Family Adventure Center, day-care center, game room, and a whirlpool with sauna/steam room.

Address: 933 Mentor Ave.
Phone: (216†) 352-3303
Season: Year-round
Hours: Mon–Fri 5 a.m.–9 p.m.; Sat 5 a.m.–4 p.m.
Prices: Vary
Direct.:   I-90 to Exit 200 (SR 44); north on SR 44 to exit for US 20/SR 84; left on US 20 (Mentor Ave.); on south side.

  Strollers   ● *Groups*   ● *Food Serv.*   ● *Parking*   ● *Birthdays*
● *Diap. Chg.*   *Picnic*   ● *Food Nearby*   ● *Pub. Trans.*   ● *Handicap. Access*

YMCA, East End Branch (Madison)
Area: **Far East**   City: **Madison**   Ages: **All**   Cost: **$$–$$$**

Swimming pool, gym, fitness and weight room, preschool center, babysitting room, outdoor recreational area, summer day camp.

Address: 730 N. Lake St.
Phone: (216†) 428-5125

SPORTS & RECREATION

Season: Year-round
Hours: Mon–Fri 5:30 a.m.–10 p.m.; Sat 8 a.m.–2:30 p.m.; 6:30–9 p.m. until early April;
              Sun 1–5 p.m.
Prices: Vary
Direct.: I-90 to Exit 212 (SR 528); north on SR 528 (N. Lake St., becomes Hubbard Rd.).

- ● Strollers   ● Groups   ● Food Serv.   ● Parking   ● Birthdays
- ● Diap. Chg.   Picnic   ● Food Nearby   ● Pub. Trans.   ● Handicap. Access

YMCA, Elyria Family
Area: **Far West**   City: **Elyria**   Ages: **All**   Cost: **$$–$$$**

Swimming, gymnastics, fitness room, day camp, preschool, and child care.

Address: 265 Washington Ave.
Phone: (216†) 323-5500
Season: Year-round
Hours: Mon–Thu 5:45 a.m.–10 p.m.; Fri 5:45 a.m.–9 p.m.; Sat 8:30 a.m.–8 p.m.; Sun 2
              p.m.–6 p.m.
Prices: Vary
Direct.: Take I-480 to SR 10; SR 10 west to Elyria; exit at SR 57; north on SR 57 to E. Broad
              St.; left (west) on E. Broad to Washington Ave.; right (north) on Washington.

-   Strollers   ● Groups   Food Serv.   ● Parking   ● Birthdays
-   Diap. Chg.   Picnic   ● Food Nearby   Pub. Trans.   ● Handicap. Access

YMCA, Euclid Family Branch
Area: **East**   City: **Euclid**   Ages: **All**   Cost: **$$–$$$**

Swimming, gymnastics, day camp, school-age day care, youth sports, tae kwon do, fitness center, and weight room.

Address: 631 Babbitt Rd.
Phone: (216) 731-7454
Season: Year-round
Hours: Mon–Fri 6 a.m.–10 p.m.; Sat 8:30 a.m.–5 p.m.; Sun 1–4 p.m.
Prices: Vary
Direct.: I-90 to exit for Babbitt Rd.; north on Babbit for 1-1/2 mile.

-   Strollers   ● Groups   ● Food Serv.   ● Parking   ● Birthdays
- ● Diap. Chg.   ● Picnic   ● Food Nearby   ● Pub. Trans.   ● Handicap. Access

YMCA, Geauga County
Area: **Far East**   City: **Newbury**   Ages: **All**   Cost: **$$–$$$**

Most of the programs here are held outside or at other locations in Geauga County. There is a basketball court and workout programs.

Address: 12121 Kinsman Rd.

Phone: (216†) 564-7158
Season: Year-round
Hours: 6:30 a.m.–6:30 p.m.
Prices: Vary
Direct.: On Kinsman Rd (SR 87) in Newbury, 1/4 mile west of SR 44 (Ravenna Rd.); across from St. Helen's Church.

| ● Strollers | Groups | Food Serv. | ● Parking | Birthdays |
| Diap. Chg. | Picnic | Food Nearby | ● Pub. Trans. | Handicap. Access |

YMCA, Glenville Branch
Area: **Near East**   City: **Cleveland**   Ages: **All**   Cost: **$$–$$$**

Swimming pool, gym, fitness room, summer day camp.

Address: 11111 St. Clair Ave.
Phone: (216) 851-4700
Season: Year-round
Hours: Mon–Fri 8:30 a.m.–8 p.m.; Sat 9 a.m.–1 p.m.
Prices: Vary
Direct.: Located on St. Clair Ave. off Eddy Rd.

| Strollers | ● Groups | Food Serv. | ● Parking | ● Birthdays |
| Diap. Chg. | Picnic | ● Food Nearby | ● Pub. Trans. | Handicap. Access |

YMCA, Heights Family Branch
Area: **East**   City: **Cleveland Hts.**   Ages: **All**   Cost: **$$–$$$**

Swimming, gymnastics, fitness room, day camp. Aerobics classes also available. Pool is not handicapped-accessible.

Address: 2340 Lee Rd.
Phone: (216) 371-2323
Season: Year-round
Hours: Mon–Fri 6:30 a.m.–10 p.m.; Sat 8:30 a.m.–5 p.m.; Sun 1–5 p.m.
Prices: Vary—call or stop by for details
Direct.: Located on Lee Rd. between Cedar and Fairmount Rds.

| Strollers | ● Groups | ● Food Serv. | ● Parking | ● Birthdays |
| Diap. Chg. | Picnic | ● Food Nearby | ● Pub. Trans. | ● Handicap. Access |

YMCA, Hillcrest Family Branch
Area: **East**   City: **Lyndhurst**   Ages: **All**   Cost: **$$–$$$**

Swimming pool, gym, fitness areas, day camp, child care and babysitting, youth and adult programming.

Address: 5000 Mayfield Rd.
Phone: (216) 382-4300
Season: Year-round

Hours: Mon–Fri 6 a.m.–10 p.m.; Sat 8 a.m.–6 p.m.
Prices: Vary
Direct.: Located on Mayfield Rd., east of Richmond Rd. in Lyndhurst.

Strollers   • Groups   Food Serv.   • Parking   • Birthdays
Diap. Chg.   Picnic   • Food Nearby   • Pub. Trans.   • Handicap. Access

YMCA, Lake County Outdoor Family Center
Area: **Far East**   City: **Perry Twp.**   Ages: **All**   Cost: **FREE–$$**

In winter, cross-country ski trails here cover nearly five miles over 180 acres of woods, fields, and scenic river valley. Overlooking the river from atop a scenic bluff is a stone-and-timber lodge with a large fireplace—a popular gathering spot. Winter activities feature sledding, moonlight ski outings, skating, and hiking. In the warmer months there is outdoor tennis, racquetball, sand volleyball, and basketball. An outdoor pool complex includes a kiddie pool and water slide. A special events calendar includes youth sports, family nights, and monthly preschool programs.

Address: 4540 River Rd.
Phone: (216†) 259-2724
Season: Lodge: year-round; cross-country ski trails: winter
Hours: Lodge Mon–Fri 9 a.m.–dusk, Sat 10 a.m.–dusk, Sun noon–dusk (hours vary by season, please call ahead)
Prices: Vary
Direct.: I-90 take Exit 205 (Vrooman Rd.); north on Vrooman for 3–4 miles; right (east) on SR 84 for 1/2 mile; right on River Rd. for 5 miles.

• Strollers   • Groups   • Food Serv.   • Parking   • Birthdays
• Diap. Chg.   • Picnic   • Food Nearby   Pub. Trans.   • Handicap. Access

YMCA, Lakewood Branch
Area: **Near West**   City: **Lakewood**   Ages: **All**   Cost: **$$–$$$**

Swimming pool, gymnasium, fitness room, day camp.

Address: 16915 Detroit Rd.
Phone: (216) 521-8400
Season: Year-round
Hours: Mon–Fri 6 a.m.–10:30 p.m.; Sat 7 a.m.–9 p.m.; Sun noon–9 p.m.
Prices: Vary
Direct.: I-90 to Exit 163 (McKinley Ave.); north on McKinley (becomes Larchmont Ave.); right (east) on Detroit Rd. for 1/3 mile; on right.

• Strollers   • Groups   • Food Serv.   • Parking   • Birthdays
• Diap. Chg.   Picnic   • Food Nearby   • Pub. Trans.   • Handicap. Access

SPORTS & RECREATION

YMCA, Lorain Family
Area: **Far West**   City: **Lorain**   Ages: **All**   Cost: **$$–$$$**

Swimming pool, gym, racquetball, summer day camp, free weight room, track, school-age and all-day child care, Toddler Center.

Branches:

Longfellow Park YMCA, 300 Longfellow Pkwy., Lorain (216†) 282-4144

North Coast YMCA (see separate listing)

Address: 1121 Tower Blvd.
Phone: (216†) 282-4414
Season: Year-round
Hours: Mon–Fri 6 a.m.–10:30 p.m.; Sat 8:00 a.m.–5 p.m.
Prices: Vary
Direct.:   SR 2 to exit for Middle Ridge Rd.; north on Middle Ridge to first light; left (west) on SR 254; right (north) on Oberlin Ave.; right (east) on Tower Blvd.; second building on right (south) side.

Strollers	● *Groups*	*Food Serv.*	● *Parking*	● *Birthdays*
Diap. Chg.	*Picnic*	● *Food Nearby*	● *Pub. Trans.*	● *Handicap. Access*

YMCA, North Coast
Area: **Far West**   City: **Avon Lake**   Ages: **All**   Cost: **$$–$$$**

Child care and preschool programs, including athletic exercise; adult fitness programs; weights and exercise equipment; racquetball courts with league competition; sauna and fully equipped locker rooms.

Address: 32796 Walker Rd.
Phone: (216†) 835-9622
Season: Year-round
Hours: Mon–Thu 6 a.m.–10 p.m., Fri 6 a.m.–9 p.m., Sat 8 a.m.–5 p.m., Sun 1 p.m.–5 p.m.; closed most major holidays
Prices: Vary
Direct.:   I-90 to Exit 153 (SR 83/Center Rd.); north on SR 83; left (west) on Walker Rd.

Strollers	*Groups*	● *Food Serv.*	● *Parking*	● *Birthdays*
Diap. Chg.	*Picnic*	● *Food Nearby*	*Pub. Trans.*	● *Handicap. Access*

YMCA, Ridgewood Branch
Area: **South**   City: **Parma**   Ages: **All**   Cost: **$$–$$$**

Swimming, gymnasium, fitness room, preschool enrichment classes, day camp.

Address: 6840 Ridge Rd.
Phone: (216†) 842-5200
Season: Year-round
Hours: Mon–Fri 6 a.m.–9:30 p.m., Sat 8 a.m.–6 p.m., Sun noon–6 p.m.

SPORTS & RECREATION

Prices: Vary
Direct.: Located near Parmatown Mall.

Strollers	• Groups	Food Serv.	• Parking	Birthdays
• Diap. Chg.	Picnic	• Food Nearby	• Pub. Trans.	• Handicap. Access

YMCA, Southeast Branch
Area: **South**   City: **Bedford**   Ages: **All**   Cost: **$$–$$$**

Swimming pool, gym, fitness room, day camp, child care programs, child and adult physical fitness programs and sports leagues.

Address: 460 Northfield Rd.
Phone: (216) 663-7522
Season: Year-round
Hours: Mon–Fri 6 a.m.–10 p.m., Sat 7:30 a.m.–4 p.m., Sun 1 p.m.–4 p.m.
Prices: Vary
Direct.: I-271 to Exit 26 (Rockside Rd.); west on Rockside to Northfield Rd.; left (south) on Northfield; on right.

• Strollers	• Groups	Food Serv.	• Parking	• Birthdays
Diap. Chg.	Picnic	• Food Nearby	Pub. Trans.	• Handicap. Access

SPORTS & RECREATION

YMCA, Southwest Branch
Area: **Southwest**   City: **Strongsville**   Ages: **All**   Cost: **$$–$$$**

Summer day camp.

Address: 8381 Pearl Rd.
Phone: (216†) 243-0750
Season: Year-round
Hours: Mon–Fri 8:30 a.m.–5 p.m.; Sat 9 a.m.–2 p.m
Prices: Vary
Direct.: I-71 to Exit 234 (Pearl Rd./US 42); south on Pearl for 1 mile.

Strollers	Groups	Food Serv.	• Parking	Birthdays
Diap. Chg.	Picnic	• Food Nearby	• Pub. Trans.	• Handicap. Access

YMCA, West End Branch (Willoughby)
Area: **East**   City: **Willoughby**   Ages: **All**   Cost: **$$–$$$**

Swimming pool, gym, fitness room, summer day camp. Babysitting free for members. Many different programs for preschoolers to seniors.

Address: 37100 Euclid Ave.
Phone: (216†) 946-1160
Season: Year-round
Hours: Vary

Prices: Vary
Direct.: I-90 to Exit 189 (SOM Center Rd./SR 91); north on SR 91; right (east) on Euclid Ave. (US 20) for 2 miles.

Strollers	• Groups	Food Serv.	• Parking	• Birthdays
• Diap. Chg.	• Picnic	• Food Nearby	• Pub. Trans.	• Handicap. Access

YMCA, West Park-Fairview Branch
Area: **Near West**   City: **Cleveland**   Ages: **All**   Cost: **$$–$$$**

Swimming pool, gym, fitness room, summer day camp.

Address: 15501 Lorain Ave.
Phone: (216) 941-5410
Season: Year-round
Hours: Mon–Fri 6 a.m.–9:30 p.m.; Sat 8 a.m.–4 p.m.; Sun 12:30 p.m.–5 p.m.
Prices: Vary
Direct.:   I-71 to Exit 240 (W. 150 St.); north on W. 150; left (west) on Lorain; on left at Triskett Rd. intersection.
I-90 to Exit 165 (Warren Rd./W. 150); south on Warren Rd. (becomes W. 150); right on Triskett Rd. to dead end at Lorain Ave; on south side of Lorain at this intersection.

• Strollers	• Groups	Food Serv.	• Parking	• Birthdays
Diap. Chg.	Picnic	• Food Nearby	• Pub. Trans.	• Handicap. Access

YMCA, West Shore Family Branch
Area: **Far West**   City: **Westlake**   Ages: **All**   Cost: **$$–$$$**

Swimming pool, gymnasium, fitness room, day camp.

Address: 1575 Columbia Rd.
Phone: (216†) 871-6885
Season: Year-round
Hours: Mon–Fri 5:30 a.m.–10 p.m.; Sat 7 a.m.–6 p.m.; Sun noon–6 p.m.
Prices: Vary
Direct.:   I-90 to Exit 159 (Columbia Rd./SR 252); south on Columbia for 1 mile.

• Strollers	• Groups	• Food Serv.	• Parking	• Birthdays
• Diap. Chg.	• Picnic	• Food Nearby	• Pub. Trans.	• Handicap. Access

YMCA, West Side Branch
Area: **Near West**   City: **Cleveland**   Ages: **All**   Cost: **$$–$$$**

Swimming pool, gym, fitness room, racquetball, day camp.

Address: 3200 Franklin Blvd.
Phone: (216) 961-3277
Season: Year-round
Hours: Mon–Fri 5:30 a.m.–9 p.m.; Sat 7 a.m.–4 p.m.; Sun 9 a.m.–1:30 p.m.
Prices: Vary

SPORTS &
RECREATION

Direct.:   I-90 to exit for W. 25 St.; north on W. 25; right (west) on Franklin Blvd.

Strollers	● *Groups*	*Food Serv.*	● *Parking*	● *Birthdays*
Diap. Chg.	*Picnic*	*Food Nearby*	● *Pub. Trans.*	*Handicap. Access*

YWCA of Lorain
Area: **Far West**   City: **Lorain**   Ages: **All**   Cost: **$$–$$$**

After-school programs, summer day camp.

Address: 200 9th St.
Phone: (216†) 244-1919
Season: Year-round
Hours: Mon–Fri 8 a.m.–4 p.m.
Prices: Vary
Direct.:   Located in downtown Lorain off Broadway Ave.

● *Strollers*	● *Groups*	● *Food Serv.*	● *Parking*	*Birthdays*
● *Diap. Chg.*	*Picnic*	● *Food Nearby*	*Pub. Trans.*	*Handicap. Access*

SPORTS & RECREATION

Spectator Sports

Clevelanders love sports. While their waistlines may not always show it, their wallets do. In 1931, residents laid out $2.5 million to build Municipal Stadium in hopes of wooing the Olympics. The Games never came, but the city got the cavernous 78,189-seat stadium anyway. In 1990, mobilized by the threat of losing the Cleveland Indians baseball team to another city, Cleveland-area residents dipped into their wallets to provide most of the funds for the $400 million Gateway sports complex including Jacobs Field and Gund Arena. Since moving to their new homes, the Indians been among the winningest teams in baseball and the Cavaliers have managed to stay in contention. New digs have also given a boost to other area teams, including the Lumberjacks (minor-league hockey) at Gund Arena, and the Crunch (indoor soccer) at the Cleveland State University Convocation Center.

So infectious is the desire for updated facilities that in 1995 area residents voted to help foot the bill for construction of a new multi-million-dollar stadium to attract a professional football franchise.

Cleveland Cavaliers

Area: **Downtown**   City: **Cleveland**   Ages: **5 & up**   Cost: **$$$**

The Cavs' new home at Gund Arena is as nice as any in the NBA. Although the seating is steep, sight lines are good. In addition to professional basketball action, Gund Arena includes a team store, two restaurants, and a food court area. With non-nosebleed seats starting at $35 a piece, many in the crowd are corporate types, who are usually pretty sedate. The same cannot be said of the arena's state-of-the-art sound system, which can be painfully loud.

Address: Gund Arena, Huron Rd. & Ontario St.
Phone: Ticket office: (216) 420-CAVS; main office: (216) 420-2000; group info: (216) 420-2153
WWW: http://www.nba.com/cavs
Season: Nov–Apr
Hours: Vary. Usually 7:30 p.m. weeknights; some weekends
Prices: Ticket prices: $16.50–$65; discounts available for groups of 20 or more

Direct.:   I-90 eastbound to Exit 171B (Ontario Ave.); north on Ontario to Gund Arena. I-90 westbound to Exit 173A (Prospect Ave.); right (west) on Prospect; left (south) on E. 20 St.; right (west) on Carnegie Ave.; on right.

Strollers	● Groups	● Food Serv.	● Parking	● Birthdays
● Diap. Chg.	Picnic	● Food Nearby	● Pub. Trans.	● Handicap. Access

Cleveland Crunch
Area: **Downtown**   City: **Cleveland**   Ages: **5 & up**   Cost: **$$–$$$**

The Cleveland Crunch offers championship indoor soccer and also sports training and advice from players and coaches, a nice change of pace for a professional sports team. Fans should watch for the Crunch's many special promotional nights throughout the season, with give-aways such as hats, posters, and tickets.

For young soccer players, summertime brings five-day Crunch soccer camps offered at various sites throughout the metro area for boys and girls ages 6–14. (A special session is also offered in December.) Fine points of the game such as ball control, shooting, and passing are taught by Crunch players. The price includes instruction, a tee-shirt, and tickets to a Camper Night home game.

Address: 2000 Prospect Ave. (Cleveland State University Convocation Center)
Phone: Main office: (216) 349-2090; Crunch Soccer Center: (216) 475-5222
Season: Oct–Apr
Hours: Home games at CSU Convocation Ctr., Fri 7:30 p.m, Sat 7:05 p.m., Sun 3:05 p.m.
Prices: Tickets: $11–$18, no charge under age 2, discounts available for groups of 25+
Direct.:   I-90 eastbound to Exit 172C (E. 22 St.); north on E. 22; left (west) on Carnegie or Prospect Aves.
            I-90 westbound to Exit 173A (Prospect Ave.); west on Prospect; on left.

● Strollers	● Groups	● Food Serv.	● Parking	● Birthdays
● Diap. Chg.	Picnic	● Food Nearby	● Pub. Trans.	● Handicap. Access

Cleveland Indians
Area: **Downtown**   City: **Cleveland**   Ages: **3 & up**   Cost: **$$–$$$**

We're hard-pressed to think of a nicer place to watch a baseball game. Modeled after more intimate ballparks such as Chicago's Wrigley Field or Baltimore's Camden Yards, Jacobs Field has nary a bad seat. Unlike these older parks, however, this one has amenities galore, from a white-linen-table-cloth restaurant to a kids' area behind right field, complete with climbing gyms and a sandbox. There are bars, TVs in the women's washroom, and seat-side food and drink service.

Getting a ticket is another story. After spending more than 40 years as major league baseball's doormat, the Indians have become the American League's hottest team, sweeping the city (and the region) with

SPECTATOR SPORTS

Tribe fever. Each of the last two seasons was sold out before Opening Day. And as long as the team continues to win, that is not likely to change.

Tours of Jacobs Field are offered Monday through Saturday from May to September and include visits to the press box, dugout, and club lounge.

Address: E. 9 St. & Eagle Ave.
Phone: Tickets: (216) 241-8888; fan info line: (216) 420-4636; office: (216) 420-4200; groups: (216) 420-4487
WWW: http://www.indians.com
Season: Apr–Oct
Hours: Games Mon–Fri usually 7:05 p.m.; Sat–Sun usually 1:05 p.m.; consult schedule
Prices: $8 (bleachers)–$25 (field box), group rates available
Direct.: I-90 eastbound to Exit 171B (Ontario Ave.); north on Ontario; on right. I-90 westbound to Exit 173A (Prospect Ave.); right (west) on Prospect; left (south) on E. 20 St.; right (west) on Carnegie Ave. to E. 9th St.

	Strollers	● Groups	● Food Serv.	● Parking	● Birthdays
● Diap. Chg.		● Picnic	● Food Nearby	● Pub. Trans.	● Handicap. Access

Photo: Gregory Drezdzon / courtesy of Cleveland Indians

SPECTATOR SPORTS

Cleveland Lumberjacks
Area: **Downtown**   City: **Cleveland**   Ages: **3 & up**   Cost: **$$–$$$**

What the city's minor-league hockey team (affiliated with the NHL's Pittsburgh Penguins) may lack in stick-handling skill they more than make up for in enthusiasm. They check hard and their slapshots reverberate off the Plexiglas. And when they score, a foghorn kicks in, followed by blaring rock music. In-between period activities include tot-hockey championships and interactive events for the fans. This franchise works very hard at getting families to show up—recent marketing pitches include Family Nights in which dinner is included in the price of the ticket. Kids can also join the on-ice action with after-game skates on Friday evenings.

Younger fans should check out the Cleveland Lumberjacks Jack Pack, a team-organized youth club. Membership includes four tickets to any regular-season home game, a team pennant, bumper sticker, and logo puck, and a private autographing event with players.

Address: 200 Huron Rd.
Phone: Office: (216) 420-0000
WWW: http://www.theihl.com/teams/cleveland; http://www.jackshockey.com
Season: Sep–Apr
Hours: Home games Sat–Sun 7:30 p.m.; some weeknights & afternoons (consult schedule)
Prices: $10, $12, $15, $20; group discounts available
Direct.: I-90 eastbound to Exit 171B (Ontario Ave.); north on Ontario to Gund Arena. I-90 westbound to Exit 173A (Prospect Ave.); right (west) on Prospect; left (south) on E. 20 St.; right (west) on Carnegie Ave.; on right.

● Strollers	● Groups	● Food Serv.	● Parking	Birthdays
● Diap. Chg.	● Picnic	● Food Nearby	● Pub. Trans.	● Handicap. Access

Photo: Jonathan Wayne

Northfield Park
Area: **South**   City: **Northfield**   Ages: **All ages**   Cost: **$**

Even with an aging clubhouse that resembles a Greyhound bus station circa 1947, owner Carl Milstein has done a bang-up job of luring spectators. The 50-year-old facility underwent a $3-million renovation in 1996. Publicity schemes include Saturday night barbeques, the sale of ownership stakes in harness horses for as little as the price of admission, and busing in elementary-school students for stable tours. Kitschy fun.

Address: 10705 Northfield Rd. (SR 8)
Phone: (216†) 467-4101

Season: Year-round
Hours: Vary; live racing Mon, Wed, Fri, Sat evenings
Prices: $1.50 (grandstand), $3 (clubhouse)
Direct.: I-480 to SR 8; south on SR 8 (Northfield Rd.); on left.
I-271 to Exit 23 (SR 14); west on Forbes Rd.; left (south) on Northfield.

- Strollers   • Groups   • Food Serv.   • Parking   • Birthdays
   Diap. Chg.   Picnic   • Food Nearby   Pub. Trans.   • Handicap. Access

Thistledown Racing Club
Area: **Southeast**   City: **North Randall**   Ages: **All**   Cost: **$-$$**

   Shopping mall developer Edward J. DeBartolo liked horse racing so much that he built a track near his Youngstown home (he would fly a private plane to the track, land it on the infield, and take his seat in the grandstand complex to watch the races). In the late 1980s, he plowed $26 million into renovating the aging facility to keep railbirds warmer in the winter and cooler in the summer (the live racing season starts March 1 and ends November 30). Simulcast betting is available January through November. Thoroughbreds run only during daylight hours. We recently took advantage of the Sunday brunch and found it to be an easy way to organize a family outing and lose money at the same time.

Address: Emery Rd.
Phone: (216) 662-8600
WWW: http://www.thistledown.com
Season: Jan–Nov
Hours: Noon–9 p.m.
Prices: $2.25, 12 & under Free, $1 seniors; Sunday brunch $13.95 per person
Direct.: I-480 to Exit 26 (Miles Ave.); west on Miles to Northfield Rd. (SR 8); left (west) on Emery Rd.; on right.

- Strollers   • Groups   • Food Serv.   • Parking   • Birthdays
   Diap. Chg.   Picnic   • Food Nearby   • Pub. Trans.   • Handicap. Access

SPECTATOR
SPORTS

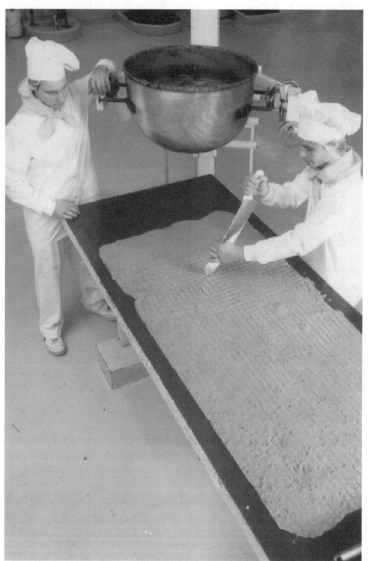

Tours

....

Ever wonder how crayons are made or chocolate molded? Curious to explore the stables of the mounted police or behind the scenes of a theater? When choosing tours for young children, keep in mind their interests. And, know the length of the tour beforehand, because children at young ages have short attention spans. Thirty minutes in one place can be much too long; a tour should keep moving. Listed here are a number of tours in the area that are both fun and educational. While some welcome walk-ins, most require at least a few weeks' notice and are open only to organized groups.

Amish Farm and Home
Area: **Farther South**　　City: **Berlin**　　　Ages: **All**　　　Cost: **$**

This privately owned farm, opened to the public in 1989, is still an actual residence. A 20-minute slide show covers the lifestyle of the Amish and is followed by a guided tour of the home. Tours are aimed at all ages and can last from 45 minutes to two hours (tailored to your group). Afterward, visitors are offered a 10-minute buggy ride around the farm grounds to see the barn animals (sheep, calves, geese, and ponies) and visit the petting area. Reservations are not required, and there is no minimum group size.

Address:	SR 39
Phone:	(330) 893-2951
Season:	Apr–Oct
Hours:	Mon–Fri 10 a.m.–5 p.m.; Sat 10 a.m.–6 p.m.; closed Sun
Prices:	Vary
Direct.:	I-77 south; take Exit 83 for SR 39 in Dover/New Philadelphia; west on SR 39; Amish Farm on SR 39 east of Berlin.

● Strollers　　　● Groups　　　● Food Serv.　　　● Parking　　　Birthdays
　Diap. Chg.　　　● Picnic　　　Food Nearby　　　Pub. Trans.　　　Handicap. Access

Cleveland Department of Water—Filtration Plants
Area: **various**　　City: **Cleveland**　　　Ages: **6 & up**　　　Cost: **FREE**

Have you ever driven by one of Cleveland's impressive-looking filtration plants and wondered what was inside? Wonder no more. The plants are open to anyone wanting to know how our water is cleansed, processed, and sent on its way to our faucets. The one-hour tour includes a walk through the plant and an 11-minute video on the history of the Cleveland Water Department, covering the early 1900s to the present. About 30 to 40 tours are given each year. Reservations are required, except during National Drinking Water Week (early May); the minimum group size is six.

Locations:

Baldwin Plant, 11216 Fairhill Rd., Cleveland
Crown Plant, 955 Clague Rd., Westlake
Garrett A. Morgan Plant, 1245 W. 45 St., Cleveland
Nottingham Plant, 1230 Chardon Rd., Euclid

Address:	(Multiple locations)
Phone:	(216) 664-2444 ext. 5663
Season:	Year-round
Hours:	Open during National Drinking Water Week (early May); other times by appt.
Prices:	FREE
Direct.:	Multiple locations. Call for directions.

Strollers	• Groups	Food Serv.	• Parking	Birthdays
Diap. Chg.	Picnic	Food Nearby	• Pub. Trans.	Handicap. Access

Cleveland Mounted Police
Area: **Near East**   City: **Cleveland**   Ages: **All**   Cost: **FREE**

The Cleveland Mounted Police have been patrolling the city's streets on horseback since 1905. Their horses, currently numbering 21, are donated from area stables. The tour lasts 45 minutes and includes a walk through the stables to learn how the horses are fed, groomed, and cared for; the blacksmith shows how they are shod.

Reservations for tours are required and can accommodate no fewer than 10 and no more than 40 people (adult supervision is a must). The barns are open for self-guided walking tours from 10 a.m. through 4 p.m.

Address:	1150 E. 38 St.
Phone:	(216) 623-5653; 623-5654
Season:	Year-round
Hours:	Tue, Wed, Thu 10 a.m. by appt. only
Prices:	FREE
Direct.:	I-90 to Exit 175 (E. 55 St.); south on E. 55; west on S. Marginal Rd. (just after eastbound exit ramp; left (south) on E. 38 St.; on right up the hill.

Strollers	• Groups	Food Serv.	• Parking	Birthdays
Diap. Chg.	• Picnic	• Food Nearby	• Pub. Trans.	• Handicap. Access

TOURS

Cleveland Postal Business Center (U.S. Postal Service)
Area: **Downtown**   City: **Cleveland**   Ages: **10 & up**   Cost: **FREE**

Want to show your kids how letters get from the mailbox to their proper destination? Visit the main post office on Orange Ave. A tour, guided by postal employees, lasts an hour and includes a 15-minute movie and a walk through the mailroom floor to see the behind-the-scenes activities, such as sorting and preparation, as well as the machinery involved in the mail service. Reservations are required and limited to groups of up to 45 people.

Address: John O. Holly Building, 2400 Orange Ave.
Phone: (216) 443-4241 or 443-4401
Season: Year-round
Hours: Daily 10 a.m.–12:30 p.m. (Mon–Thu mornings preferred)
Prices: FREE
Direct.: Located 3 blocks south of Jacobs Field on Orange Ave. (Ontario Ave. becomes Orange Ave. south of the Inner Belt). Children 10 and over preferred.

Strollers	● Groups	● Food Serv.	● Parking	Birthdays
Diap. Chg.	Picnic	● Food Nearby	● Pub. Trans.	● Handicap. Access

Dixon Ticonderoga Crayon Factory
Area: **Farther West**   City: **Sandusky**   Ages: **6 & up**   Cost: **FREE**

This century-old business merged in 1984 with the American Crayon Company but continues to delight children with free samples and an up-close look at crayon manufacturing. Tours last one hour and include a walk through the factory to see how crayons are mixed, molded, labeled, and packaged. Reservations are required and are typically booked up to a year in advance. Tours are for groups of 8–30 and are open only to schools, scout troops, and other organized groups.

Address: 1706 Hayes Ave.
Phone: (419) 625-9545
WWW: http://www.dixonticonderoga.com
Season: Sep–Jun
Hours: Tue, Wed, Thu 10 a.m.
Prices: FREE
Direct.: SR 2 to SR 4 (Sandusky exit); north on SR 4 (Hayes Ave.).

Strollers	● Groups	Food Serv.	● Parking	● Birthdays
Diap. Chg.	Picnic	● Food Nearby	Pub. Trans.	● Handicap. Access

TOURS

Garrett's Mill
Area: **Far East**   City: **Garrettsville**   Ages: **All**   Cost: **FREE**

The 190-year-old wheel at Garrett's Mill (formerly Hopkins Old Water Mill) is the largest working water wheel in the world. It has stopped only once (after a 1940 fire) since the mill opened in 1804. The tour involves a walk through the mill to watch as two sets of 3,000-pound granite stones work with the wheel's power to turn grain into flour. The upstairs was recently renovated to create a restaurant, brewery, gift shop, and ice-cream shop. There is no minimum group size. Tours (guided) are by appointment.

Address: 8148 Main St. (SR 82)
Phone: (330) 527-2705
Season: Year-round
Hours: Daily 11 a.m.–dark
Prices: FREE
Direct.: I-271 to Exit 27 (US 422); east on US 422; right (south) on SR 88 to Garretsville; at intersection of SR 82 and SR 88.

Strollers	• Groups	• Food Serv.	• Parking	Birthdays
Diap. Chg.	• Picnic	• Food Nearby	Pub. Trans.	• Handicap. Access

Goodyear World of Rubber Museum
Area: **Far South**   City: **Akron**   Ages: **School-age**   Cost: **FREE**

As company museums go, this is way above the norm. For starters, there is a replica of Charles Goodyear's kitchen gum workshop where he discovered how to vulcanize rubber, giving birth to the tire industry, not to mention Akron's former moniker (the "Rubber City").

As manufacturing history, it is packed with good stuff: enter the museum through a small grove of rubber trees and get a visual idea of how tires got their start. (These days, of course, tires come from petroleum products and modern chemistry; for details to satisfy the most inquisitive of six-year-old minds there is an entire exhibit devoted to how tires are now made.) In addition to tires, Goodyear has gotten a lot of mileage out of its blimps, to which the museum also devotes a large amount of attention with pictures and entire sections of dirigible frames.

Also on display are Indianapolis 500 race cars, an artificial heart, a moon rover tire, and a short history of the beginnings of the interstate trucking industry. Film segments accompany many exhibits.

Fighter jocks (both young and old) will like the open cockpit of a World War II–era Corsair, also made by Goodyear.

The small gift shop is worth checking out for its mini-blimps and logo-adorned items.

Address: 1144 E. Market St.
Phone: (330) 796-7117
Season: Year-round
Hours: Mon–Fri 8:00 a.m.–4:30 p.m.; closed holidays; reservations required for groups of 10 or more
Prices: FREE

10 Great Things to Do...

That Your Kids Never Thought of:

- Place bets on the bug races at the Penitentiary Glen Reservation Bug Day festival. (p. 120)

- Bring your own letter and see where it goes on a tour of the U.S. Postal Service. (p. 199)

- Take a day trip to Conneaut Lake or Geneva-on-the-Lake. (p. 17, 99)

- Rent cross-country skis or snowshoes at the Cuyahoga Valley National Recreation Area. (p. 87)

- Watch youngsters show their animals in the ring at the Cuyahoga County Fair. (p. 229)

- Explore the underground river at the Seneca Caverns. (p. 126)

- Learn about trolleys from all over the world at Trolleyville. (p. 69)

- Sign up for a canoe trip with Lake Metroparks. (p. 109)

- Attend a Cleveland Orchestra concert in the Key Concert series for young people. (p. 143)

- See how flour is made at Garrett's Mill. (p. 199)

Direct.: I-77 to I-76 east; take Exit 24C (Kelly/Goodyear Blvd.); left (north) on Kelly; right (east) on 3rd Ave.; left (north) on Martha Ave.; left on E. Market; on right.

- *Strollers*   ● *Groups*   *Food Serv.*   ● *Parking*   *Birthdays*
  Diap. Chg.   *Picnic*   ● *Food Nearby*   ● *Pub. Trans.* ● *Handicap. Access*

Goodtime III
Area: **Downtown**   City: **Cleveland**   Ages: **3 & up**   Cost: **$$**

Goodtime sightseeing boats have been cruising the Cuyahoga River since 1958. The current boat, the *Goodtime III*, tours the Cleveland lakefront and 6-1/2 miles of the 100-mile-long Cuyahoga in two hours. A highlight for most kids is seeing the 21 different bridges that span the crooked river. The tour guide who accompanies the trip is armed with little-known historical facts, discussing the river's hand-dug mouth, its original entrance (by Edgewater Park), and the early inhabitants of its shorelines. The *Goodtime III* sails rain or shine but is sometimes constrained by lake and river traffic.

No food or beverages may be brought on board. Reservations are required; there is no minimum group size.

Address: 825 E. 9 St. (on the E. 9 St. Pier)
Phone: (216) 861-5110
Season: Jun 15–Labor Day (also weekends Memorial Day–Jun 15)
Hours: Mon–Sat 12 p.m. & 3 p.m.; Sun 12 p.m., 3 p.m., & 6 p.m.
Prices: $10, $9.50 seniors, $6 ages 2–11, no charge under age 2
Direct.: I-90 eastbound to exit 171B (E. 9 St.); north on E. 9 through downtown to North Coast Harbor.
I-90 westbound to SR 2 split; continue west on SR 2 to exit for E. 9 St.; right on E. 9 to North Coast Harbor.

- ● *Strollers*   ● *Groups*   ● *Food Serv.*   ● *Parking*   *Birthdays*
  ● *Diap. Chg.*   *Picnic*   ● *Food Nearby*   ● *Pub. Trans.* ● *Handicap. Access*

TOURS

Courtesy of Cleveland Convention & Visitors Bureau

Lolly the Trolley
Area: **Downtown**   City: **Cleveland**   Ages: **All**   Cost: **$$-$$$**

A fast-growing and popular city institution, this family-owned trolley service offers a variety of tours, including a one-hour city sights tour of Cleveland's North Coast Harbor and the Rock and Roll Hall of Fame and Museum, downtown Cleveland, the Flats and the Warehouse District, Ohio City, and the West Side Market. The two-hour tour also includes Playhouse Square, University Circle, and a drive along the Lake Erie shore. Children under age 5 are not permitted on the two-hour tour.

Address: Departs from the Powerhouse at Nautica, on the Flats' west bank
Phone: (216) 771-4484; (800) 848-0173
Season: Year-round
Hours: Vary, reservations required
Prices: Vary
Direct.: I-90 eastbound to Exit 170A (W. 25 St.); north on W. 25 under Detroit-Superior Bridge; right on Main Ave.; follow signs to Nautica.
I-90 westbound to Exit 171C (Abbey/W. 14); left (west) on Abbey over bridge; right (north) on W. 20 St.; left (west) on Lorain Ave. to W. 25; right on Main Ave.; follow signs to Nautica.

| *Strollers* | ● *Groups* | *Food Serv.* | ● *Parking* | *Birthdays* |
| *Diap. Chg.* | *Picnic* | ● *Food Nearby* | *Pub. Trans.* | ● *Handicap. Access* |

Courtesy of Trolley Tours of Cleveland

Malley's Chocolates
Area: **South**   City: **Cleveland**   Ages: **All**   Cost: **$**

The Malley family has been producing sweets in the Cleveland area since 1935. In 1990, the Brookpark plant was designed specifically with factory tours in mind. The tour lasts 30 to 45 minutes and includes a look at nut roasting, chocolate making, filling preparation, coating, designing, and packaging, all in the order of production. Guides' commentaries are tailored to the ages and interests of the group. In theory, three chocolate samples are given: one to get kids going at the beginning, one to move them out at the finish, and a candy bar to take home. Our son, however, consumed seven. Reservations are required; group size is limited to 15–45.

Address: 13400 Brookpark Rd.
Phone: (216) 362-8700; (800) 835-5684
WWW: http://www.grouptour.com/Oh/malleys.html
Season: Seasonal
Hours: Mon–Fri 10 a.m.–3 p.m. by appt.
Prices: $2, $1 ages 4–11, no charge age 3 and under
Direct.: I-480 to exit for W. 130 St./Brookpark Rd.; west on Brookpark.

• Strollers   • Groups   Food Serv.   • Parking   Birthdays
  Diap. Chg.   Picnic   • Food Nearby   • Pub. Trans.   • Handicap. Access

Old Stone Church (First Presbyterian Society of Cleveland)
Area: **Downtown**   City: **Cleveland**   Ages: **All**   Cost: **FREE**

A venerable institution on Public Square for more than 175 years, the Old Stone Church is in the process of an extensive restoration. (The oldest building on the Square has suffered over the years, including fire damage in 1857 and 1884.) With its stained glass windows, frescoed walls, and stunning vaulted wooden ceiling, the church is very much worth rescuing. Tours and regular musical events offer a glimpse of the historic interior of this "spiritual lighthouse of Cleveland."

Address: 91 Public Square
Phone: (216) 241-6145
Season: Year-round
Hours: Mon–Fri 11:30 a.m.–4:30 p.m. (self-guided); by reservation for guided tours
Prices: FREE
Direct.: I-90 eastbound to Exit 171B (Ontario Ave.); north on Ontario to Public Square.
          I-90 westbound to Exit 173C (Superior Ave.); west on Superior to Public Square.

• Strollers   • Groups   Food Serv.   Parking   Birthdays
  Diap. Chg.   Picnic   • Food Nearby   • Pub. Trans.   Handicap. Access

Olympia Gourmet Chocolates
Area: **Southwest**   City: **Strongsville**   Ages: **4 & up**   Cost: **$**

A fixture at East 55 St. and Broadway for 85 years, Olympia Candies changed ownership and location six years ago and now makes gourmet caramel corn in addition to fancy chocolates. Birthday parties and tours are offered at the new Strongsville factory. The one-hour tour for kids allows them to make and take home a molded chocolate. Special clothing is also included: Olympia provides hats, aprons, and gloves for party-goers to wear while creating their confections.

Address: 15155 Pearl Rd. (in back of Town Center complex)
Phone: (216†) 572-7747
Season: Oct–Nov, Jan–Feb, Apr–May
Hours: By arrangement
Prices: Tour : $3 under age 8, $5 ages 8–13
Direct.: I-71 to Exit 231 (SR 82/Royalton Rd.); west on SR 82; left (south) on Pearl Rd. (US 42); on right.

| Strollers | ● Groups | Food Serv. | ● Parking | ● Birthdays |
| Diap. Chg. | ● Picnic | ● Food Nearby | ● Pub. Trans. | ● Handicap. Access |

Courtesy of Olympia Gourmet Chocolates

Terminal Tower Observation Deck
Area: **Downtown**　　City: **Cleveland**　　Ages: **All**　　Cost: **$**

TOURS

The observation deck offers a fine 360-degree view of the city (on clear days). It also has some displays with historical information about the Terminal Tower and the downtown area.

Address: Terminal Tower, 42nd floor, 50 Public Square
Phone: (216) 621-7981
Season: Year-round
Hours: (Sat–Sun) Oct–Apr 11 a.m.–3:30 p.m.; May–Sep 11 a.m.–4:30 p.m.
Prices: $2 adults, $1 ages 6–16, Free age 5 & under
Direct.: I-90 eastbound to Exit 171B (Ontario Ave.); north on Ontario to Public Square. I-90 westbound to Exit 173C (Superior Ave.); west on Superior to Public Square. Parking on street level around Terminal Tower complex or at the Avenue at Tower City shopping mall.

| ● Strollers | ● Groups | Food Serv. | ● Parking | Birthdays |
| Diap. Chg. | Picnic | ● Food Nearby | ● Pub. Trans. | ● Handicap. Access |

The Plain Dealer Production & Distribution Ctr.
Area: **Near West**   City: **Brooklyn**   Ages: **8 & up**   Cost: **FREE**

Want to know what $220 million buys these days? For *The Plain Dealer*, it buys a state-of-the-art printing and distribution center. Inside the Brooklyn compound, trains pull up to drop off huge rolls of newsprint. From there, robots take the rolls to the presses, and entire sections of the paper wait in adjoining rooms before being put together. There, they are moved into tractor trailers that spill out onto I-480. Because production of *The Plain Dealer* occurs late at night, call first to see if you'll find the place humming with activity. Regardless, it's an impressive factory tour.

Address: 4800 Tiedeman Rd.
Phone: (216) 999-5665
Season: Year-round
Hours: Tue, Thu–Sat at 9 a.m., 11 a.m., 1 p.m., and 3 p.m.; registration required
Prices: FREE
Direct.:   I-480 to Exit 13 for Tiedeman Rd.; north on Tiedeman; on left.

• Strollers	• Groups	Food Serv.	• Parking	Birthdays
Diap. Chg.	Picnic	• Food Nearby	• Pub. Trans.	Handicap. Access

United States Coast Guard Station
Area: **Downtown**   City: **Cleveland**   Ages: **5 & up**   Cost: **FREE**

At the Coast Guard Station you can take either a 20-minute tour (station only) or about an hour-long tour (station and boat). In the station you will see the emergency room and living quarters of the Coast Guard. Down on the water are the ice breaker *Neah Bay*, which is the most popular feature here (when it is docked), and the emergency rescue boats. Reservations are required two to three weeks in advance (ask if the boat will be in). There is no limit on group size.

Address: 1055 E. 9 St.
Phone: (216) 522-4412
Season: Mid-May–mid-September
Hours: Vary (Fri–Sat afternoons preferred)
Prices: FREE
Direct.:   I-90 to SR 2 west to exit for E. 9 St.; right (north) on E. 9 St.; in North Coast Harbor, across from the Rock and Roll Hall of Fame and Museum.

Strollers	• Groups	Food Serv.	• Parking	Birthdays
Diap. Chg.	Picnic	• Food Nearby	• Pub. Trans.	• Handicap. Access

TOURS

West Side Market
Area: **Near West**   City: **Cleveland**   Ages: **All**   Cost: **FREE**

The West Side Market is the bustling home to hundreds of produce vendors representing the dozens of ethnic groups that have helped shape Cleveland. The building, constructed in 1912 in the European market-hall tradition, is a designated National Historic Landmark. It is also filled with a delicious and exotic assortment of foods.

There is no guided tour here, but the possibilities are terrific for sampling ethnic flavors and getting a feel for shopping in an open-air market. No reservations are required, but be prepared for a packed house on the weekends and before holidays. (Although parents do bring kids in strollers and backpacks, be aware that this really is a crowded place, especially outside in the produce arcades.)

Address: 1979 W. 25 St. (at Lorain Ave.)
Phone: (216) 664-3386
Season: Year-round
Hours: Mon, Wed 7 a.m.–4 p.m.; Fri–Sat 7 a.m.–6 p.m.
Prices: FREE
Direct.: I-90 eastbound to Exit 170A (W. 25 St.); north on W. 25.
I-90 westbound to Exit 171C (Abbey/W. 14); left (west) on Abbey over bridge; right (north) on W. 20 St.; left (west) on Lorain Ave. to W. 25; on right.

| • Strollers | Groups | • Food Serv. | • Parking | Birthdays |
| Diap. Chg. | Picnic | • Food Nearby | • Pub. Trans. | Handicap. Access |

TOURS

Libraries: Storytimes & More

Reading aloud is one of the most pleasant and educational things you can do with your children. Still, some of us aren't comfortable with storytelling, or we can't seem to satisfy our children's appetite for "one more story." Don't fear, there's help out there. What follows is a comprehensive list of area libraries, with specific information on storytimes and other regular programming designed for youngsters.

Of course, area libraries have never been just about books—many have regular craft activities (especially around the holidays), family film series, and special programs for both parents and children.

These days more and more library children's areas are equipped with computers, and quite a few allow access to the internet and World Wide Web. Families without computers should take advantage of this resource. And whether or not you have a computer at home, the library can be a great place to sample software titles. Many libraries also offer computer classes for students of all ages. A list of select computer and related "new media" resources are featured in each library's general listing.

Akron-Summit County Public Library
Area: **Far South**   City: **Akron**   Ages: **All**   Cost: **FREE**

Each branch of the library system offers storytimes and after-school activities as well as special holiday events. The Main Library and branches also often host Saturday films for children. Of special note, Science Corner activity kits rotate between branches, offering hands-on project ideas. **Branches:**

Ayres: 1765 W. Market St., (330) 836-1081
Chamberlain: 760 E. Archwood Ave., (330) 724-2126
East: 60 Goodyear Blvd., (330) 784-2019
Ellet: 485 Canton Rd., (330) 784-2019
Green: 4759 Massillon Rd., (330) 896-9074
Kenmore: 2200 14th St., SW, (330) 745-6126
McDowell: 3101 Smith Rd., (330) 666-4888
Main Library: 55 S. Main St., (330) 643-9000
Maple Valley: 1293 Copley Rd., (330) 864-5721
Mogadore: 1 S. Cleveland Ave., (330) 628-9228

Nordonia Hills: 9458 Olde Eight Rd., (216†) 467-8595
North: 183 E. Cuyahoga Falls Ave., (330) 535-9423
Norton: 3930 S. Cleve-Mass Rd., (330) 825-7800
Portage Lakes: 4261 Manchester Rd., (330) 644-7050
Richfield: 4400 W. Streetsboro Rd., (216†) 659-4343
Tallmadge: 32 South Ave., (330) 633-4345
West Hill: 807 W. Market St., (330) 376-2927
Wooster: 600 Wooster Ave., (330) 434-8726

Address: 55 S. Main St. (Main Library)
Phone: (330) 643-9000
Season: Year-round
Hours: Main Library: Mon–Thu 9 a.m.–9 p.m., Fri 9 a.m.–6 p.m., Sat 9 a.m.–5 p.m., Sun
1–5 p.m.; Branches: Mon & Wed 10 a.m.–8:30 p.m., Tue & Thu noon–8:30 p.m.,
Fri noon–6 p.m., Sat 10 a.m.–5 p.m., closed Sun
Prices: FREE
Direct.: I-77 to Exit 22A (Main St.); north on Main.
SR 8 to exit for Perkins St.; left on Union St.; right on Market St.; left on High St.;
use alternate entrance on High St.

Computers & Internet Access:
Catalog terminal only / Internet / CD ROM
Computer phone: dial-up access: (330) 643-9900
CD-ROM collection quickly growing.

| ● Strollers | ● Groups | Food Serv. | ● Parking | Birthdays |
| Diap. Chg. | Picnic | ● Food Nearby | ● Pub. Trans. | ● Handicap. Access |

Avon Lake Public Library
Area: **West**   City: **Avon Lake**   Ages: **All**   Cost: **FREE**

Preschool storytimes (ages 3–5) run in 10-week sessions in fall, winter, and spring. A summer reading program is open to all readers. Three children's groups, the Explorers Club (grades K–2), the Adventure Club (grade 3 and up), and the Junior Friends Group (grade 3 and up) offer stories, crafts, and activities throughout the year.

Discovery Works is a great resource for neighborhood parents, especially on rainy and wintry days. While programs are scheduled occasionally, most kids just like to come play. Favorites are the floor-to-ceiling bubblemaker and the small appliance take-apart area. Budding Mr. and Ms. Fix-its have a field day.

Address: 32649 Electric Dr.
Phone: (216†) 933-8128
Season: Year-round
Hours: Mon–Thu 9 a.m.–9 p.m., Fri–Sat 9 a.m.–5 p.m., Sun 1–5 p.m. (Sep–May);
Discovery Works (Sep–May): Tue 10 a.m.–noon, Wed 3 p.m.–5 p.m., Thu
10 a.m.–noon and 3 p.m.–5 p.m., Sat noon–4 p.m., Sun 2 p.m.–4 p.m.
Prices: FREE
Direct.: SR 2 to Exit 153 (SR 83/Center Rd.); north on SR 83 to Electric Dr.; right on
Electric for 1/4 mile; on right.

Computers & Internet Access:
IBM & Mac / Internet / CD ROM / Reservations: recommend. / Time limit: 1/2 hr.
Computer phone: (216†) 933-8128

| ● Strollers | ● Groups | ● Food Serv. | ● Parking | Birthdays |
| Diap. Chg. | ● Picnic | ● Food Nearby | ● Pub. Trans. | ● Handicap. Access |

LIBRARIES

Burton Public Library
Area: **Far East**   City: **Burton**   Ages: **All**   Cost: **FREE–$$**

Storytimes begin with toddlers (ages 2–3 with an adult) and preschoolers (ages 3–5). A special series of activities kicks off the annual Summer Reading Program. After-school craft programs and events for school-age children are usually scheduled four or five times during the year, as is family programming. A newsletter is sent out to all residents of the Berkshire school district and is available at the library.

Address: 14588 W. Park St.
Phone: (216†) 834-4466; Dial-A-Story: (216†) 834-0707
Season: Year-round
Hours: Mon–Thu 9 a.m.–9 p.m.; Fri–Sat 9 a.m.–5 p.m.; Sun 1–5 p.m. (school year)
Prices: FREE; fees for some programs
Direct.: SR 87, on the west side of the Burton Town Square.
Computers & Internet Access:
IBM / Internet / CD ROM / Reservations avail. / Time limit: 1 hr.
Computer phone: dial-up access: (216†) 834-0628

● *Strollers* ● *Groups* *Food Serv.* ● *Parking* *Birthdays*
● *Diap. Chg.* *Picnic* ● *Food Nearby* ● *Pub. Trans.* ● *Handicap. Access*

Cleveland Hts.-University Hts. Public Library
Area: **East**   City: **Cleveland Hts.**   Ages: **All**   Cost: **FREE–$$**

Each branch holds storytimes and programs for toddlers (30–36 months with parent) and preschool-age children (3–5), as well as for school-age kids (6 and up). Programs run from one day to 10 weeks. Special events are scheduled throughout the year and include holiday storytelling, games, and crafts. (Most programs require pre-registration.) A guide to events—"Check Us Out"—is published four times a year.

Branches:
Coventry Village: 1925 Coventry Rd., (216) 321-3400 (no parking); (216) 321-0739 (tty)
Noble Neighborhood: 2800 Noble Rd., (216) 291-5665
University Heights: 13866 Cedar Rd., (216) 321-4700

Address: 2345 Lee Rd. (Main Library)
Phone: (216) 932-3600
WWW: http://www.chuhpl.lib.oh.us/
Season: Year-round
Hours: Mon–Fri 9 a.m.–9 p.m.; Sat 9 a.m.–5:30 p.m.; Sun 1–5 p.m. (branch hrs. vary)
Prices: FREE
Direct.: Main Library located on Lee Rd., 3 blocks south of Cedar Rd.
Computers & Internet Access:
IBM & Mac / Internet (limited) / CD ROM (limited) / Reservations for game terminal. Computer phone: 932-3600

Strollers ● *Groups* *Food Serv.* ● *Parking* *Birthdays*
● *Diap. Chg.* *Picnic* ● *Food Nearby* ● *Pub. Trans.* ● *Handicap. Access*

LIBRARIES

Cleveland Public Library
Area: **Various**   City: **Cleveland**   Ages: **All**   Cost: **FREE–$$**

Each branch of the library system offers preschool storytimes and after-school activities such as crafts and movies. All of the branches have a summer reading club that runs from mid-June to August. Throughout the year the library system works with the Cleveland Indians and Cleveland Lumberjacks to provide inspiration and incentives (such as game tickets) to keep reading. **Branches:**

Addison: 6901 Superior Ave., (216) 623-6906
Broadway: 5417 Broadway, (216) 623-6913
Brooklyn: 3706 Pearl Rd., (216) 623-6920
Carnegie West: 1900 Fulton Rd., (216) 623-6927
Collinwood: 856 E. 152 St., (216) 623-6934
East 131: 3830 E. 131 St., (216) 623-6941
Eastman: 11602 Lorain Rd., (216) 623-6955
Fleet: 7224 Broadway, (216) 623-6962
Fulton: 3545 Fulton Rd., (216) 623-6969
Garden Valley: 7100 Kinsman Rd., (216) 623-6976
Glenville: 11900 St. Clair Ave., (216) 623-6983
Harvard-Lee: 16918 Harvard Ave., (216) 623-6990
Hough: 1566 Crawford Ave., (216) 623-6997
Jefferson: 850 Jefferson Ave., (216) 623-7004

Lorain: 8216 Lorain Ave., (216) 623-7011
Martin Luther King Jr.: 1962 E. 107 St. (Stokes Blvd.), (216) 623-7018
Memorial: 17109 Lakeshore Blvd., (216) 623-7039
Mt. Pleasant: 14000 Kinsman Rd., (216) 623-7032
Rice: 2820 E. 116 St., (216) 623-7046
Rockport: 4421 W. 140 St., (216) 623-7053
South: 3096 Scranton Rd., (216) 623-7060
South Brooklyn: 4303 Pearl Rd., (216) 623-7067
Sterling: 2200 E. 30 St., (216) 623-7074
Union: 3463 E. 93 St., (216) 623-7088
Walz: 7910 Detroit Ave., (216) 623-7095
West Park: 3805 W. 157 St., (216) 623-7102
Woodland: 5806 Woodland Ave., (216) 623-7109

Address: 325 Superior Ave. (Admin. office)
Phone: (216) 623-2800; Children's Services: (216) 623-2834
WWW: http://www.cpl.org
Season: Year-round
Hours: Mon–Sat 9 a.m.–6 p.m.; Sun 1–5 p.m. (branch hrs. vary)
Prices: FREE; fee for some classes
Direct.:   Main Branch: I-90 to Exit 173C (Superior Ave.); west on Superior; 1 block east of Public Square; on right. Call for directions to other branches.
Computers & Internet Access:
                IBM / Internet / CD ROM / Reservations avail. / Time limit: none
                Computer phone: (216) 623-2955; (216) 623-0623 (modem)
                Includes all 27 branches

● *Strollers*   ● *Groups*   *Food Serv.*   ● *Parking*   *Birthdays*
   Diap. Chg.   *Picnic*   ● *Food Nearby*   ● *Pub. Trans.*   ● *Handicap. Access*

Cuyahoga County Public Libraries
Area: **Various**   City: **Parma (Admin. office)**   Ages: **All**   Cost: **FREE–$$**

Each branch of the Cuyahoga County library system offers activities, such as storytimes, crafts, shows, and after-school events. The system also participates in Project LEAP, which provides storytime book kits and puppet shows based on a theme of your choice and designed specifically for preschool teachers, care providers, and parents. Of special interest to parents, the Brooklyn branch has a toy lending library. With a library card, patrons can borrow blocks, puzzles, puppets, and other items to encourage learning about science, nature, the arts, and language.

For specific information and a schedule for all programs, request a copy of *The Corridor*, which is published quarterly. **Branches:**

Bay Village: 502 Cahoon Rd., (216†) 871-6392
Beachwood: 25501 Shaker Blvd., (216) 831-6868
Berea: 7 Berea Commons, (216†) 234-5475
Brecksville: 9089 Brecksville Rd., (216†) 526-1102
Brook Park: 6155 Engle Rd., (216) 267-5250
Brooklyn: 4480 Ridge Rd., (216) 398-4600
Chagrin Falls: 100 E. Orange., (216†) 247-3556
Fairview Park: 4449 W. 213 St., (216†) 333-4700
Garfield Heights: 5409 Turney Rd., (216) 475-8178
Gates Mills: 7580 Old Mill Rd., (216†) 423-4808
Independence: 6361 Selig Dr., (216) 447-0160
Maple Heights: 5225 Library Lane, (216) 475-5000
Mayfield: 6080 Wilson Mills Rd., (216†) 473-0350
Middleburg Hts. 15600 E. Bagley Rd., (216†) 234-3600

N. Olmsted: 27425 Butternut Ridge Rd., (216†) 777-6211
North Royalton: 14600 State Rd., (216†) 237-3800
Olmsted Falls: 7850 Main St., (216†) 235-1150
Orange: 31300 Chagrin Blvd., (216) 831-4282
Parma Heights: 6206 Pearl Rd., (216†) 884-2313
Parma: 7335 Ridge Rd., (216†) 885-5362
Parma-Ridge: 5850 Ridge Rd., (216†) 888-4300
Parma-Snow: 2121 Snow Rd., (216) 661-4240
Richmond Mall: 691 Richmond Rd., (216†) 449-2666
Solon: 33800 Inwood Dr., (216†) 248-8777
S. Euclid-Lyndhurst: 4645 Mayfield Rd., (216) 382-4880
Southeast: 70 Columbus Rd., (216†) 439-4997
Strongsville: 13213 Pearl Rd., (216†) 238-5530
Warrensville: 22035 Clarkwood Pkwy., (216) 464-5280

Address: 2111 Snow Rd.
Phone: (216) 398-1800; Children's Services: (216) 749-9353
Season: Year-round
Hours: Vary
Prices: FREE; fee for some classes
Direct.: (Call for directions to each location.)
Computers & Internet Access:
        IBM / Internet / CD ROM (limited) / No reservations / Time limit: 1 hr.
        Includes all 28 branches; CD ROM available only at Fairview, Maple Hts.,
        Mayfield, and Parma.

● Strollers	● Groups	Food Serv.	● Parking	Birthdays
● Diap. Chg.	Picnic	● Food Nearby	● Pub. Trans.	● Handicap. Access

East Cleveland Public Libraries

Area: **Near East**   City: **Cleveland**   Ages: **All**   Cost: **FREE**

The East Cleveland public library system offers storytimes for toddlers (ages 2–3) at the Main and North branches and for preschoolers (ages 3–5) at the Caledonia branch. Sessions run for 10 weeks. There are also activities and workshops for school-age children throughout the year. Most require pre-registration. A printed list of programs is available at the branches.

Branches:
Caledonia: 960 Caledonia Ave., (216) 268-6280 (no stroller access)
North: 1425 Hayden Ave., (216) 268-6283

Address: 14101 Euclid Ave.

Phone: (216) 541-4128
Season: Year-round
Hours: Vary by season
Prices: FREE
Direct.: I-90 to Exit 178 (Eddy Rd.); south on Eddy; right (west) on Euclid Ave. (US 20); across the street from the RTA Windermere station.
Computers & Internet Access:
              Mac / Internet / CD ROM / Reservations recommended / Time limit: 1 hr. Includes both branches

● Strollers   ● Groups   Food Serv.   ● Parking   Birthdays
  Diap. Chg.   Picnic   ● Food Nearby   ● Pub. Trans.   ● Handicap. Access

Elyria Public Library
Area: **Far West**   City: **Elyria**   Ages: **All**   Cost: **FREE–$$**

Storytimes are offered seasonally for children of all ages (some require an accompanying adult). Divisions include Toddler (under 3) and PreSchool (3–5). Special events are usually planned around the holidays for older kids and families. Registration is necessary for some programs. Elyria also offers a round-the-clock telephone storyline.

Branch:

1194 W. River Rd. North, (440) 324-2270

Address: 320 Washington Ave. (Main Branch)
Phone: (216†) 323-5747 (Main); Dial-A-Story: (216†) 323-3333
Season: Year-long
Hours: Mon–Thu 9 a.m.–8:30 p.m., Fri–Sat 9 a.m.–5:30 p.m., Sun 1–4 p.m.; branch hours vary.
Prices: FREE
Direct.:   Located off Broadway Ave. in downtown Elyria.
Computers & Internet Access:
                IBM & Mac / Internet / CD ROM / Reservations recommended / Time limit: 1 hr. Computer phone: (216†) 323-5747; dial-up access: (216†) 323-8212

● Strollers   ● Groups   Food Serv.   ● Parking   Birthdays
● Diap. Chg.   Picnic   ● Food Nearby   ● Pub. Trans.   ● Handicap. Access

Euclid Public Libraries
Area: **East**   City: **Euclid**   Ages: **All**   Cost: **FREE**

Storytime sessions start young, with "Lap Sit" sessions for newborns and new walkers accompanied by an adult; there are also sessions for toddlers (ages 2-1/2–3-1/2) and preschoolers (ages 3-1/2–5). For school-age children there is a summer reading program. Registration is required for storytimes and other library activities.

Address: 631 E. 222 St. (Main Branch)
Phone: (216) 261-5300
Season: Year-round

Hours: Main Branch: Mon–Thu 9 a.m.–9 p.m.; Fri–Sat 9 a.m.–5 p.m.; Sun 1–5 p.m.
(during school year)
Prices: FREE
Direct.: I-90 to Exit 183 (E. 222 St.); north on E. 222 for 1 mile; on right, adjacent to Euclid
High School and Euclid City Hall.
Computers & Internet Access:
IBM / Internet / CD ROM (limited) / Reservations recommend./ Time limit: 1 hr.
Computer phone: (216) 261-5300

- *Strollers*   • *Groups*   *Food Serv.*   • *Parking*   *Birthdays*
  Diap. Chg.   *Picnic*   *Food Nearby*   • *Pub. Trans.*   • *Handicap. Access*

Geauga County Public Library
Area: **Far East**   City: **Chardon (Admin. office)**   Ages: **All**   Cost: **FREE–$$**

There are storytimes for infants, toddlers (ages 2–3), and preschoolers (ages 3–5). The length of the sessions varies throughout the year. The summer reading program includes activities for school-age children, teenagers (middle school–high school), and adults. Registration is preferred. Special events and programs are prepared seasonally by the individual branches, so call to see if a printed list of activities is available. Also contact each location for branch hours.

Branches:
Bainbridge: 17222 Snyder Rd., (216†) 543-5611
Chardon: 110 E. Park, (216†) 285-7601
Geauga West: 13455 Chillicothe Rd., (216†) 729-4250
Middlefield: 15982 E. High, (216†) 632-1961
Newbury: 14775 Auburn, (216†) 564-7552
Thompson: 16700 Thompson Rd., (216†) 298-3831

Address: 121 South St.
Phone: (216†) 286-6811
Season: Year-round
Hours: Mon–Thu 9 a.m.–9 p.m., Fri–Sat 9 a.m.–6 p.m., Sun 1–5 p.m.; branches vary
Prices: FREE; fee for some classes
Direct.: (Multiple branches. Please call for directions.)

- • *Strollers*   • *Groups*   *Food Serv.*   • *Parking*   *Birthdays*
  • *Diap. Chg.*   • *Picnic*   • *Food Nearby*   *Pub. Trans.*   • *Handicap. Access*

LIBRARIES

Lakewood Public Libraries
Area: **West**   City: **Lakewood**   Ages: **All**   Cost: **FREE–$$**

There are storytimes for toddlers (ages 2-1/2–3 with parents), preschoolers (ages 3–5), and kindergartners in six-week sessions. Also for younger pre-readers, Weekend Wonders programs are scheduled every weekend year-round at both branches; these include stories and make-and-take projects that are perfect for creating enthusiasm about the library and reading.

For school-age children, After-School Sensations are offered daily during the school year and Summer Sensations in the summertime. Activities relating to a variety of study areas are organized by weekly topics, with each day offering something new. For example, during the World Geography focus, South of the Equator week featured a trip down the Congo on Monday and a day in Cairo on Tuesday. After-School Sensations and Weekend Wonders programs are free, and there is no need to register in advance. Registration is required for children's storytimes.

The Lakewood Public Library has a number of new-media programs for children of all ages, including seasonal computer camps (offered for seniors as well) and weekday computer use, which complements other library reading and learning programs. In addition, the Madison branch recently opened the KidKiosk, a kiosk display featuring samples of educational and entertainment software that promote kindergarten reading readiness skills.

Lakewood Public Library program listings are published twice a year (fall/winter and spring/summer).

Branches:

Madison Branch: 13229 Madison Ave., (216) 228-7428. (Sunday hours: 1–5 p.m.)

Address:	15425 Detroit Ave. (Main Branch)
Phone:	(216) 226-8275
WWW:	http://www.lkwdpl.org
Season:	Year-round
Hours:	Main: Mon–Fri 9 a.m.–9 p.m., Sat 9 a.m.–6 p.m., Sun 1 p.m.–9 p.m.
Prices:	FREE
Direct.:	I-90 to Exit 165 (Warren Rd.); right (north) on Warren; left (west) on Detroit Ave. for 1/3 mile; on left at corner of Detroit and Arthur Ave.

Computers & Internet Access:

IBM / Internet / CD ROM / Reservations recommended / Time limit: 1 hr., 15 min. on Internet Express
Computer phone: (216) 226-8275, x127
Includes both branches

● *Strollers*	● *Groups*	*Food Serv.*	● *Parking*	*Birthdays*
● *Diap. Chg.*	*Picnic*	● *Food Nearby*	● *Pub. Trans.*	● *Handicap. Access*

Mentor Public Library

Area: **Far East**	City: **Mentor**	Ages: **All**	Cost: **FREE**

There are storytimes for toddlers (age 2 with adult) and preschoolers (ages 3–5). Sessions run six to eight weeks. The All-Aboard Express storytime runs every Thursday at 1:30 p.m. and is designed for children 3 and up with an adult. Mother Goose Time, an infant story hour, requires advance registration. For ages 6 and up, there is the after-

10 Great Things to Do...

On a Snowy Day:

◉ Mount your own puppet show with materials borrowed from the public library. (p. 209)

◉ Skate on the rink at Public Square or indoors at your neighborhood ice rink. (p. 175)

◉ Head for the nearest Discovery Zone or other indoor playground to work off some stress. (p. 18)

◉ Rent cross-country skis or snowshoes at Lake Metroparks' Chapin Forest Pine Lodge. (p. 82)

◉ Bundle up and take on the toboggan run at the Cleveland Metroparks' Mill Stream Run Reservation. (p. 114)

◉ Sign up for a cooking class through a community college.

◉ Take a ski lesson at Alpine Valley or Boston Hills/Brandywine. (p. 157)

◉ Check out a Lumberjacks game and stay for a post-game skate with a team member. (p. 193)

◉ Sign up for a dance or gymnastics class and blow off some steam.

◉ Stargaze at one of the area's planetariums.

school Book Break program. Call for information. For school-age children, the summer reading program begins the Monday after school lets out and runs until the end of July. Watch for seasonal specials and make-and-take activities in the winter months. Ask for the seasonal schedule.

Branches:

Headlands: 4669 Corduroy Rd., (216†) 257-2000

Lake: 5828 Andrews Rd., (216†) 257-2512

Address: 8215 Mentor Ave.
Phone: (216†) 255-8811
WWW: http://www.mentor.lib.oh.us
Season: Year-round
Hours: Mon–Fri 9 a.m.–9 p.m., Sat 9 a.m.–5 p.m., Sun noon–4 p.m. (branches vary)
Prices: FREE
Direct.: SR 2 to exit for SR 615; south on SR 615; right (west) on Mentor Ave. (US 20) for 2 blocks; on north side.

Computers & Internet Access:
Catalog terminal only

● Strollers	● Groups	Food Serv.	● Parking	Birthdays
Diap. Chg.	Picnic	● Food Nearby	● Pub. Trans.	● Handicap. Access

Rocky River Public Library

Area: **West**   City: **Rocky River**   Ages: **All**   Cost: **FREE–$$**

There are storytimes for toddlers (ages 2-1/2–3), preschoolers (ages 4–5) and school-age groups. Registration is required for all storytimes. The newsletter *Ex Libris*, which contains class and special event information, is sent to Rocky River residents three times a year. Also, the Cowan Pottery Collection is on display throughout the library.

Address: 1600 Hampton Rd.
Phone: (216†) 333-7610; (216†) 333-3219 (tty); online access (216†) 333-5098
WWW: http://www.ne-ohio.net/rrpl
Season: Year-round
Hours: Mon–Thu 9 a.m.–9 p.m.; Fri–Sat 9 a.m.–6 p.m.; Sun (during school year) 1–5 p.m.
Prices: FREE; fees for some programs
Direct.: I-90 westbound to exit for Hilliard Blvd. (stay in right lane); right on Westway Blvd.; right on Lakeview Ave.; right on Riverview Ave.; right on Hampton Rd. I-90 eastbound to exit for Detroit Rd.; left (east) on Detroit Rd. over I-90; right on Lakeview Ave.; left on Riverview Ave.; right on Hampton Rd.

Computers & Internet Access:
IBM & Mac / CD ROM / Reservations recommended / Time limit: 1-1/2 hrs. Computer phone: 333-7610

● Strollers	● Groups	Food Serv.	● Parking	Birthdays
● Diap. Chg.	Picnic	● Food Nearby	● Pub. Trans.	● Handicap. Access

LIBRARIES

Shaker Heights Public Library

Area: **East**   City: **Shaker Hts.**   Ages: **All**   Cost: **FREE–$$**

There are storytimes for infants (12 months and up with parent), toddlers (age 2), preschoolers (ages 3–5), and Book Bugs (grades K–3) throughout the school year.

After School Specials for school-age children feature a book-related activity and sometimes a craft. A summer reading club is open to readers of any age and runs from mid-June through early August. Pre-teen (ages 9–12), teenage, and family programs are offered. The library also features large-print books and books on tape for children and adults.

Registration is requested for most of the activities. Call either branch for listings.

Branch:
Bertram Woods: 20600 Fayette Rd. (216) 991-2421 (no Sun hours or diaper-changing)

Address: 16500 Van Aken Blvd. (Main Branch)
Phone: (216) 991-2030
Season: Year-round
Hours: Mon–Thu 9 a.m.–9 p.m.; Fri 9 a.m.–6 p.m.; Sat 9 a.m.–5:30 p.m.; Sun 1–5 p.m.
               (Sep–Jun, at Main only); branch hours same but closed Sun
Prices: FREE; fees for some programs
Direct.:   Main Branch is located at Lee Rd. and Van Aken Blvd. between Van Aken &
               Chagrin; access is off Lee Rd. (corner of Lee & Chagrin).
Computers & Internet Access:
               IBM & Mac / Internet / CD ROM / Reservations required / Time limit: 1 hr.
               Computer phone: (216) 991-2030
               Includes both branches

- Strollers   ● Groups   Food Serv.   ● Parking   Birthdays
- Diap. Chg.   Picnic   ● Food Nearby   ● Pub. Trans.   ● Handicap. Access

Westlake Porter Public Library

Area: **West**   City: **Westlake**   Ages: **All**   Cost: **FREE–$$**

Storytimes are offered for preschoolers (ages 3–5) in 10-week sessions each fall and winter. Family summer reading programs run June through August. A special Summer Reading Team recruits volunteers to help beginning readers. Look for arts-and-crafts instruction, theater presentations, special programs, and other activities throughout the year.

Address: 27333 Center Ridge Rd.
Phone: (216†) 871-2600
WWW: http://www.ohionet.org/porter-public-library
Season: Year-round
Hours: Mon–Thu 9 a.m.–9 p.m.; Fri–Sat 9 a.m.–5 p.m.; Sun (school year) 1–5 p.m.
Prices: FREE; fees for some classes
Direct.:   I-90 to Exit 159 (Columbia Rd./SR 252); south on Columbia ; right (west) on
               Center Ridge Rd.; parking lot on left just past Dover Center Rd.

LIBRARIES

Computers & Internet Access:
IBM & Mac / Internet / CD ROM / No reservations / Time limit: 1/2 hr.
Computer phone: (216) 871-2600
12 in-house CD ROMs for preschoolers

● Strollers   ● Groups   Food Serv.   ● Parking   Birthdays
  Diap. Chg.   Picnic   ● Food Nearby   ● Pub. Trans.   ● Handicap. Access

Wickliffe Public Library
Area: **East**   City: **Wickliffe**   Ages: **All**   Cost: **FREE**

Seasonal storytimes (fall, winter, and spring) are held for toddlers (ages 2-1/2–3-1/2) and preschoolers (ages 3-1/2–5). A Summer Reading Program is offered to all readers and non-reading preschoolers. Special craft events usually take place around the holidays. Pre-registration is required for storytimes and special events. A schedule of events can be picked up at the library.

Branch:
Wickliffe Civic Branch: 900 Warden Rd., (216†) 944-6010

Address: 1713 Lincoln Rd. (Main Branch)
Phone: (216†) 944-6010
Season: Year-round
Hours: Mon–Thu 9 a.m.–9 p.m.; Fri 9 a.m.–6 p.m.; Sat 9 a.m.–5 p.m.; Sun 1–5 p.m.
Prices: FREE
Direct.: SR 2 to exit for Lloyd Rd.; right on Lakeland Blvd.; left (south) on Lloyd Rd. across Euclid Ave. (US 20); Lloyd Rd. becomes Lincoln Rd.; on left.

Computers & Internet Access:
IBM / Internet / CD ROM / Reservations recommended / Time limit: 1 hr.
Computer phone: (216†) 944-6010

● Strollers   ● Groups   Food Serv.   ● Parking   Birthdays
● Diap. Chg.   Picnic   ● Food Nearby   ● Pub. Trans.   ● Handicap. Access

Willoughby-Eastlake Public Libraries
Area: **East**   City: **Willowick**   Ages: **All**   Cost: **FREE**

Seasonal (fall, winter, and spring) storytimes run in eight-week sessions for preschoolers (ages 3–5), toddlers (ages 2–3), and babies (up to 24 months). Pre-registration is required. Reading Buddies (on Wednesdays) and Twilight Tales (on Thursdays) are offered for school-age children. Special storytimes are scheduled around holidays. Summer Reading programs for children, young adults, and adults begin in June. Each library releases a schedule three times a year (Jan–May, Jun–Aug, and Sep–Dec).

Branches:
Eastlake Public Library: 36706 Lakeshore Blvd., Eastlake, (216) 942-7880
Willoughby Public Library: 30 Public Square, Willoughby, (216) 942-3200

Willowick Public Library: 263 E. 305 St., Willowick, (216) 943-4151

Address: 263 E. 305 St.
Phone: (216†) 943-4151
Season: Year-round
Hours: Mon–Thu 9 a.m.–9:00 p.m.; Fri–Sat 9 a.m.–5 p.m.; Sun 1 p.m.–5 p.m. Apr–Oct
at Willowick Public Library only.
Prices: FREE
Direct.: Main Library (Willowick branch): just south of Lakeshore Blvd. and E. 305, across
from Shoregate Shopping Center. Call other branches for directions.
Computers & Internet Access:
Catalog terminal only / Internet / No reservations / Time limit: 15 min.
Computer phone: (216) 943-2203
Includes 3 branches; graphic internet access provided by OPLIN—Ohio Public
Library Information Network, available at all locations.

● Strollers	● Groups	Food Serv.	● Parking	Birthdays
● Diap. Chg.	Picnic	Food Nearby	● Pub. Trans.	● Handicap. Access

Favorite Family Events

JANUARY

Hand-feed chickadees at the Cleveland Metroparks Brecksville Nature Center (216†-526-1012). This annual tradition dates back to the 1930s. If you stand still, the small birds will land right on your hand. Metroparks staff provide the birdseed. Weekends; FREE.

Winter Expo at The Chalet (216†-572-9990) in the Cleveland Metroparks Mill Stream Run Reservation traditionally includes dogsled and cross-country ski demonstrations and ice sculpture. The toboggan run is also open, and there is a warm-up fire inside the Chalet. Sat–Sun; FREE, fee for tobogganing.

If you're craving colors other than gray, check out the annual **winter flower displays** at the Rockefeller Park Greenhouse (216-664-3103). Traditionally, poinsettias are out until mid-January, followed by a lush display of primroses. Daily; FREE.

Martin Luther King, Jr. is remembered each year at the Western Reserve Historical Society (216-721-5722) with a special program. For other observances, check with the Rainbow Children's Museum (216-791-KIDS) and Cuyahoga Community College (216-987-4527).

Free Family Activity: Storytelling. Cleveland's dismal winter weather makes this the perfect time of year to explore offerings at area libraries. Children of all ages love to hear a story read out loud—even older ones who are reading themselves. This month is typically registration time for formal storytime sessions. Special groups are available for toddlers (ages 2–3), preschoolers (ages 3–5) and beginning readers (grades K–3). (See our listings in the "Libraries: Storytimes and More" section.)

Of course, libraries offer much more than storytimes, including such family-oriented activities as puppet shows, films, crafts, and holiday celebrations, as well as an array of family education programs. For a selection of read-aloud books, consult the list published by the American Library Association; for a free copy call (312) 280-2153.

FEBRUARY

Black History Month brings a variety of special programs to area libraries and colleges, including storytelling, music, film festivals, and puppet shows. Look for announcements. Month-long.

Winter Days Festival at the Lorain County Metroparks (800-LCM-PARK) celebrates the longer days of a waning winter with horse-drawn-wagon rides, sled dog demonstrations, and ice sculpting. Fri–Sun; FREE.

Valentine's Day, February 14, is observed at area parks, museums, and libraries with tea parties, special storytimes, and craft programs.

Free Family Activity: Museum Visits. For an economical outing, visit area museums on their free day. The Cleveland Museum of Natural History is free on Tuesday and Thursday from 3 to 5 p.m. The Cleveland Metroparks Zoo is free on Monday mornings until noon to residents of Cuyahoga County and Hinckley Township. (Admission to the RainForest is not free but is reduced during these hours.)

And take advantage of the following places that are always free for the under-6 set: the Dunham Tavern Museum, the Inland Seas Maritime Museum, the Health Museum, Holden Arboretum, Lawnfield, and the Western Reserve Historical Society.

MARCH

If you like a parade, check out the **St. Patrick's Day Parade** (216-621-4110), held downtown each year along Euclid Avenue, with area bands and floats attracting crowds. St. Patrick's Day (March 17); FREE.

Buzzard Day at the Cleveland Metroparks Hinckley Reservation (216-351-6300) celebrates the annual migration of the turkey vulture. These large, garish birds perch on the rock ledges of this reservation. The event features a pancake breakfast, exhibits, and activities, but be forewarned: participants rarely see a bird. Sat; FREE.

Free Family Activity: Maple Sugaring. Mid-February to mid-March is maple sugaring time. The exact season depends on the weather, with the ideal combination being cold nights followed by warmish (40-degree) days.

Stirring, tapping, guided hikes, and pancake tasting are part of the tradition on Maple Sugaring Weekends, held at the Cleveland Metroparks Maple Grove Picnic Area in the Rocky River Reservation (216†-734-6660). Sat–Sun; FREE.

The log cabin on the Square in Burton (216†-834-1119) is open for viewing maple syrup making and maple candy stirring. Month-long; FREE.

EVENTS

Visitors are asked to help with the drilling and tapping at the Lorain County Metroparks (800-LCM-PARK). Sat–Sun; FREE.

Folk music, sugarhouse tours, and crafts are part of Sap's-A-Risin' Day at Geauga Park District's Swine Creek Reservation (216†-286-9504). Sat; FREE.

(Remember to dress in warm clothing and add some boots—trekking to maple trees often includes some muddy trails.)

APRIL

National Library Week is observed at area libraries with special storytimes, activities, and book sales. It is observed all month. Really.

The **Geauga Maple County Festival** (216†-286-3007) features syrup making and maple candy making, along with contests, food, and rides. Sat and Sun; FREE.

Each year, the Earth Day Coalition sponsors an **Earth Day festival** (216-281-6468), a day of environmentally oriented education, information, activities, and performances. The Cleveland Metroparks Zoo is usually the place to be for the area's largest Earth Day celebration. Sat or Sun; FREE.

The **Cleveland International Film Festival**, (Tower City Cinemas, 216-349-FILM) typically devotes a portion of its schedule to family films. Week-long; fee.

The **Cleveland Performance Art Festival** (216-221-6017 or 216-491-4555), the biggest such fest in the country, includes several performances suitable for kids each year. Month-long; fee.

The **Tri-C Jazz Fest** (216-987-4814) showcases national jazz talent as well as young performers in concerts at Cuyahoga Community College's Metro campus and at other area locations. Month-long; some shows FREE, some charge a fee.

The **Very Special Arts Festival** combines the talented staffs of the Beck Center, the Health Museum, and the Cleveland Play House to present activities for adults and kids with disabilities, including performances, demonstrations, and hands-on activities. Sat & Sun; FREE.

Free Family Activity: Get Down to Earth. Celebrate Earth Day—along with the sense of anticipation that accompanies the early days of spring—by taking some time to appreciate nature.

One good way to satisfy a child's seemingly endless curiosity about the world is to consult with people who know the answers—at one of the area's many nature centers. (See our listings in the Nature and Outdoor Recreation section.) Visit and learn more about local plants and

EVENTS

animals. Check out the sky and do some star-gazing or cloud-gazing on your own—or visit one of the area's planetariums. Get personal with the earth and plant a tree, explore a new park, or come up with a family plan to do more recycling or composting.

MAY

Familyland Fair at the Mandel Jewish Community Center (216-831-0700) offers a day filled with entertainment, arts and crafts, and exhibits from the Zoo and nature centers, specifically for children. Sun; FREE.

May Day Festival at the Cuyahoga Valley National Recreation Area (800-433-1986) features music, crafts, traditional May Pole dancing, and early games such as lawn bowling and croquet. Sat; FREE.

Free Family Activity: Gardening. Ask any experienced young gardener—it's fun to dig in the dirt, watering is never a chore, and nothing tastes as wonderful as something you have grown yourself!

If your child is just getting started (or for that matter, so are you) try limiting a first venture to a container. This is a good way to create a patch that is manageable for smaller children (or smaller yards). Then, collect a few smaller tools (for smaller hands); plant a few well-chosen seeds; and conduct a weekly hunt for slugs, moths, and earthworms. Don't forget to let the water flow.

For expert help, consult the Cleveland Botanical Garden, Holden Arboretum, or one of the Cleveland Metroparks nature centers.

JUNE

Lorain International Fest, in the Centre of Sheffield (216†-244-2292), features music and food from around the world with three tents, a parade, and a princess pageant. Fri–Sun; FREE.

Parade the Circle Celebration (216-421-7340) presented by University Circle, Inc., features a wildly non-traditional parade organized by the Cleveland Museum of Art that is filled with handmade, people-powered floats. The rest of the day includes continuous entertainment, puppet shows, and craft activities. Sat; FREE.

For older kids and anyone interested in modern art, check out the **Summer Art Walk** in Little Italy (Murray Hill and Mayfield Rds., 216-791-1622; 216-621-1601). During this public walking tour, private galleries exhibit many works of art and crafts, including some works in progress. Fri–Sun; FREE.

Very Square Affair (216-751-9204) on Shaker Square presents a

10 Great Things to Do...

During the Winter Holidays:

- ◉ Dress up and attend a performance of the Cleveland Ballet's *Nutcracker*. (p. 140)

- ◉ Take in the decorations at Tower City; skate on the Public Square ice rink and enjoy the lights. (p. 175)

- ◉ Tour the Western Reserve Historical Society during the annual Family Day Celebration. (p. 70)

- ◉ Enjoy a holiday story hour at your local library.

- ◉ Visit the Cleveland Botanical Garden's lavish annual holiday display. (p. 34)

- ◉ Skate with Frosty or Santa at an area ice rink.

- ◉ Ride the Polar Bear Express on the Cuyahoga Valley Scenic Railway. (p. 88)

- ◉ Visit an open house at the Benjamin Bacon Museum in the Lorain County Metroparks for caroling and hot cider. (p. 113)

- ◉ Try your hand at early American crafts at Lake County History Center's annual celebration. (p. 52)

- ◉ Explore scenic trails by snowshoe or cross-country skis at Kendall Lake Area (CVNRA). (p. 107)

very family-friendly day with entertainment, kid's activities, and food. Sat; FREE.

Free Family Activity: Create a Family Tree. Children love to hear stories about their own families. And, since we all have ancestors, we all have some stories to tell.

If you think you don't have much to tell, or don't know where to get started, just look around. The most obvious family histories are told in photos and letters. But what about recipes, furniture, jewelry, trophies? Just remembering who passed these things on can help you think of things to tell about that person.

Then, next time you have a family gathering, encourage your children to "interview" their family. Or sit down and arrange a photo album together.

If your kids want to know more, and you want to pursue a serious family tree, ask the librarians at the Western Reserve Historical Society (216-721-5722) or the Fairview Park Regional Library (216†-333-4700) for help. The Western Reserve Historical Society also offers workshops.

JULY

The annual **Cain Park Arts Festival** (216-291-2828) brings this Cleveland Heights park alive with music, art demonstrations, and arts and crafts projects for children. Fri–Sun; FREE.

Cleveland Cool Kidsfest (216†-247-2722), planned by the New Cleveland Campaign, combines a lineup of nationally known children's entertainers such as Parachute Express and Thomas the Tank Engine with a slew of local exhibitors, a Fun Run, sandcastle building, and a scavenger hunt. Sat–Sun; fee.

The Parade of Lights, a lighted nighttime boat parade, illuminates an annual downtown weekend of music, games, and small rides held along the banks of the winding Cuyahoga River. Fri–Sun; FREE; fees for most activities. (Greater Cleveland Growth Assoc.: 216-621-3300)

The **E. 185th Street Festival** (216-692-8981, Northeast Shores Development Corp.), on E. 185th between Pawnee and Chickasaw, has celebrated Euclid's ethnic heritage since 1977 with German, Italian, Croatian, and Lithuanian food; three bandstands; a parade; rides; and dancing. Fri–Sun; FREE.

Free Family Activity: Camping Out. Can you think of a better way to spend a summer evening than toasting marshmallows over a campfire? Children love to explore and try new things, and living and sleeping outdoors for a night or two opens up a whole new world for them (often for their parents, too). Of course, camping does require preparation: bring appropriate equipment and have plenty of sunscreen and insect repellent. With kids along, don't forget some games and books. Many area parks have a variety of activities, such as swimming, boat rentals, and naturalist programs; others are truly out in the middle of nowhere. A few are free, but most charge a minimal fee for a night's stay.

Check out our reviews of various state parks in the Nature and Outdoor Recreation section. For general camping information, the National Association of RV Parks and Campgrounds offers a camping vacation planner; for a free copy, call 1-800-47-SUNNY.

AUGUST

The Slavic Village Heritage Festival (216-271-5591, Slavic Village Broadway Development Corp.) runs along 10 blocks of Fleet Ave. in a historic Polish neighborhood. This street fair has ethnic food, crafts, a Kielbasa Cook-Off, dancing, games, and rides. Sat–Sun; FREE.

Celebrations of the **Feast of the Assumption** in mid-August include food, rides, music, fireworks, and a parade in Little Italy at Mayfield Rd. and Murray Hill Rd. (216-421-2995, Holy Rosary Church).

The **Glenville Neighborhood Fest** (216-851-8724, Glenville Development Office) brings families to a park on St. Clair Ave. for food, games, and local talent featuring African-American & Puerto Rican dancing and singing. Fri–Sun; FREE.

The nationally known **Twins Day Fest** (216-425-3652) at Glenn Chamberlain Park, is the nation's largest gathering of twins, with contests and entertainment. Fri–Sun; registration fee for twins; $1 non-twins ages 4 and up.

This is the month for **County Fairs**:

Cuyahoga County Fair, Berea, 216†-243-0090

Ashtabula County Fair, Jefferson, 216†-576-7626

Lorain County Fair, Wellington, 216†-647-2781

Lake County Fair, Painesville, 216†-354-3339

Medina County Fair, Medina, 330-723-9633

Summit County Fair, Tallmadge, 330-633-6200

County fairs typically run from four to five days; fees vary.

Free Family Activity: Festivals. What better way to explore different cultures and ethnic backgrounds with your kids than by sampling foods, music, and customs at a neighborhood ethnic festival?

EVENTS

You need not venture far in this city to explore a world rich with cultural diversity. The Cleveland area is filled with ethnic grocery stores, restaurants, and markets. This time of the year, the city literally is alive with fairs and festivals.

For a complete list of this year's fair dates all over the state call 1-800-BUCKEYE.

SEPTEMBER

Labor Day Weekend offers many choices for family outings. Some of the most popular are:

The **Renaissance Fayre** at Baycrafters in the Cleveland Metroparks Huntington Reservation (216†-871-5678) with arts, music, jesters, jugglers, and puppets. Sat–Sun; fee.

The **National Air Show** at Burke Lakefront Airport (216-781-0747) has five-hour shows each day featuring precision-flying displays by groups such as the Blue Angels, Thunderbirds, or Golden Knights, and fly-bys of unusual and vintage aircraft. Many aircraft are parked and open to view, touch, and sometimes even sit in. Sat–Mon; fee.

The **Geauga County Fair** in Burton (216†-834-1846) includes a heritage village of craft demonstrations, country music, a frog-jumping contest, and hot air balloons. Days vary; fees vary.

The **Pioneer Days Festival** at Lorain County Metroparks' Mill Hollow-Bacon Woods Memorial Park (216†-458-5121) celebrates our past with crafts, music, and hands-on activities for children. Fri–Sun; FREE.

The **Geneva Area Grape Jamboree** in downtown Geneva (216†-466-JAMB) celebrates the harvest of the grape with grape tasting, grape-juice making, parades, food, and rides. Sat–Sun; FREE.

Free Family Activity: Go Fly a Kite. Everyone can fly a kite, or at least help put one together and take part in the chase to catch the wind.

It can be fun just to watch, too. Every second Sunday throughout kite-flying season (roughly April through October), you will find members of the Ohio Society for the Elevation of Kites gathered at Edgewater Park testing winds of over 25 miles per hour. Kites these days are downright acrobatic, and flyers perfect kite ballets in the skies above Lake Erie.

OCTOBER

The **Apple Butter Festival** in Century Village, Burton (216†-834-

EVENTS

4012) includes apple butter simmering in kettles over an outside fire, fritters to eat, and cider to drink. Fri–Sun; FREE.

For Halloween fun, check out the annual **Boo at the Zoo** at the Cleveland Metroparks Zoo (216-661-6500), with costume parades, treats, and children's activities. Week-long; fee.

Fall Festival Family Fun Day at the Lake Erie Science and Nature Center (216†-871-2900), offers a hands-on afternoon filled with crafts, pumpkin decorating, and games. Sat; FREE.

Children's Fest, presented by the Lorain County Metroparks at the French Creek Nature Center (216†-526-7275) offers live entertainment, hands-on crafts, and games. Fri–Sun; FREE.

The **Huntsberg Pumpkin Fest** in Geauga County (800-775-8687) includes a pumpkin contest and games. Fri–Sun; FREE.

The city of Vermilion traditionally hosts the **Woolly Bear Fest** (216†-967-4477) to forecast the length of the coming winter. It features a parade, a woolly bear (fat caterpillar) costume contest, food, games, rides, and entertainment. Sat; FREE; fees for some activities.

Free Family Activity: Leaf Peeping. One of the best parts of living in Northeast Ohio is witnessing the change of seasons. And fall, with its colorful foliage, may well be the most visually dramatic time of year.

While it's hard to miss the colors wherever you are, take some time to visit a leafy place this month. A walk through any of the area's metropark reserves, arboretums, or nature centers, or through the Cuyahoga Valley National Recreation Area, will fit the bill. (See our listings for these in the section titled Nature and Outdoor Recreation.)

A number of places even have official driving tours: the Burton Fall Drive Tour (800-775-8687, Geauga Tourism Council) has a map available at the log cabin in the center of town; the Lorain County Fall Farm Tour (800-334-1673, Lorain County Visitors Bureau) includes stops at area farms for tours, machinery demonstrations, and snacks.

Short train rides offered through Lake Metroparks (216†-256-1404) are also designed for fall foliage sightings.

NOVEMBER

The annual **Children's Fest** at the Lorain County Metroparks (800-LCM-PARK) includes a variety of family entertainment as well as hands-on activities for kids. Sat–Sun; FREE.

Family Day at the Western Reserve Historical Society (216-751-5722), held Thanksgiving Weekend, showcases the Society's exhibits with craft demonstrations, entertainment, workshops, and children's activities. Fri–Sun; fee.

The annual **Thanksgiving Day Parade** downtown is followed by the official holiday lighting of Public Square. Sat; FREE. (216-621-3300, Greater Cleveland Growth Assoc.)

Free Family Activity: Baking. Is cookie baking a part of your holiday tradition? Perhaps this is the year to start.

One of the biggest challenges to overcome when cooking with youngsters is making something that's not too complicated. Preparation is also important to ensure a fun-filled baking session. Clear a large work space and provide plenty of aprons, paper towels, and clean-up equipment.

What are kids especially good at? Rolling dough into balls and then flattening them, using cutters to make shapes, and adding icing and sprinkles. (Of course they are particularly good at the tasting part, too.)

If you're looking for more formal training, many community recreation departments and area community colleges offer baking classes at this time of year.

DECEMBER

Holiday Programs are scheduled at most area libraries to celebrate Christmas, Chanukah, and Kwanzaa. They offer storytimes, crafts, puppet shows, and music. Usually, these are all-ages activities and are FREE.

First Night, an annual celebration of New Year's Eve for families, is celebrated in North Ridgeville (216†-327-3737) with music, dance, fireworks, and comedy along Center Ridge Rd. Dec. 31, 7 p.m.–midnight; fee.

First Night—Akron. A New Year's Eve party for all ages with activities beginning at 5 p.m. and ending (with fireworks) at midnight. The first, held in 1996, took place in several locations around downtown. It brought together short performances by the Akron Symphony Orchestra and the Ohio Ballet, and included mimes, jugglers, and ice-carving. Tickets (one price included the entire evening) sold out fast. In fact, the event was such a hit that some activities ran out of supplies. For more information, please call the Downtown Akron Partnership (330-762-9550 or 330-972-7570).

The **Family New Year's Eve Party** at the Cuyahoga Valley National Recreation Area's Happy Days Visitor Center (216†-650-4636) includes storytelling, crafts for kids, music, and night hikes. 8:30–midnight; $4; $1 children 12 and under.

EVENTS

Stream Run Reservation, Strongsville (216†-572-9990). Two 1,000-foot refrigerated ice chutes offer a thrilling plunge that is not for the weak of heart (or short of stature—riders must be at least 42 inches tall). Thu–Sun.

Free Family Activity: Snowy Outings. Even if winter is not your favorite time of year, take some time for a fresh-air walk in the snow, perhaps stopping to feed birds at a frozen pond or park and winding up with some hot cocoa at home.

If you are up for more invigorating winter fun, try skating, cross-country skiing, sledding, or winter hiking. Many area parks have designated winter recreation areas as well as equipment rental and guided excursions. (See our listings in the Nature and Outdoor Recreation section.)

A formal winter solstice celebration at the Swine Creek Reservation of the Geauga Park District (216†-286-9504) includes an evening walk.

OTHER EVENTS

For a current listing of other family-oriented events, refer to the monthly calendar in every issue of *Cleveland Parent*, which is available free at many locations all over Greater Cleveland, or by subscription (216†-899-2511).

The Following organizations listed elsewhere in this guide host annual special events (see individual listings for details):

African American Museum, 31
Akron Art Museum, 32
Akron Zoological Park, 73
Alpine Valley, 157
Ashtabula Arts Center, 135
Ashtabula, Carson & Jefferson Scenic Line, 33
Baycrafters, 136
Beck Center for the Cultural Arts, 137
Brooklyn Recreation Center, 160
Buzzard Cove, 16
Cain Park, 138
Carlisle Reservation and Visitors Center, 81
Century Village, 33
Cleveland Ballet, 140
Cleveland Botanical Garden, 34
Cleveland Center for Contemporary Art, 35
Cleveland Heights Pavilion, 163
Cleveland Heights-University Heights Public Library, 211
Cleveland Metroparks Zoo and RainForest, 85
Cleveland Museum of Art, 36
Cleveland Museum of Natural History, 37

Conneaut Lake Park, 17
Crawford Auto-Aviation Museum, 40
Cuyahoga Valley National Recreation Area, 87
Cuyahoga Valley Scenic Railroad, 88
Dobama Theatre, 146
Edgewater Park, 90
Elyria Public Library, 214
Euclid Orr Ice Rink, 166
Fairport Harbor Lakefront Park, 92
Fine Arts Association, 147
Frostville Museum, 44
Geauga County Public Library, 215
Hale Farm and Village, 46
Happy Days Visitor Center, 101
Hoover Historical Center, 47
Hower House Victorian Mansion, 48
I-X Center Indoor Amusement Park, 22
Jewish Community Center, 170-171
Lake County History Center, 52
Lake Erie Nature and Science Center, 108
Lake Farmpark, 108
Mill Hollow-Bacon Woods Memorial Park, 113

EVENTS

Other Events (continued)

General Index

Geographical Index

INDEXES

Idea Index

Looking for something in particular? Can't decide what to do? Here are some specific activities and the places listed in this book where you can find them. While this is not a complete list, it should help get you started....

Animals on Site
Akron Zoological Park, 73
Amish Farm and Home, 197
Big Creek Park and Meyer Nature Center, 75
Big Creek Reservation, 75
Burnett's Pet Farm, 79
Children's Schoolhouse Nature Park, 83
Cleveland Metroparks Zoo and RainForest, 85
Cleveland Museum of Natural History, 37
F. A. Seiberling Naturealm, 92
French Creek Nature Center, 94
Garfield Park Nature Center, 96
I-X Center Indoor Amusement Park, 22
Lake Erie Nature and Science Center, 108
Lake Farmpark, 108
McKinley Museum of History, Science, and Industry, 55
Mentor Marsh State Nature Preserve, 111
North Chagrin Nature Center, 116
Penitentiary Glen Reservation and Nature Center, 120
Rocky River Nature Center, 123
Sauder Farm and Craft Village, 65
Sea World of Ohio, 26
Sippo Lake Park, 127

Arts Instruction
Ashtabula Arts Center, 135
Baycrafters, 136
Beck Center for the Cultural Arts, 137
Brecksville Center for the Arts, 138
Cain Park, 138
Cleveland Center for Contemporary Art, 35
Cleveland Institute of Art, 36
Cleveland Museum of Art, 36
Cudell Fine Arts Center, 145
Fairmount Fine Arts Center, 147
Fine Arts Association, 147
Firelands Association for the Visual Arts, 148
Lakeland Community College, 172
Lorain County Community College, 151
Shore Cultural Centre, 154
Wildwood Cultural Center, 155

Camping
Cedar Point, 16
East Harbor State Park, 89
Findley State Park, 93
Geneva State Park, 99
Kelleys Island State Park, 106
Mosquito Lake State Park, 114
Portage Lakes State Park, 120
Punderson State Park, 121
Pymatuning State Park, 122
Quail Hollow State Park, 122
Riverview Park, 123
South Bass Island State Park, 127
West Branch State Park, 132

Canoeing
Camp Hi Canoe Livery, 162
Eldon Russell Park, 91
Grand River Canoe Livery, 167
Hidden Valley Park, 103
Mason's Landing Park, 111
Punderson State Park, 121
Wildwood Water Park, 28

Caving
Kendall Lake Area, 107
Seneca Caverns, 126

Climbing
Cleveland Rock Gym, 164
Hinckley Reservation, 104

Cross-Country Skiing
Bedford Reservation, 74
Big Creek Park and Meyer Nature Center, 75
Bradley Woods Reservation, 76
Brookside Reservation, 79
Cascade Valley Metro Park, 81
Chapin Forest, 82
Cuyahoga Valley National Recreation Area, 87
East Harbor State Park, 89
Eldon Russell Park, 91
Euclid Creek Reservation, 91
Findley State Park, 93

INDEXES

INDEXES

Appendix—Tourism & Visitor's Info

Convention and Visitors Bureau of Greater Cleveland
3100 Terminal Tower, Cleveland, OH 44113; (216) 621-4110
Weekly events recording: (216) 621-8860; (800) 321-1004
Pick up a self-guided tour brochure at any Visitor Information Center or at the Convention and Visitors Bureau office.

Visitor Information Centers:
Tower City Center, (216) 621-4110
Cleveland Hopkins International Airport, (216) 265-3729
Nautica Boardwalk, The Flats, 623-4442 (Memorial Day–Labor Day)
Terminal Tower Observation Deck, (216) 621-7981 (see p. 205)

Cleveland Activity Line: (216) 899-1555

Event Tickets
Advantix: (216) 348-5323
Mailtix: (216) 694-ARTS
Ticketmaster: (216) 241-5555

RTA (Regional Transit Authority)
Customer Service Center: 315 Euclid Ave., Cleveland, OH 44114
Rideline: (216) 623-0180 (touch-tone phones only)
Answerline: (216) 621-9500 (Mon–Fri 5:30 a.m.–10 p.m.; Sat 8 a.m.–5 p.m.)
Special rates: Children age 6 & under ride FREE with a paying adult.

University Circle, Inc.
10831 Magnolia Dr., Cleveland, OH 44106; (216) 791-3900

Akron/Summit County Tourism Information
Cascade Plaza, Akron, OH 44308; (330) 376-4254

Geauga County Tourism Information
PO Box 62, Chardon, OH 44024; (216†) 564-7625

Lake County Tourism Information
1670 Mentor Ave., Painesville, OH 44077; (216†) (800) 368-LAKE; (216†) 951-5700

Lorain County Tourism Information
611 Broadway Ave., Lorain, OH 44052, (800) 334-1673; (216†) 245-5282

Ohio Tourism Information
1-800-BUCKEYE; "Ohio—The Heart of it All!" is a free quarterly calendar of events.

Portage County Tourism Information
173 S. Chillicothe Rd., Aurora, OH 44202; (800) 648-6342; (216†) 562-3355

Road & Lake Condition Information
Cuyahoga County Highway Patrol: (216) 587-4305
Ohio Turnpike Commission: (216†) 234-2030
Coast Guard: (216) 522-4412